M

AUG 2 9 2007

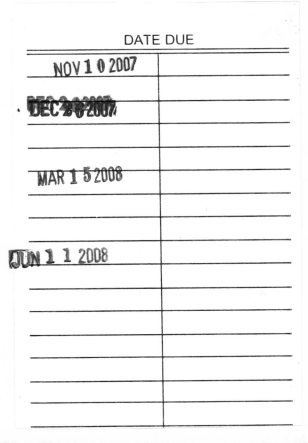

Mike Davis lives in San Diego. He is the author of *Buda's Wagon*, *Prisoners of the American Dream*, *City of Quartz*, *Ecology of Fear*, *Magical Urbanism*, *Late Victorian Holocausts*, and *Dead Cities*.

Further praise for *Planet of Slums*

"There can be no doubt about the achievement of *Planet of Slums* ... it forces us, angrily, to confront the deplorable realities of slum existence and the limitations of slum policies in many developing countries."   *The Times*

"The astonishing facts hit like anvil blows ... Davis has produced a heartbreaking book that hammers the reader a little further into the ground with the blow of each new and shocking statistic."   *Financial Times*

"The Raymond Chandler of urban geography ... In *Planet of Slums*, Davis's genre is the global disaster movie, as directed by the chroniclers of Victorian poverty: Engels, Booth and Dickens. The scale of modern squalor revealed in his brilliant survey dwarfs its predecessors ... [a] coruscating tragedy."
Independent

"Packed with rigorous analysis and heart-stopping facts this is a brilliant exploration of how millions of poor city-dwellers worldwide are being driven to the squalid periurban shadowlands of today's megaslums ... Davis's book is absolutely vital reading."   *Big Issue*

"Davis's descriptions of the conditions endured by slum-dwellers provide reason enough to read this book. His analysis is full of gripping stories from globalisation's frontline."   *New Statesman*

"While many case studies have described what it means to reside in a *favela*, *basti*, *kampung*, *gecekondu* or *bidonville*, Davis provides a properly global portrait ... And whereas urban specialists have focused on questions of space and land use in their discussions of slums, and developmentalists on the issue of their 'informal' economies, *Planet of Slums* commands our attention as a broader historical synthesis of the two."   *New Left Review*

Planet of Slums

◆

MIKE DAVIS

VERSO
London • New York

First published by Verso 2006
This paperback edition published by Verso 2007
© Mike Davis 2006, 2007
All rights reserved

1 3 5 7 9 10 8 6 4 2

Verso
UK: 6 Meard Street, London W1F 0EG
USA: 180 Varick Street, New York, NY 10014-4606
www.versobooks.com

Verso is the imprint of New Left Books

ISBN-13: 978-1-84467-160-1

British Library Cataloguing in Publication Data
A catalogue record for this book is available from the British Library

Library of Congress Cataloging-in-Publication Data
A catalog record for this book is available from the Library of Congress

Printed in the USA by Quebecor World, Fairfield

for my darlin' Roisin

Slum, semi-slum, and superslum ...
to this has come the evolution of cities.

Patrick Geddes[1]

1 Quoted in Lewis Mumford, *The City in History: Its Origins, Its Transformations, and Its Prospects*, New York 1961, p. 464.

Contents

1

The Urban Climacteric

We live in the age of the city. The city is everything to
us – it consumes us, and for that reason we glorify it.

Onookome Okome[1]

Sometime in the next year or two, a woman will give birth in the Lagos
slum of Ajegunle, a young man will flee his village in west Java for the
bright lights of Jakarta, or a farmer will move his impoverished family
into one of Lima's innumerable *pueblos jovenes*. The exact event is unim-
portant and it will pass entirely unnoticed. Nonetheless it will constitute
a watershed in human history, comparable to the Neolithic or
Industrial revolutions. For the first time the urban population of the
earth will outnumber the rural. Indeed, given the imprecisions of Third
World censuses, this epochal transition has probably already occurred.

The earth has urbanized even faster than originally predicted by the
Club of Rome in its notoriously Malthusian 1972 report *Limits of
Growth*. In 1950 there were 86 cities in the world with a population of
more than one million; today there are 400, and by 2015 there will be
at least 550.[2] Cities, indeed, have absorbed nearly two-thirds of the

1 Onookome Okome, "Writing the Anxious City: Images of Lagos in Nigerian
Home Video Films," in Okwui Enwezor et al. (eds), *Under Siege: Four African Cities –
Freetown Johannesburg, Kinshasa, Lagos*, Ostfildern-Ruit 2002, p. 316.
2 UN Department of Economic and Social Affairs, Population Division, *World
Urbanization Prospects*, the 2001 Revision, New York 2002.

global population explosion since 1950, and are currently growing by
a million babies and migrants each week.[3] The world's urban labor
force has more than doubled since 1980, and the present urban population – 3.2 billion – is larger than the total population of the world
when John F. Kennedy was inaugurated.[4] The global countryside,
meanwhile, has reached its maximum population and will begin to
shrink after 2020. As a result, cities will account for virtually all future
world population growth, which is expected to peak at about 10 billion
in 2050.[5]

Megacities and *Desakotas*

Ninety-five percent of this final buildout of humanity will occur in the
urban areas of developing countries, whose populations will double to
nearly 4 billion over the next generation.[6] Indeed, the combined urban
population of China, India, and Brazil already roughly equals that of
Europe and North America. The scale and velocity of Third World
urbanization, moreover, utterly dwarfs that of Victorian Europe.
London in 1910 was seven times larger than it had been in 1800, but
Dhaka, Kinshasa, and Lagos today are each approximately *forty* times
larger than they were in 1950. China – urbanizing "at a speed unprecedented in human history" – added more city-dwellers in the 1980s than
did all of Europe (including Russia) in the entire nineteenth century![7]

3 Population Information Program, Center for Communication Programs, the
Johns Hopkins Bloomburg School of Public Health, *Meeting the Urban Challenge*,
Population Reports, vol. 30, no. 4, Baltimore 2002 (Fall), p. 1.
4 Dennis Rondinelli and John Kasarda, "Job Creation Needs in Third World
Cities," in John D. Kasarda and Allan M. Parnell (eds), *Third World Cities: Problems,
Policies and Prospects*, Newbury Park 1993, p. 101.
5 Wolfgang Lutz, Warren Sanderson, and Sergei Scherbov, "Doubling of World
Population Unlikely," *Nature* 387 (19 June 1997), pp. 803–04. However, the populations of sub-Saharan Africa will triple, and of India, double.
6 Although the velocity of global urbanization is not in doubt, the growth rates
of specific cities may brake abruptly as they encounter the frictions of size and
congestion. A famous instance of such a "polarization reversal" is Mexico City, widely
predicted to achieve a population of 25 million during the 1990s (the current population is between 19 and 22 million). See Yue-man Yeung, "Geography in an Age of
Mega-Cities," *International Social Sciences Journal* 151 (1997), p. 93.
7 *Financial Times*, 27 July 2004; David Drakakis-Smith, *Third World Cities*, 2nd ed.,
London 2000.

Figure 1
World Population Growth

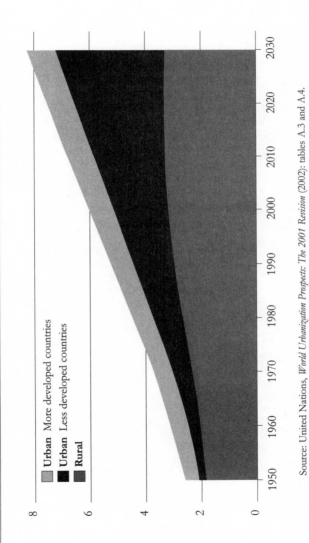

Urban More developed countries
Urban Less developed countries
Rural

BILLIONS

1950   1960   1970   1980   1990   2000   2010   2020   2030

0   2   4   6   8

Source: United Nations, *World Urbanization Prospects: The 2001 Revision* (2002): tables A.3 and A.4.

Figure 2[8]
Third World Megacities
(population in millions)

	1950	2004
Mexico City	2.9	22.1
Seoul-Injon	1.0	21.9
(*New York*	*12.3*	*21.9*)
São Paulo	2.4	19.9
Mumbai (Bombay)	2.9	19.1
Delhi	1.4	18.6
Jakarta	1.5	16.0
Dhaka	0.4	15.9
Kolkata (Calcutta)	4.4	15.1
Cairo	2.4	15.1
Manila	1.5	14.3
Karachi	1.0	13.5
Lagos	0.3	13.4
Shanghai	5.3	13.2
Buenos Aires	4.6	12.6
Rio de Janeiro	3.0	11.9
Tehran	1.0	11.5
Istanbul	1.1	11.1
Beijing	3.9	10.8
Krung Thep (Bangkok)	1.4	9.1
Gauteng (Witwatersrand)	1.2	9.0
Kinshasa/Brazzaville	0.2	8.9
Lima	0.6	8.2
Bogotá	0.7	8.0

8 Composite of UN-HABITAT Urban Indicators Database (2002); Thomas Brinkhoff "The Principal Agglomerations of the World", www.citypopulation.de/World.html (May 2004).

The most celebrated phenomenon, of course, is the burgeoning of new megacities with populations in excess of 8 million and, even more spectacularly, hypercities with more than 20 million inhabitants – the estimated urban population of the world at the time of the French Revolution. In 2000, according to the UN Population Division, only metropolitan Tokyo had incontestably passed that threshold (although Mexico City, New York, and Seoul-Injon made other lists).[9] The *Far Eastern Economic Review* estimates that by 2025 Asia alone might have ten or eleven conurbations that large, including Jakarta (24.9 million), Dhaka (25 million), and Karachi (26.5 million). Shanghai, whose growth was frozen for decades by Maoist policies of deliberate underurbanization, could have as many as 27 million residents in its huge estuarial metro-region. Mumbai (Bombay), meanwhile, is projected to attain a population of 33 million, although no one knows whether such gigantic concentrations of poverty are biologically or ecologically sustainable.[10]

The exploding cities of the developing world are also weaving extraordinary new urban networks, corridors, and hierarchies. In the Americas, geographers already talk about a leviathan known as the Rio/São Paulo Extended Metropolitan Region (RSPER) which includes the medium-sized cities on the 500-kilometer-long transport axis between Brazil's two largest metropolises, as well as the important industrial area dominated by Campinas; with a current population of 37 million, this embryonic megalopolis is already larger than Tokyo–Yokohama.[11] Likewise, the giant amoeba of Mexico City, already having consumed Toluca, is extending pseudopods that will eventually incorporate much of central Mexico, including the cities of Cuernavaca, Puebla, Cuautla, Pachuca, and Queretaro, into a single megalopolis with a mid-twenty-first-century population of approximately 50 million – about 40 percent of the national total.[12]

Even more surprising is the vast West African conurbation rapidly coalescing along the Gulf of Guinea with Lagos (23 million people by

9 UN-HABITAT Urban Indicators Database (2002).

10 *Far Eastern Economic Review*, Asia 1998 Yearbook, p. 63.

11 Hamilton Tolosa, "The Rio/São Paulo Extended Metropolitan Region: A Quest for Global Integration," *The Annals of Regional Science* 37:2 (September 2003), pp. 480, 485.

12 Gustavo Garza, "Global Economy, Metropolitan Dynamics and Urban Policies in Mexico," *Cities* 16:3 (1999), p. 154.

2015 according to one estimate) as its fulcrum. By 2020, according to an OECD study, this network of 300 cities larger than 100,000 will "have a population comparable to the U.S. east coast, with five cities of over one million ... [and] a total of more than 60 million inhabitants along a strip of land 600 kilometers long, running east to west between Benin City and Accra."[13] Tragically, it probably will also be the biggest single footprint of urban poverty on earth.

Figure 3[14]
Urbanization of the Gulf of Guinea

Cities	1960	1990	2020
over 100,000	17	90	300
over 5000	600	3500	6000

The largest-scale posturban structures, however, are emerging in East Asia. The Pearl River (Hong Kong–Guangzhou)[15] and the Yangze River (Shanghai) deltas, along with the Beijing–Tianjin corridor, are well on their way to becoming urban-indusrial megapolises comparable to Tokyo–Osaka, the lower Rhine, or New York–Philadelphia. Indeed, China, unique amongst developing countries, is aggressively planning urban development at a super-regional scale using Tokyo–Yokohama and the US eastern seaboard as its templates. Created in 1983, the Shanghai Economic Zone is the biggest subnational planning entity in the world, encompassing the metropolis and five adjoining provinces with an aggregate population almost as large as that of the United States.[16]

These new Chinese megalopolises, according to two leading researchers, may be only the first stage in the emergence of "a

13 Jean-Marie Cour and Serge Snrech (eds), *Preparing for the Future: A Vision of West Africa in the Year 2020*, Paris 1998, p. 94.

14 Ibid., p. 48.

15 See Yue-man Yeung, "Viewpoint: Integration of the Pearl River Delta," *International Development Planning Review* 25:3 (2003).

16 Aprodicio Laquian, "The Effects of National Urban Strategy and Regional Development Policy on Patterns of Urban Growth in China," in Gavin Jones and Pravin Visaria (eds), *Urbanization in Large Developing Countries: China, Inonesia, Brazil, and India*, Oxford 1997, pp. 62–63.

continuous urban corridor stretching from Japan/North Korea to West Java."[17] As it takes shape over the next century, this great dragon-like sprawl of cities will constitute the physical and demographic culmination of millennia of urban evolution. The ascendency of coastal East Asia, in turn, will surely promote a Tokyo–Shanghai "world city" dipole to equality with the New York–London axis in the control of global flows of capital and information.

The price of this new urban order, however, will be increasing inequality within and between cities of different sizes and economic specializations. Chinese experts, indeed, are currently debating whether the ancient income-and-development chasm between city and countryside is now being replaced by an equally fundamental gap between small, particularly inland cities and the giant coastal metropolises.[18] However, the smaller cities are precisely where most of Asia will soon live. If megacities are the brightest stars in the urban firmament, three-quarters of the burden of future world population growth will be borne by faintly visible second-tier cities and smaller urban areas: places where, as UN researchers emphasize, "there is little or no planning to accommodate these people or provide them with services."[19] In China – officially, 43 percent urban in 1993 – the number of official "cities" has soared from 193 to 640 since 1978, but the great metropolises, despite extraordinary growth, have actually declined in relative share of urban population. It is, instead, the small- to medium-sized cities and recently "city-ized" towns that have absorbed the majority of the rural labor-power made redundant by post-1979 market reforms.[20] In part, this is the result of conscious planning: since the 1970s the Chinese state has embraced policies designed to promote a more balanced urban hierarchy of industrial investment and population.[21]

17 Yue-man Yeung and Fu-chen Lo, "Global restructuring and emerging urban corridors in Pacific Asia," in Lo and Yeung (eds), *Emerging World Cities in Pacific Asia*, Tokyo 1996, p. 41.

18 Gregory Guldin, *What's a Peasant To Do? Village Becoming Town in Southern China*, Boulder 2001, p. 13.

19 UN-HABITAT, *The Challenge of Slums: Global Report on Human Settlements 2003*, [henceforth: *Challenge*], London 2003, p. 3.

20 Guldin, *What's a Peasant To Do?*

21 Sidney Goldstein, "Levels of Urbanization in China," in Mattei Dogon and John Kasarda (eds), *The Metropolis Era: Volume One – A World of Giant Cities*, Newbury Park 1988, pp. 210–21.

In India, by contrast, small cities and towns have lost economic traction and demographic share in the recent neoliberal transition – there is little evidence of Chinese-style "dual-track" urbanization. But as the urban ratio soared in the 1990s from one quarter to one third of total population, medium-sized cities, such as Saharanpur in Uttar Pradesh, Ludhiana in the Punjab, and, most famously, Visakhapatnam in Andhra Pradesh, have burgeoned. Hyderabad, growing almost 5 percent per annum over the last quarter century, is predicted to become a megacity of 10.5 million by 2015. According to the most recent census, 35 Indian cities are now above the one million threshold, accounting for a total population of nearly 110 million.[22]

In Africa, the supernova growth of a few cities like Lagos (from 300,000 in 1950 to 13.5 million today) has been matched by the transformation of several dozen small towns and oases like Ouagadougou, Nouakchott, Douala, Kampala, Tanta, Conakry, Ndjamena, Lumumbashi, Mogadishu, Antananarivo, and Bamako into sprawling cities larger than San Francisco or Manchester. (Most spectacular, perhaps, has been the transformation of the bleak Congolese diamond-trading center of Mbuji-Mayi from a small town of 25,000 in 1960 into a contemporary metropolis of 2 million, with growth occurring mostly in the last decade.[23]) In Latin America, where primary cities long monopolized growth, secondary cities such as Santa Cruz, Valencia, Tijuana, Curitiba, Temuco, Maracay, Bucaramanga, Salvador, and Belem are now booming, with the most rapid increase in cities of fewer than 500,000 people.[24]

Moreover, as anthropologist Gregory Guldin has emphasized, urbanization must be conceptualized as structural transformation along, and intensified interaction between, every point of an urban–rural continuum. In Guldin's case study of southern China, he found that the

22 *Census 2001*, Office of the Registrar General and Census Commissioner, India; and Alain Durand-Lasserve and Lauren Royston, "International Trends and Country Contexts," in Alain Durand-Lasserve and Lauren Royston (eds), *Holding Their Ground: Secure Land Tenure for the Urban Poor in Developing Countries*, London 2002, p. 20.

23 Mbuji-Mayi is the center of the "ultimate company state" in the Kaasai region run by the Société Minière de Bakwanga. See Michela Wrong, *In the Footsteps of Mr. Kurtz: Living on the Brink of Disaster in the Congo*, London 2000, pp. 121–23.

24 Miguel Villa and Jorge Rodríguez, "Demographic Trends in Latin America's Metropolises, 1950–1990," in Alan Gilbert (ed.), *The Mega-City in Latin America*, Tokyo and New York 1996, pp. 33–34.

countryside is urbanizing *in situ* as well as generating epochal migrations; "Villages become more like market and *xiang* towns, and county towns and small cities become more like large cities." Indeed, in many cases, rural people no longer have to migrate to the city: it migrates to them.[25]

This is also true in Malaysia, where journalist Jeremy Seabrook describes the fate of Penang fishermen "engulfed by urbanization without migrating, their lives overturned, even while remaining on the spot where they were born." After the fishermen's homes were cut off from the sea by a new highway, their fishing grounds polluted by urban waste, and neighboring hillsides deforested to build apartment blocks, they had little choice but to send their daughters into nearby Japanese-owned sweatshop factories. "It was the destruction," Seabrook emphasizes, "not only of the livelihood of people who had always lived symbiotically with the sea, but also of the psyche and spirit of the fishing people."[26]

The result of this collision between the rural and the urban in China, much of Southeast Asia, India, Egypt, and perhaps West Africa is a hermaphroditic landscape, a partially urbanized countryside that Guldin argues may be "a significant new path of human settlement and development ... a form neither rural nor urban but a blending of the two wherein a dense web of transactions ties large urban cores to their surrounding regions."[27] German architect and urban theorist Thomas Sieverts⁶ proposes that this diffuse urbanism, which he calls *Zwischenstadt* ("in-between city"), is rapidly becoming the defining landscape of the twenty-first century in rich as well as poor countries, regardless of earlier urban histories. Unlike Guldin, however, Sieverts conceptualizes these new conurbations as polycentric webs with neither traditional cores nor recognizable peripheries.

25 Guldin, *What's a Peasant To Do?*, pp. 14–17.

26 Jeremy Seabrook, *In the Cities of the South: Scenes from a Developing World*, London 1996, pp. 16–17.

27 Guldin, *What's a Peasant To Do?*, pp. 14–17. See also Jing Neng Li, "Structural and Spatial Economic Changes and Their Effects on Recent Urbanization in China," in Jones and Visaria, *Urbanization in Large Developing Countries*, p. 44. Ian Yeboah finds a *desakota* ("city village") pattern developing around Accra, whose sprawling form (188 percent increase in surface area in 1990s) and recent automobilization he attributes to the impact of structural adjustment policies. Yeboah, "Demographic and Housing Aspects of Structural Adjustment and Emerging Urban Form in Accra, Ghana," *Africa Today*, 50: 1 (2003), pp. 108, 116–17.

Across all cultures of the entire world, they share specific common characteristics: a structure of completely different urban environments
which at first sight is diffuse and disorganized with individual islands of
geometrically structured patterns, a structure without a clear centre, but
therefore with many more or less sharply functionally specialized areas,
networks and nodes.[28]

Such "extended metropolitan regions," writes geographer David
Drakakis-Smith, referring specifically to Delhi, "represent a fusion of
urban and regional development in which the distinction between what
is urban and rural has become blurred as cities expand along corridors
of communication, by-passing or surrounding small towns and villages
which subsequently experience *in situ* changes in function and occupation."[29] In Indonesia, where a similar process of rural/urban
hybridization is far advanced in Jabotabek (the greater Jakarta region),
researchers call these novel landuse patterns *desakotas* ("city villages")
and argue whether they are transitional landscapes or a dramatic new
species of urbanism.[30]

An analogous debate is taking place amongst Latin American urbanists as they confront the emergence of polycentric urban systems
without clear rural/urban boundaries. Geographers Adrian Aguilar and
Peter Ward advance the concept of "region-based urbanization" to characterize contemporary peri-urban development around Mexico City, São
Paulo, Santiago, and Buenos Aires. "Lower rates of metropolitan
growth have coincided with a more intense circulation of commodities,
people and capital between the city center and its hinterland, with ever
more diffuse frontiers between the urban and the rural, and a manufacturing deconcentration towards the metropolitan periphery, and in

28 Thomas Sieverts, *Cities Without Cities: An Interpretation of the Zwischenstadt*,
London 2003, p. 3.

29 Drakakis-Smith, *Third World Cities*, p. 21.

30 See overview in T. G. McGee, "The Emergence of *Desakota* Regions in Asia:
Expanding a Hypothesis," in Norton Ginsburg, Bruce Koppel, and T. G. McGee
(eds), *The Extended Metropolis: Settlement Transition in Asia*, Honolulu 1991. Philip Kelly,
in his book on Manila, agrees with McGee about the specificity of the Southeast
Asian path of urbanization, but argues that *desakota* landscapes are unstable, with
agriculture slowly being squeezed out. Kelly, *Everyday Urbanization: The Social Dynamics
of Development in Manila's Extended Metropolitan Region*, London 1999, pp. 284–86.

particular beyond into the peri-urban spaces or penumbra that surround mega-cities." Aguilar and Ward believe that "it is in this peri-urban space that the reproduction of labor is most likely to be concentrated in the world's largest cities in the 21st century."[31]

In any case, the new and old don't easily mix, and on the *desakota* outskirts of Colombo "communities are divided, with the outsiders and insiders unable to build relationships and coherent communities."[32] But the process, as anthropologist Magdalena Nock points out in regard to Mexico, is irreversible: "Globalization has increased the movement of people, goods, services, information, news, products, and money, and thereby the presence of urban characteristics in rural areas and of rural traits in urban centers."[33]

Back to Dickens

The dynamics of Third World urbanization both recapitulate and confound the precedents of nineteenth- and early-twentieth-century Europe and North America. In China the greatest industrial revolution in history is the Archimedean lever shifting a population the size of Europe's from rural villages to smog-choked, sky-climbing cities: since the market reforms of the late 1970s it is estimated that more than 200 million Chinese have moved from rural areas to cities. Another 250 or 300 million people – the next "peasant flood" – are expected to follow in coming decades.[34] As a result of this staggering influx, 166 Chinese

31 Adrián Aguilar and Peter Ward, "Globalization, Regional Development, and Mega-City Expansion in Latin America: Analyzing Mexico City's Peri-Urban Hinterland," *Cities* 20:1 (2003), pp. 4, 18. The authors claim that *desakota*-like development does not occur in Africa: "Instead city growth tends to be firmly urban and large-city based, and is contained within clearly defined boundaries. There is not meta-urban or peri-urban development that is tied to, and driven by, processes, in the urban core," p. 5. But certainly Gauteng (Witwatersrand) must be accounted as an example of "regional urbanization" fully analogous to Latin American examples.

32 Ranjith Dayaratne and Raja Samarawickrama, "Empowering Communities: The Peri-Urban Areas of Colombo," *Environment and Urbanization* 15:1 (April 2003), p. 102. (See also, in the same issue, L. van den Berg, M. van Wijk, and Pham Van Hoi, "The Transformation of Agricultural and Rural Life Downsteam of Hanoi.")

33 Magdalena Nock, "The Mexican Peasantry and the *Ejido* in the Neo-liberal Period," in Deborah Bryceson, Cristóbal Kay, and Jos Mooij (eds), *Disappearing Peasantries? Rural Labour in Africa, Asia and Latin America*, London 2000, p. 173.

34 *Financial Times*, 16 December 2003, 27 July 2004.

cities in 2005 (as compared to only 9 US cities) had populations of more than 1 million.[35] Industrial boomtowns such as Dongguan, Shenzhen, Fushan City, and Chengchow are the postmodern Sheffields and Pittsburghs. As the *Financial Times* recently pointed out, within a decade "China [will] cease to be the predominantly rural country it has been for millennia."[36] Indeed, the great oculus of the Shanghai World Financial Centre may soon look out upon a vast urban world little imagined by Mao or, for that matter, Le Corbusier.

Figure 4[37]
China's Industrial Urbanization
(percent urban)

	Population	GDP
1949	11	–
1978	13	–
2003	38	54
2020 (*projected*)	63	85

It is also unlikely that anyone fifty years ago could have envisioned that the squatter camps and war ruins of Seoul would metamorphose at breakneck speed (a staggering 11.4 percent per annum during the 1960s) into a megalopolis as large as greater New York – but, then again, what Victorian could have envisioned a city like Los Angeles in 1920? However, as unpredictable as its specific local histories and urban miracles, contemporary East Asian urbanization, accompanied by a tripling of per capita GDP since 1965, preserves a quasi-classical relationship between manufacturing growth and urban migration.

35 *New York Times*, 28 July 2004.

36 Wang Mengkui, Director of the Development Research Center of the State Council, quoted in the *Financial Times*, 26 November 2003.

37 Goldstein, "Levels of Urbanizaton in China," table 7.1, p. 201; 1978 figure from Guilhem Fabre, "La Chine," in Thierry Paquot, *Les Monde des Villes: Panorama Urbain de la Planète*, Brussels 1996, p. 187. It is important to note that the World Bank's time series differs from Fabre's, with a 1978 urbanization rate of 18 percent, not 13 percent. (See World Bank, *World Development Indicators*, 2001, CD-ROM version.)

Eighty percent of Marx's industrial proletariat now lives in China or somewhere outside of Western Europe and the United States.[38]

In most of the developing world, however, city growth lacks the powerful manufacturing export engines of China, Korea, and Taiwan, as well as China's vast inflow of foreign capital (currently equal to half of total foreign investment in the entire developing world). Since the mid-1980s, the great industrial cities of the South – Bombay, Johannesburg, Buenos Aires, Belo Horizonte, and São Paulo – have all suffered massive plant closures and tendential deindustrialization. Elsewhere, urbanization has been more radically decoupled from industrialization, even from development *per se* and, in sub-Saharan Africa, from that supposed *sine qua non* of urbanization, rising agricultural productivity. The size of a city's economy, as a result, often bears surprisingly little relationship to its population size, and vice versa. Figure 5 illustrates this disparity between population and GDP rankings for the largest metropolitan areas.

Figure 5[39]

Population versus GDP: Ten Largest Cities

	(1) by 2000 population	(2) by 1996 GDP (2000 pop. rank)
1.	Tokyo	Tokyo (1)
2.	Mexico City	New York (3)
3.	New York	Los Angeles (7)
4.	Seoul	Osaka (8)
5.	São Paulo	Paris (25)
6.	Mumbai	London (19)
7.	Delhi	Chicago (26)
8.	Los Angeles	San Francisco (35)
9.	Osaka	Düsseldorf (46)
10.	Jakarta	Boston (48)

38 World Bank, *World Development Report 1995: Workers in an Integrating World*, New York 1995, p. 170.

39 Population rank from Thomas Brinkhoff (www.citypopulation.de); GDP rank from Denise Pumain, "Scaling Laws and Urban Systems," *Santa Fe Institute Working Paper* 04-02-002, Santa Fe 2002, p. 4.

Some would argue that urbanization without industrialization is an expression of an inexorable trend: the inherent tendency of silicon capitalism to delink the growth of production from that of employment. But in Africa, Latin America, the Middle East and much of South Asia, urbanization without growth, as we shall see later, is more obviously the legacy of a global political conjuncture – the worldwide debt crisis of the late 1970s and the subsequent IMF-led restructuring of Third World economies in the 1980s – than any iron law of advancing technology.

Third World urbanization, moreover, continued its breakneck pace (3.8 percent per annum from 1960 to 1993) throughout the locust years of the 1980s and early 1990s, in spite of falling real wages, soaring prices, and skyrocketing urban unemployment.[40] This perverse urban boom surprised most experts and contradicted orthodox economic models that predicted that the negative feedback of urban recession would slow or even reverse migration from the countryside.[41] "It appears," marveled developmental economist Nigel Harris in 1990, "that for low-income countries, a significant fall in urban incomes may not necessarily produce in the short term a decline in rural–urban migration."[42]

The situation in Africa was particularly paradoxical: How could cities in Côte d'Ivoire, Tanzania, Congo-Kinshasa, Gabon, Angola, and elsewhere – where economies were contracting by 2 to 5 percent per year – still support annual population growth of 4 to 8 percent?[43] How could Lagos in the 1980s grow twice as fast as the Nigerian population, while its urban economy was in deep recession?[44] Indeed, how has Africa as a whole, currently in a dark age of stagnant urban employment and stalled agricultural productivity, been able to sustain

40 Josef Gugler, "Introduction – II. Rural–Urban Migration," in Gugler (ed.), *Cities in the Developing World: Issues, Theory and Policy*, Oxford 1997, p. 43.

41 Sally Findley emphasizes that everyone in the 1980s underestimated levels of continuing rural–urban migration and resulting rates of urbanization. Findley, "The Third World City," in Kasarda and Parnell, *Third World Cities: Problems*, p. 14.

42 Nigel Harris, "Urbanization, Economic Development and Policy in Developing Countries," *Habitat International* 14:4 (1990), pp. 21–22.

43 David Simon, "Urbanization, Globalization and Economic Crisis in Africa," in Carole Rakodi (ed.), *The Urban Challenge in Africa: Growth and Management in Its Large Cities*, Tokyo 1997, p. 95. For growth rates of English industrial cities 1800–50, see Adna Weber, *The Growth of Cities in the Nineteenth Century: A Study in Statistics*, New York 1899, pp. 44, 52–53.

44 A. S. Oberai, *Population Growth, Employment and Poverty in Third-World Mega-Cities: Analytical Policy Issues*, London 1993, p. 165.

an annual urbanization rate (3.5 to 4.0 percent) considerably higher
than the average of most European cities (2.1 percent) during peak
Victorian growth years?[45]

Part of the secret, of course, was that policies of agricultural dereg-
ulation and financial discipline enforced by the IMF and World Bank
continued to generate an exodus of surplus rural labor to urban slums
even as cities ceased to be job machines. As Deborah Bryceson, a
leading European Africanist, emphasizes in her summary of recent
agrarian research, the 1980s and 1990s were a generation of unprecedented upheaval in the global countryside:

> One by one national governments, gripped in debt, became subject to
> structural adjustment programmes (SAPs) and International Monetary
> Fund (IMF) conditionality. Subsidized, improved agricultural input
> packages and rural infrastructural building were drastically reduced. As
> the peasant "modernization" effort in Latin American and African
> nations was abandoned, peasant farmers were subjected to the interna-
> tional financial institutions' "sink-or-swim" economic strategy. National
> market deregulation pushed agricultural producers into global commod-
> ity markets where middle as well as poor peasants found it hard to
> compete. SAPs and economic liberalization policies represented the con-
> vergence of the worldwide forces of de-agrarianization and national
> policies promoting de-peasantization.[46]

As local safety nets disappeared, poor farmers became increasingly
vulnerable to any exogenous shock: drought, inflation, rising interest
rates, or falling commodity prices. (Or illness: an estimated 60 percent
of Cambodian small peasants who sell their land and move to the city
are forced to do so by medical debts.[47])

45 United Nations Economic Programme (UNEP), *African Environment Outlook:
Past, Present and Future Perspectives*, quoted in *Al Ahram Weekly* (Cairo), 2–8 October
2003; Alain Jacquemin, *Urban Development and New Towns in the Third World: Lessons from
the New Bombay Experience*, Aldershot 1999, p. 28.

46 Deborah Bryceson, "Disappearing Peasantries? Rural Labour Redundancy in
the Neo-Liberal Era and Beyond," in Bryceson, Kay, and Mooij, *Disappearing
Peasantries?*, pp. 304–05.

47 Sébastien de Dianous, "Les Damnés de la Terre du Cambodge," *Le Monde diplo-
matique* (September 2004), p. 20.

At the same time, rapacious warlords and chronic civil wars, often spurred by the economic dislocations of debt-imposed structural adjustment or foreign economic predators (as in the Congo and Angola), were uprooting whole countrysides. Cities – in spite of their stagnant or negative economic growth, and without necessary investment in new infrastructure, educational facilities or public-health systems – have simply harvested this world agrarian crisis. Rather than the classical stereotype of the labor-intensive countryside and the capital-intensive industrial metropolis, the Third World now contains many examples of capital-intensive countrysides and labor-intensive deindustrialized cities. "Overurbanization," in other words, is driven by the reproduction of poverty, not by the supply of jobs. This is one of the unexpected tracks down which a neoliberal world order is shunting the future.[48]

From Karl Marx to Max Weber, classical social theory believed that the great cities of the future would follow in the industrializing footsteps of Manchester, Berlin, and Chicago – and indeed Los Angeles, São Paulo, Pusan, and today, Ciudad Juárez, Bangalore, and Guangzhou have roughly approximated this canonical trajectory. Most cities of the South, however, more closely resemble Victorian Dublin, which, as historian Emmet Larkin has stressed, was unique amongst "all the slumdoms produced in the western world in the nineteenth century ... [because] its slums were not a product of the industrial revolution. Dublin, in fact, suffered more from the problems of de-industrialization than industrialization between 1800 and 1850."[49]

Likewise, Kinshasa, Luanda, Khartoum, Dar-es-Salaam, Guayaquil, and Lima continue to grow prodigiously despite ruined import-substitution industries, shrunken public sectors, and downwardly mobile middle classes. The global forces "pushing" people from the countryside – mechanization of agriculture in Java and India, food imports in Mexico, Haiti, and Kenya, civil war and drought throughout Africa, and everywhere the consolidation of small holdings into

48 See Josef Gugler, "Overurbanization Reconsidered," in Gugler, *Cities in the Developing World*, pp. 114–23.
49 Foreword to Jacinta Prunty, *Dublin Slums, 1800–1925: A Study in Urban Geography*, Dublin 1998, p. ix. Larkin, of course, forgets Dublin's Mediterranean counterpart: Naples.

large ones and the competition of industrial-scale agribusiness – seem to sustain urbanization even when the "pull" of the city is drastically weakened by debt and economic depression. As a result, rapid urban growth in the context of structural adjustment, currency devaluation, and state retrenchment has been an inevitable recipe for the mass production of slums. An International Labour Organization (ILO) researcher has estimated that the formal housing markets in the Third World rarely supply more than 20 percent of new housing stock, so out of necessity, people turn to self-built shanties, informal rentals, pirate subdivisions, or the sidewalks.[50] "Illegal or informal land markets," says the UN, "have provided the land sites for most additions to the housing stock in most cities of the South over the last 30 or 40 years."[51]

Since 1970, slum growth everywhere in the South has outpaced urbanization *per se*. Thus, looking back at late-twentieth-century Mexico City, urban planner Priscilla Connolly observes that "as much as 60 percent of the city's growth is the result of people, especially women, heroically building their own dwellings on unserviced peripheral land, while informal subsistence work has always accounted for a a large proportion of total employment."[52] São Paulo's *favelas* – a mere 1.2 percent of total population in 1973, but 19.8 percent in 1993 – grew throughout the 1990s at the explosive rate of 16.4 percent per year.[53] In the Amazon, one of the world's fastest-growing urban frontiers, 80 percent of city growth has been in shantytowns largely unserved by established utilities and municipal transport, thus making "urbanization" and "favelization" synonymous.[54]

The same trends are visible everywhere in Asia. Beijing police authorities estimate that 200,000 "floaters" (unregistered rural

50 Oberai, *Population Growth, Employment and Poverty in Third-World and Mega-Cities*, p. 13.

51 UN-HABITAT, *An Urbanising World: Global Report on Human Settlements*, Oxford 1996, p. 239.

52 Priscilla Connolly, "Mexico City: Our Common Future?," *Environment and Urbanization* 11:1 (April 1999), p. 56.

53 Ivo Imparato and Jeff Ruster, *Slum Upgrading and Participation: Lessons from Latin America*, Washington, D.C. 2003, p. 333.

54 John Browder and Brian Godfrey, *Rainforest Cities: Urbanization, Development, and Globalization of the Brazilian Amazon*, New York 1997, p. 130.

migrants) arrive each year, many of them crowded into illegal slums on the southern edge of the capital.[55] In South Asia, meanwhile, a study of the late 1980s showed that up to 90 percent of urban household growth took place in slums.[56] Karachi's sprawling *katchi abadi* (squatter) population doubles every decade, and Indian slums continue to grow 250 percent faster than overall population.[57] Mumbai's estimated annual housing deficit of 45,000 formal-sector units translates into a corresponding increase in informal slum dwellings.[58] Of the 500,000 people who migrate to Delhi each year, it is estimated that fully 400,000 end up in slums; by 2015 India's capital will have a slum population of more than 10 million. "If such a trend continues unabated," warns planning expert Gautam Chatterjee, "we will have only slums and no cities."[59]

The African situation, of course, is even more extreme. Africa's slums are growing at twice the speed of the continent's exploding cities. Indeed, an incredible 85 percent of Kenya's population growth between 1989 and 1999 was absorbed in the fetid, densely packed slums of Nairobi and Mombasa.[60] Meanwhile any realistic hope for the mitigation of Africa's urban poverty has faded from the official horizon. At the annual joint meeting of the IMF and World Bank in October 2004, Gordon Brown, UK Chancellor of the Exchequer and heir apparent to Tony Blair, observed that the UN's Millennium Development Goals for Africa, originally projected to be achieved by 2015, would not be attained for generations: "Sub-Saharan Africa will not achieve universal primary education until 2130, a 50 percent reduction in poverty in 2150

55 Yang Wenzhong and Wang Gongfan, "Peasant Movement: A Police Perspective," in Michael Dutton (ed.), *Streetlife China*, Cambridge 1998, p. 89.

56 Dileni Gunewardena, "Urban Poverty in South Asia: What Do We Know? What Do We Need To Know?", working paper, Conference on Poverty Reduction and Social Progress, Rajendrapur, Bangladesh, April 1999, p. 1.

57 Arif Hasan, "Introduction," in Akhtar Hameed Khan, *Orangi Pilot Project: Reminiscences and Reflections*, Karachi 1996, p. xxxiv.

58 Suketu Mehta, *Maximum City: Bombay Lost and Found*, New York 2004, p. 117.

59 Gautam Chatterjee, "Consensus versus Confrontation," *Habitat Debate* 8:2 (June 2002), p. 11. Statistic for Delhi from Rakesh K. Sinha, "New Delhi: The World's Shanty Capital in the Making," *OneWorld South Asia*, 26 August 2003.

60 Harvey Herr and Guenter Karl, "Estimating Global Slum Dwellers: Monitoring the Millenium Development Goal 7, Target 11," UN-HABITAT working paper, Nairobi 2003, p. 19.

and the elimination of avoidable infant deaths until 2165."[61] By 2015 Black Africa will have 332 million slum-dwellers, a number that will continue to double every fifteen years.[62]

Thus, the cities of the future, rather than being made out of glass and steel as envisioned by earlier generations of urbanists, are instead largely constructed out of crude brick, straw, recycled plastic, cement blocks, and scrap wood. Instead of cities of light soaring toward heaven, much of the twenty-first-century urban world squats in squalor, surrounded by pollution, excrement, and decay. Indeed, the one billion city-dwellers who inhabit postmodern slums might well look back with envy at the ruins of the sturdy mud homes of Çatal Hüyük in Anatolia, erected at the very dawn of city life nine thousand years ago.

61 Gordon Brown quoted in *Los Angeles Times*, 4 October 2004.
62 UN statistics quoted in John Vidal, "Cities Are Now the Frontline of Poverty," *Guardian*, 2 February 2005.

2

The Prevalence of Slums

> He let his mind drift as he stared at the city, half
> slum, half paradise. How could a place be so ugly
> and violent, yet beautiful at the same time?
>
> *Chris Abani*[1]

The astonishing prevalence of slums is the chief theme of *The Challenge of Slums*, a historic and somber report published in October 2003 by the United Nations Human Settlements Programme (UN-HABITAT). This first truly global audit of urban poverty, which follows in the famous footsteps of Friedrich Engels, Henry Mayhew, Charles Booth, and Jacob Riis, culminates two centuries of the scientific reconnaisance of slum life that began with James Whitelaw's 1805 *Survey of Poverty in Dublin*. It is also the long-awaited empirical counterpart to the World Bank's warnings in the 1990s that urban poverty would become the "most significant, and politically explosive, problem of the next century."[2]

The Challenge of Slums, a collaboration of more than one hundred researchers, integrates three novel sources of analysis and data. First, it is based on synoptic case-studies of poverty, slum conditions, and housing policy in 34 metropolises from Abidjan to Sydney; this project

---

1 Chris Abani, *Graceland*, New York 2004, p. 7.
2 Anqing Shi, "How Access to Urban Potable Water and Sewerage Connections Affects Child Mortality," Finance, Development Research Group, working paper, World Bank, January 2000, p. 14.

was coordinated for UN-HABITAT by the Development Planning Unit at University College London.[3] Secondly, it utilizes a unique comparative database for 237 cities worldwide created by the UN-HABITAT Urban Indicators Programme for the 2001 Istanbul + 5 Urban Summit.[4] And thirdly, it incorporates global household survey data that breaks new ground by including China and the ex-Soviet bloc. The UN authors acknowledge a particular debt to Branko Milanovic, the World Bank economist who pioneered these surveys as a powerful microscope for studying global inequality. (In one of his papers, Milanovic explains: "For the first time in human history, researchers have reasonably accurate data on the distribution of income or welfare [expenditures or consumption] amongst more than 90 percent of the world population."[5]) If the reports of the Intergovernmental Panel on Climate Change represent an unprecedented scientific consensus on the dangers of global warming, then *The Challenge of Slums* sounds an equally authoritative warning about the worldwide catastrophe of urban poverty.

But what is a "slum"? The first published definition reportedly occurs in the convict writer James Hardy Vaux's 1812 *Vocabulary of the Flash Language*, where it is synonymous with "racket" or "criminal trade."[6] By the cholera years of the 1830s and 1840s, however, the poor were living in slums rather than practicing them. Cardinal Wiseman, in his writings on urban reform, is sometimes given credit for transforming "slum" ("room in which low goings-on occurred") from street slang into a term comfortably used by genteel writers.[7] By mid-century slums were identified in France, America, and India, and were generally recognized as an international phenomenon. Connoisseurs and *flâneurs* debated where human degradation was most awful: Whitechapel or

3 University College London Development Planning Unit and UN-HABITAT, *Understanding Slums: Case Studies for the Global Report on Human Settlements* 2003, available at www.ucl.ac.uk/dpu-projects/Global_Report. Most of these studies are summarized in an appendix at the back of *The Challenge of Slums*. Missing, however, is the brilliant survey of Khartoum by Galal Eldin Eltayeb, deleted, one supposes, because of his characterization of the "Islamist, totalitarian regime."

4 See *Challenge*, p. 245.

5 Branko Milanovic, "True World Income Distribution, 1988 and 1993: First Calculation Based On Household Survey Alone," working paper, World Bank, New York 1999, n.p.

6 Prunty, *Dublin Slums*, p. 2.

7 J. A. Yelling, *Slums and Slum Clearance in Victorian London*, London 1986, p. 5.

La Chapelle, the Gorbals or the Liberties, Pig Alley or Mulberry Bend. In an 1895 survey of the "poor in the great cities," *Scribner's Magazine* voted Naples's *fondaci* as "the most ghastly human dwellings on the face of the earth," but Gorky was certain that Moscow's notorious Khitrov district was actually the "lower depths," while Kipling laughed and took his readers "deeper and deeper still" to Coolootollah, the "lowest sink of all" in Calcutta's "city of dreadful night."[8]

These classic slums were notoriously parochial and picturesquely local places, but reformers generally agreed with Charles Booth – the Dr. Livingstone of outcast London – that all slums were characterized by an amalgam of dilapidated housing, overcrowding, disease, poverty, and vice. For nineteenth-century liberals, of course, the moral dimension was decisive, and the slum was first and above all envisioned as a place where an incorrigible and feral social "residuum" rots in immoral and often riotous splendor; indeed, a vast literature titillated the Victorian middle classes with lurid tales from the dark side of town. "Savages," rhapsodized the Reverend Chapin in *Humanity in the City* (1854), "not in gloomy forests, but under the strength of gas-light, and the eyes of policemen; with war-whoops and clubs very much the same, and garments as fantastic and souls as brutal as any of their kindred at the antipodes."[9] Forty years later, the new US Department of Labor, in the first "scientific" survey of American tenement life (*The Slums of Baltimore, Chicago, New York, and Philadelphia*, 1894), still defined a slum as "an area of dirty back streets, especially when inhabited by a squalid and criminal population."[10]

A Global Slum Census

The authors of *The Challenge of Slums* discard these Victorian calumnies but otherwise preserve the classical definition of a slum, characterized

8 Robert Woods et al., *The Poor in Great Cities: Their Problems and What is Being Done to Solve Them*, New York 1895, p. 305 (*Scribners Magazine*); Blair Ruble, *Second Metropolis: Pragmatic Pluralism in Gilded Age Chicago, Silver Age Moscow, and Meiji Osaka*, Cambridge 2001, pp. 266–67 (Khitrov); Rudyard Kipling, *The City of Dreadful Night, and Other Poems*, London 1891, p. 71.

9 Rev. Edwin Chapin, *Humanity in the City*, New York 1854, p. 36.

10 See Carroll D. Wright, *The Slums of Baltimore, Chicago, New York, and Philadelphia*, Washington 1894, pp. 11–15.

by overcrowding, poor or informal housing, inadequate access to safe water and sanitation, and insecurity of tenure. This operational definition, officially adopted at a UN meeting in Nairobi in October 2002, is "restricted to the physical and legal characteristics of the settlement," and eschews the more difficult-to-measure "social dimensions," although it equates under most circumstances to economic and social marginality.[11] Encompassing peri-urban shantytowns as well as archetypal inner-city tenements, this multidimensional approach is in practice a very conservative gauge of what qualifies as a slum; many readers will be surprised by the UN's counter-experiential finding that only 19.6 percent of urban Mexicans live in slums (it is generally conceded by local experts that almost two-thirds of Mexicans live in *colonias populares* or older tenements). Even using this restrictive definition, the UN researchers estimate that there were at least 921 million slum-dwellers in 2001 and more than one billion in 2005: nearly equal to the population of the world when the young Engels first ventured onto the mean streets of St. Giles and Old Town Manchester in 1844.[12]

Indeed, neoliberal capitalism since 1970 has multiplied Dickens's notorious slum of Tom-all-Alone's in *Bleak House* by exponential powers. Residents of slums, while only 6 percent of the city population of the developed countries, constitute a staggering 78.2 percent of urbanites in the least-developed countries; this equals fully a third of the global urban population.

According to UN-HABITAT, the world's highest percentages of slum-dwellers are in Ethiopia (an astonishing 99.4 percent of the urban population), Chad (also 99.4 percent), Afghanistan (98.5 percent), and Nepal (92 percent). Bombay, with 10 to 12 million squatters and tenement-dwellers, is the global capital of slum-dwelling, followed by Mexico City and Dhaka (9 to 10 million each), and then Lagos, Cairo, Karachi, Kinshasa-Brazzaville, São Paulo, Shanghai, and Delhi (6 to 8 million each).[13]

11 *Challenge*, pp. 12–13.

12 UN-HABITAT executive director Anna Tibaijuka quoted in "More than One Billion People Call Urban Slums Their Home," *City Mayors Report*, February 2004: www.citymayors.com/report/slums.html.

13 UN-HABITAT, "Slums of the World: The Face of Urban Poverty in the New Millennium?," working paper, Nairobi 2003, annex 3.

Figure 6[14]
Largest Slum Populations by Country

	Slum % urban pop.	Number (millions)
China	37.8	193.8
India	55.5	158.4
Brazil	36.6	51.7
Nigeria	79.2	41.6
Pakistan	73.6	35.6
Bangladesh	84.7	30.4
Indonesia	23.1	20.9
Iran	44.2	20.4
Philippines	44.1	20.1
Turkey	42.6	19.1
Mexico	19.6	14.7
South Korea	37.0	14.2
Peru	68.1	13.0
USA	5.8	12.8
Egypt	39.9	11.8
Argentina	33.1	11.0
Tanzania	92.1	11.0
Ethiopia	99.4	10.2
Sudan	85.7	10.1
Vietnam	47.4	9.2

The fastest-growing slums are in the Russian Federation (especially ex-"socialist company towns" dependent on a single, now-closed industry) and the former Soviet republics, where urban dereliction has been bred at the same stomach-churning velocity as economic inequality and civic disinvestment. In 1993 the UN Urban Indicators Programme reported poverty rates of 80 percent or higher in both Baku (Azerbaijan)

14 These estimates are derived from the 2003 UN-HABITAT case-studies and an averaging of dozens of diverse sources too numerous to cite.

and Yerevan (Armenia).[15] Likewise, the concrete-and-steel Soviet-era urban core of Ulaanbaatar is now surrounded by a sea of 500,000 or more impoverished, former pastoralists living in tents called *gers*, few of whom manage to eat more than once a day.[16]

The poorest urban populations, however, are probably found in Luanda, Maputo, Kinshasa, and Cochabamba (Bolivia), where two-thirds or more of residents earn less than the cost of their minimum required daily nutrition.[17] In Luanda, where one quarter of the households have per capita consumptions of less than 75 cents per day, child mortality (under five) was a horrifying 320 per thousand in 1993 – the highest in the world.[18]

Not all urban poor, to be sure, live in slums, nor are all slum-dwellers poor; indeed, *The Challenge of Slums* underlines that in some cities the majority of the poor actually live outside the slums *stricto sensu*.[19] Although the two categories obviously overlap in their majority, the number of urban poor is considerably greater: at least one half of the world's urban population as defined by relative national poverty thresholds.[20] Approximately one quarter of urbanites (as surveyed in 1988), moreover, live in barely imaginable "absolute" poverty – somehow surviving on one dollar or less per day.[21] If UN data are accurate, the household per-capita income differential between a rich

15 Christiaan Grootaert and Jeanine Braithwaite, "The Determinants of Poverty in Eastern Europe and the Former Soviet Union," in Jeanine Braithwaite, Christiaan Grootaert, and Branko Milanovic (eds), *Poverty and Social Assistance in Transition Countries*, New York 2000, p. 49; UNCHS Global Indicators Database 1993.

16 Office of the Mayor, Ulaanbaatar City, "Urban Poverty Profile," submitted to World Bank, n.d., infocity.org/F2F/poverty/papers2/UB(Mongolia)%20Poverty. pdf.

17 Simon, 'Urbanization, Globalization, and Economic Crisis in Africa," p. 103; Jean-Luc Piermay, "Kinshasa: A Reprieved Mega-City?," in Rakodi, p. 236; and Carmen Ledo García, *Urbanization and Poverty in the Cities of the National Economic Corridor in Bolivia*, Delft 2002, p. 175 (60% of Cochabamba on dollar per day or less).

18 Alternately, Luanda's child mortality is *400* times higher than that of Rennes, France, the city with the lowest under-5-years death rate (Shi, "How Access to Urban Portable Water Sewerage Connections Affects Child Mortality," p. 2).

19 *Challenge*, p. 28.

20 Kavita Datta and Gareth A. Jones, "Preface," in Datta and Jones (eds), *Housing and Finance in Developing Countries*, London 1999, p. xvi. In Kolkata, for example, the poverty line is defined as the monetary equivalent of 2,100 calories of nutrition per day. Thus the poorest man in Europe would most likely be a rich man in Kolkata and vice versa.

21 World Bank report quoted in Ahmed Soliman, *A Possible Way Out: Formalizing Housing Informality in Egyptian Cities*, Lanham (md) 2004, p. 125.

city like Seattle and a very poor city like Ibadan is as great as *739 to 1* – an incredible inequality.[22]

Accurate statistics are in fact difficult to come by, because poor and slum populations are often deliberately and sometimes massively under-counted by officials. In the late 1980s, for example, Bangkok had an official poverty rate of only 5 percent, yet surveys found nearly a quarter of the population (1.16 million) living in 1000 slums and squatter camps.[23] Likewise the government of Mexico claimed in the 1990s that only one in ten urbanites was truly poor, despite uncontested UN data that showed nearly 40 percent living on less than $2 per day.[24] Indonesian and Malaysian statistics are also notorious for disguising urban poverty. The official figure for Jakarta, where most researchers estimate that one quarter of the population are poor *kampung* dwellers, is simply absurd: less than 5 percent.[25] In Malaysia, geographer Jonathan Rigg complains that the official poverty line "fails to take account of the higher cost of urban living" and deliberately undercounts the Chinese poor.[26] Urban sociologist Erhard Berner, meanwhile, believes that poverty estimates for Manila are purposefully obfuscated, and that at least one eighth of the slum population is uncounted.[27]

A Slum Typology

There are probably more than 200,000 slums on earth, ranging in pop-ulation from a few hundred to more than a million people. The five great metropolises of South Asia (Karachi, Mumbai, Delhi, Kolkata, and Dhaka) alone contain about 15,000 distinct slum communities whose total population exceeds 20 million. "Megaslums" arise when shanty-towns and squatter communities merge in continuous belts of informal housing and poverty, usually on the urban periphery. Mexico City, for

22 Shi, "How Access to Urban Potable Water and Sewerage Connections Affects Child Mortality," Appendix 3, derived from UNCHS Global Urban Indicators Database, 1993. A decimal point may be misplaced in the Ibadan figure.

23 Jonathan Rigg, *Southeast Asia: A Region in Transition*, London 1991, p. 143.

24 Imparato and Ruster, *Slum Upgrading and Participation*, p. 52.

25 Paul McCarthy, "Jakarta, Indonesia," UN-HABITAT Case Study, London 2003, pp. 7–8.

26 Rigg, *Southeast Asia*, p. 119.

27 Erhard Berner, *Defending a Place in the City: Localities and the Struggle for Urban Land in Metro Manila*, Quezon City 1997, pp. 21, 25, 26.

example, in 1992 had an estimated 6.6 million low-income people living contiguously in 348 square kilometers of informal housing.[28] Most of the poor in Lima, likewise, live in three great peripheral *conos* radiating from the central city; such huge spatial concentrations of urban poverty are also common in Africa and the Middle East. In South Asia, on the other hand, the urban poor tend to live in a much larger number of distinct slums more widely dispersed throughout the urban fabric in patterns with an almost fractal complexity. In Kolkata, for instance, thousands of *thika bustees* – nine hutments of five huts each, with 45-square-meter rooms shared, on average, by an incredible 13.4 people – are intermixed with a variety of other residential statuses and landuses.[29] In Dhaka, it probably makes more sense to consider the nonslum areas as enclaves in an overwhelming matrix of extreme poverty.

Although some slums have long histories – Rio de Janeiro's first *favela*, Morro de Providencia, was founded in the 1880s – most megaslums have grown up since the 1960s. Ciudad Nezahualcóyotl, for example, had barely 10,000 residents in 1957; today this poor suburb of Mexico City has three million inhabitants. Sprawling Manshiet Nasr, outside Cairo, originated as a camp for construction workers building the suburb of Nasr City in the 1960s, while Karachi's vast hill slum of Orangi/Baldia, with its mixed population of Muslim refugees from India and Pathans from the Afghan border, was founded in 1965. Villa El Salvador – one of Lima's biggest *barriadas* – was established in 1971 under the sponsorship of Peru's military government, and within a few years had a population of more than 300,000.

Everywhere in the Third World, housing choice is a hard calculus of confusing trade-offs. As the anarchist architect John Turner famously pointed out, "Housing is a verb." The urban poor have to solve a complex equation as they try to optimize housing cost, tenure security, quality of shelter, journey to work, and sometimes, personal safety. For some people, including many pavement-dwellers, a location near a job – say, in a produce market or train station – is even more important than a roof. For others, free or nearly free land is worth epic commutes from the edge to the center. And for everyone the worst situation is a

28 Keith Pezzoli, *Human Settlements and Planning for Ecological Sustainability: The Case of Mexico City*, Cambridge 1998, p. 13.
29 Nitai Kundu, "Kolkata, India," UN-HABITAT Case Study, London 2003, p. 7.

Figure 7 30 Largest Megaslums (2005)[30]

	(Millions)			(Millions)
1. Neza/Chalco/Izta (Mexico City)[31]	4.0	16. Dharavi (Mumbai)		0.8
2. Libertador (Caracas)	2.2	17. Kibera (Nairobi)		0.8
3. El Sur/Ciudad Bolívar (Bogotá)	2.0	18. El-Alto (La Paz)		0.8
4. San Juan de Lurigancho (Lima)[32]	1.5	19. City of the Dead (Cairo)		0.8
5. Cono Sur (Lima)[33]	1.5	20. Sucre (Caracas)		0.6
6. Ajegunle (Lagos)	1.5	21. Islamshahr (Tehran)[35]		0.6
7. Sadr City (Baghdad)	1.5	22. Tlalpan (Mexico City)		0.6
8. Soweto (Gauteng)	1.5	23. Inanda INK (Durban)		0.5
9. Gaza (Palestine)	1.3	24. Manshiet Nasr (Cairo)		0.5
10. Orangi Township (Karachi)	1.2	25. Altindağ (Ankara)		0.5
11. Cape Flats (Cape Town)[34]	1.2	26. Mathare (Nairobi)		0.5
12. Pikine (Dakar)	1.2	27. Aguas Blancas (Cali)		0.5
13. Imbaba (Cairo)	1.0	28. Agege (Lagos)		0.5
14. Ezbet El-Haggana (Cairo)	1.0	29. Cité-Soleil (Port-au-Prince)		0.5
15. Cazenga (Luanda)	0.8	30. Mastna (Kinshasa)		0.5

30 Scores of sources were consulted and median figures were chosen over extremes.

31 Includes Nezahualcoyotl (1.5 million), Chimalhuacan (250,000), Chalco (300,000), Iztapalapa (1.5 million), Chimalhuacan (250,000), and 14 other contiguous delegations and *municipios* in the southeast quadrant of the metropolis.

32 Includes S. J. de L. (750,000), Comas (500,000), and Independencia (200,000).

33 "Cono Sur" = Villa El Salvador (350,000), San Juan de Miraflores (400,000) and Villa María de Triunfo (400,000).

34 "Cape Flats", Khayelitsha (400,000), Mitchell's Plain (250,000), Crossroads (180,000), and smaller townships (from 1996 Census).

35 Islamshahr (350,000) plus Chahar Dangeh (250,000).

bad, expensive location without municipal services or security of tenure. In Turner's celebrated model, based on his work in Peru in the 1960s, rural migrants first move from the province to the city center – location at any price – to find jobs; then, with employment security, they move to the periphery, where ownership is attainable. This progress from (in his terminology) "bridgeheader" to "consolidator" is, of course, an idealization that may only reflect a historically transient situation in one continent or country.[36]

In a more sophisticated analysis, housing expert Ahmed Soliman discusses four basic shelter strategies for the poor in Cairo. First, if access to central job markets is paramount, the household can consider renting an apartment; the rental tenements offer centrality and security of tenure, but are expensive and hold out no hope of eventual ownership. The second option is centrally located but informal shelter: a situation described by Soliman as "a very small room or rooftop with a location with a poor quality environment and a cheap rent, or no rent at all, with good access to job opportunities but with no hope of secure tenure. Such illegal dwellers will eventually be forced to move to squatter camps or semi-informal housing."[37]

The third and cheapest housing solution is to squat on publicly owned land, usually on Cairo's desert outskirts and almost always downwind of pollution; negative trade-offs include the very high cost of commuting to work and the government's neglect of infrastructure. "For example, the squatter area in El Dekhila district has been a settlement for 40 years with no public action or intervention from the local authority." The fourth solution, eventually preferred by most poor Cairenes, is to buy a house site in one of the vast semi-informal developments (often on land purchased from Bedouins or peasant villages) with legal tenure but without official building authorization. Although far from jobs, such sites are secure and, after considerable community mobilization and political negotiation, are usually provided with basic municipal services.[38]

36 See John Turner, "Housing Priorities, Settlement Patterns and Urban Development in Modernizing Countries," *Journal of the American Institute of Planners* 34 (1968), pp. 354–63; and "Housing as a Verb," in John Turner and Robert Fichter (eds), *Freedom to Build: Dweller Control of the Housing Process*, New York 1972.

37 Soliman, *A Possible Way Out*, pp. 119–20

38 Ibid.

Similar rational-choice models can be specified for all cities, generating a huge array of locally specific tenure and settlement types. The typology displayed in Figure 8 is an analytic simplification that abstracts from locally important features for the sake of global comparability. Other analysts might give priority to legal housing status (*formal* versus *informal*), but I think most urban newcomers' first decision is whether or not they can afford to locate near the principal job concentrations (*core* versus *periphery*).

Figure 8
Slum Typology

A. Metro Core

---

    1. *Formal*
        (a) tenements
            (i) hand-me-downs
            (ii) built for poor
        (b) public housing
        (c) hostels, flophouses, etc.

    2. *Informal*
        (a) squatters
            (i) authorized
            (ii) unauthorized
        (b) pavement-dwellers

B. Periphery

---

    1. *Formal*
        (a) private rental
        (b) public housing

    2. *Informal*
        (a) pirate subdivisions
            (i) owner-occupied
            (ii) rental
        (b) squatters
            (i) authorized (including site-and-service)
            (ii) unauthorized

    3. *Refugee Camps*

In the First World, of course, there is an archetypal distinction between "donut"-shaped American cities, with poor people concentrated in derelict cores and inner suburbs, and European "saucer" cities, with immigrant and unemployed populations marooned in highrise housing on the urban outskirts. The American poor, so to speak, live on Mercury; the European poor, on Neptune or Pluto. As Figure 9 illustrates, Third World slum-dwellers occupy a variety of urban orbits, with the greatest concentration in lowrise peripheries. In contrast to Europe, public housing for the poor in the South is an exception – Hong Kong, Singapore, China – rather than the rule. Somewhere between one fifth and one third of the urban poor live within or close to the urban core, mainly in older rental multifamily housing.

1. Inner-City Poverty

In North American and European cities, there is a basic distinction between "hand-me-down" housing, such as Harlem brownstones and Dublin Georgians, and built-for-the-poor tenements, such as Berlin's

Figure 9
Where the Poor Live[39]
(percent of poor population)

	Inner-city slums	Peripheral slums
Karachi	34	66
Khartoum	17	83
Lusaka	34	66
Mexico City	27	73
Mumbai	20	80
Rio de Janeiro	23	77

39   Keith Pezzoli, "Mexico's Urban Housing Environments," in Brian Aldrich and Ranvinder Sandhu (eds.), *Housing the Urban Poor: Policy and Practice in Developing Countries*, London 1995, p. 145; K. Sivaramakrishnan, "Urban Governance: Changing Realities," in Michael Cohen et al., (eds), *Preparing for the Urban Future: Global Pressures and Local Forces*, Washington, D.C. 1997, p. 229; Mariana Fix, Pedro Arantes, and Giselle M. Tanaka, "São-Paulo, Brazil," UN-HABITAT Case Study, London 2003, p. 9; Jacquemin, *Urban Development and New Towns in the Third World*, p. 89.

Mietskaserne and the Lower East Side's notorious "dumbbells." Although rare in the newer cities of Africa, hand-me-down housing, including converted colonial mansions and Victorian villas, is quite common in Latin America and in some Asian cities. Whatever their former splendor, most of Guatemala City's *palomares*, Rio's *avenidas*, Buenos Aires's and Santiago's *conventillos*, Quito's *quintas*, and Old Havana's *cuarterias* are now dangerously dilapidated and massively overcrowded. Architect David Glasser visited a former single-family villa in Quito, for example, that housed 25 families and 128 people but had no functioning municipal services.[40] Although rapidly being gentrified or torn down, some of Mexico City's *vecindades* are still as crowded as Casa Grande, the famous tenement block housing 700 people which anthropologist Oscar Lewis made famous in *The Children of Sanchez* (1961).[41] In Asia the equivalents are the decayed (and now municipalized) *zamindar* mansions of Kolkata and the poetically named "slum gardens" of Colombo which constitute 18 percent of the city's rundown housing.[42] The largest-scale instance, although now reduced in size and population by urban renewal, is probably Beijing's inner slum, the Old City, which consists of Ming and Qing courtyard housing lacking modern facilities.[43]

Often, as in São Paulo's once-fashionable Campos Eliseos or parts of Lima's colonial cityscape, whole bourgeois neighborhoods have devolved into slums. In Algiers's famous seaside district of Bab-el-Oued, on the other hand, the indigenous poor have replaced the *colon* working class. Although the dominant global pattern is the eviction of the poor from the center, some Third World cities reproduce US-style urban segregation, with the postcolonial middle classes fleeing from the core to gated suburbs and so-called "edge cities." This has long been the case in Kingston, where one quarter of a million poor people inhabit the crime-ridden but culturally dynamic Downtown, while the middle

40 David Glasser, "The Growing Housing Crisis in Ecuador" in Carl Patton (ed.), *Spontaneous Shelter: International Perspectives and Prospects*, Philadelphia 1988, p. 150.

41 Oscar Lewis, *The Children of Sanchez: Autobiography of a Mexican Family*, New York 1961.

42 Kalinga Tudor Silva and Karunatissia Athukorala, *The Watta-Dwellers: A Sociological Study of Selected Urban Low-Income Communities in Sri Lanka*, Lanham (Md.) 1991, p. 20.

43 Feng-hsuan Hsueh, *Beijing: The Nature and the Planning of the Chinese Capital City*, Chichester 1995, pp. 182–84.

classes live Uptown. Likewise, as the rich began to abandon the center of Montevideo in the 1970s and 1980s for the more attractive neighborhoods of the east coast, homeless people moved into abandoned homes and derelict hotels. This succession dynamic occurred much earlier in Lima: the middle and upper classes began leaving the historic city center after the large earthquake of 1940; a crackdown on street vending in 1996, however, supposedly inaugurated a government-led *reconquista* of the area from the Andean working classes.[44] In Johannesburg, meanwhile, corporate offices and upscale stores have fled in recent years to the mainly white northern suburbs. With its mixture of slum tenements and middle-class apartment complexes, the central business district – once the financial capital of the entire continent – has become a center of informal trading and African micro-enterprises.[45]

The most unusual example of an inherited housing supply is undoubtedly Cairo's City of the Dead, where one million poor people use Mameluke tombs as prefabricated housing components. The huge graveyard, the burial site of generations of sultans and emirs, is a walled urban island surrounded by congested motorways. The original residents, in the eighteenth century, were tombkeepers for rich Cairene families, followed by quarry workers, and then, in the modern era, by refugees uprooted from Sinai and Suez during the 1967 war. "The invaders," observes Jeffrey Nedoroscik, a researcher at the American University in Cairo, "have adapted the tombs in creative ways to meet the needs of the living. Cenotaphs and grave markers are used as desks, headboards, tables, and shelves. String is hung between gravestones to set laundry to dry."[46] Elsewhere in Cairo (formerly a city with 29 synagogues), smaller groups of squatters have taken over abandoned Jewish cemeteries. "On a visit in the 1980s," writes journalist Max Rodenbeck, "I found a young couple with four children cozily installed in a particularly splendid neopharaonic vault. The tomb dwellers had unsealed the columbarium inside, finding it made convenient

44 Hans Harms, "To Live in the City Centre: Housing and Tenants in Central Neighborhoods of Latin American Cities," *Environment and Urbanization* 9:2 (October 1997), pp. 197–98.

45 See Jo Beall, Owen Crankshaw, and Susan Parnell, *Uniting a Divided City: Governance and Social Exclusion in Johannesburg*, London 2002, esp. chapter 7.

46 Jeffrey Nedoroscik, *The City of the Dead: A History of Cairo's Cemetary Communities*, Westport 1997, p. 43.

built-in shelving for clothes, cooking pots, and a color TV set."[47]

In most of the Third World, however, hand-me-down housing is less common than tenements and purpose-built rental housing. In colonial India, the tightfisted refusal of the Raj to provide minimal water supplies and sanitation to urban Indian neighborhoods went hand in hand with a *de facto* housing policy that relied on the greed of local landlord elites, who built the horribly overcrowded, unsanitary, but highly profitable tenements that still house millions of Indians.[48] In Mumbai the typical *chawl* (75 percent of the city's formal housing stock) is a dilapidated, one-room rental dwelling that crams a household of six people into 15 square meters; the latrine is usually shared with six other families.[49]

Like Mumbai's *chawls*, Lima's *callejones* were built specifically to be rented to the poor, many by the city's leading slumlord, the Catholic Church.[50] In the main they are miserable dwellings made out of adobe or *quincha* (wood frames filled with mud and straw), which deteriorate rapidly and are often dangerously unstable. One study of *callejones* showed 85 people sharing a water tap and 93 using the same latrine.[51] Likewise, until the peripheral *favela* boom that began in the early 1980s, most of São Paulo's poor were traditionally housed in rented rooms in inner-city tenements known as *cortiços*, half of which were built as tenements, the other half hand-me-downs from the urban bourgeoisie.[52]

Buenos Aires's wood-and-sheetmetal *inquilinatos* were originally built for poor Italian immigrants in dockland *barrios* such as La Boca and Barracas. Since the last debt crisis, however, many formerly middle-class families have been forced out of their private apartments and now crowd into a single *inquilinato* room, sharing a communal kitchen and bathroom with five or more other families. Buenos Aires over the last crisis-ridden decade has also acquired an estimated 100,000-plus squatters in abandoned buildings and factories in the central Federal District alone.[53]

47 Max Rodenbeck, *Cairo: The City Victorious*, New York 1999, pp. 158–59.

48 See Nandini Gooptu, *The Politics of the Urban Poor in Early Twentieth-Century India*, Cambridge (UK) 2001, pp. 91–102.

49 Jacquemin, *Urban Development and New Towns in the Third World*, p. 89.

50 Geert Custers, "Inner-city Rental Housing in Lima: A Portrayal and an Explanation," *Cities* 18:1 (2001), p. 252.

51 Ibid, p. 254.

52 Fix, Arantes, and Tanaka, "São Paulo, Brazil."

53 David Keeling, *Buenos Aires: Global Dreams, Local Crises*, Chichester 1996, p. 100.

In sub-Saharan Africa, in contrast, older inner-city tenement housing is more or less absent. "In the ex-British colonies," geographer Michael Edwards points out, "tenements are rare because cities lack a historic urban core. Although renting was near universal among Africans prior to independence, tenants lived in hostels (if single men) or township houses (if families) rather than in tenements."[54] In older parts of Accra and Kumasi, customary landownership is still common; and while renting is dominant, clan ties usually preclude the rack-renting so pervasive in Lagos and Nairobi. Indeed, the kinship-based housing compound, where poor people dwell in extended family houses with wealthier kinfolk, makes most Ghanaian neighborhoods more economically diverse than their counterparts in other African cities.[55]

Other inner-city housing options, both formal and informal, include an ingenious spectrum of illegal additions, flophouses, squats, and mini-shantytowns. In Hong Kong one quarter of a million people live in illegal additions on rooftops or filled-in airwells in the center of buildings. The worst conditions, however, are endured by the so-called "caged men" – "a local term referring to bedspaces for singles, the 'cage' suggested by the tendency of these tenants to erect wire covering for their bed spaces to prevent theft of their belongings. The average number of residents in one of these bedspace apartments is 38.3 and the average per capita living space is 19.4 square feet."[56] Variants on the old-fashioned American "flophouse" are also familiar in most Asian big cities. In Seoul, for example, evictees from the city's traditional squatter settlements, as well as unemployed people, have crowded into the estimated 5000 *Jjogbang* which rent beds by the day and provide only one toilet per 15 residents.[57]

Some impoverished inner-city-dwellers live in the air. One out of ten inhabitants of Phnom Penh sleeps on a roof, as do an incredible

54 Michael Edwards, "Rental Housing and the Urban Poor" in Philip Amis and Peter Lloyd (eds), *Housing Africa's Urban Poor*, Manchester 1990, p. 263.

55 A. Graham Tipple and David Korboe, "Housing Poverty in Ghana," in Aldrich and Sandhu, *Housing the Urban Poor*, pp. 359–61.

56 Alan Smart, *Making Room: Squatter Clearance in Hong Kong*, Hong Kong 1992, p. 63.

57 Seong-Kyu Ha, "The Urban Poor, Rental Accomodation, Housing Policy in Korea," *Cities* 19:3 (2002), pp. 197–98.

1.5 million Cairenes and 200,000 Alexandrians.[58] It is cooler in Cairo's so-called "second city" than inside the tenements, but roof-dwellers are more exposed to air pollution from traffic and cement plants, as well as dust from the desert. Floating slums, meanwhile, although still common in Southeast Asia, are rapidly disappearing in Hong Kong, where boats once provided 10 percent of the Crown Colony's shelter, mainly for Tanka and Hakka people considered inferior by the majority Han.[59]

Finally, there is the street itself. Los Angeles is the First World capital of homelessness, with an estimated 100,000 homeless people, including an increasing number of families, camped on downtown streets or living furtively in parks and amongst freeway landscaping. The biggest population of pavement-dwellers in the Third World is probably in Mumbai, where 1995 research estimated one million living on the sidewalks.[60] The traditional stereotype of the Indian pavement-dweller is a destitute peasant, newly arrived from the countryside, who survives by parasitic begging, but as research in Mumbai has revealed, almost all (97 percent) have at least one breadwinner, 70 percent have been in the city at least six years, and one third had been evicted from a slum or a *chawl*.[61] Indeed, many pavement-dwellers are simply workers – rickshaw men, construction laborers, and market porters – who are compelled by their jobs to live in the otherwise unaffordable heart of the metropolis.[62]

Living in the street, however, is rarely free. As Erhard Berner emphasizes, "even sidewalk dwellers in India or the Philippines have to pay regular fees to policemen or syndicates."[63] In Lagos entrepreneurs

58 Asian Coalition for Housing Rights, "Building an Urban Poor People's Movement in Phnom Penh, Cambodia," *Environment and Urbanization* 12:2 (October 2001), p. 63; Soliman, *A Possible Way Out*, p. 119.
59 Bruce Taylor, "Hong Kong's Floating Settlements," in Patton, *Spontaneous Shelter*, p. 198.
60 Minar Pimple and Lysa John, "Security of Tenure: Mumbai's Experience," in Durand-Lasserve and Royston, *Holding Their Ground*, p. 78.
61 Jacquemin, *Urban Development and New Towns in the New World*, p. 90.
62 Frederic Thomas, *Calcutta Poor: Elegies on a City Above Pretense*, Armonk (NY) 1997, pp. 47, 136.
63 Erhard Berner, "Learning from Informal Markets," in David Westendorff and Deborah Eade (eds), *Development and Cities: Essays from Development Practice*, Oxford 2002, p. 233.

rent out wheelbarrows, borrowed from construction sites, as ersatz beds for the homeless.[64]

2. Pirate Urbanization

The majority of the world's urban poor no longer live in inner cities. Since 1970 the larger share of world urban population growth has been absorbed by slum communities on the periphery of Third World cities. Sprawl has long ceased to be a distinctively North American phenomenon, if it ever was. The "horizontalization" of poor cities is often as astonishing as their population growth: Khartoum in 1988, for example, was *48* times larger in developed area than in 1955.[65] Indeed, the suburban zones of many poor cities are now so vast as to suggest the need to rethink *peripherality*. In Lusaka, for example, the outlying shantytowns house two thirds of the city's population – leading one writer to suggest that "these compounds are called 'peri-urban' but in reality it is the city proper that is peripheral."[66] The Turkish sociologist Çağlar Keyder makes a similar point about the *gecekondus* that surround Istanbul: "In fact, it would not be too inaccurate to think of Istanbul as a conglomerate of such *gecekondu* districts with limited organic unity. As new *gecekondu* areas are added – inevitably to the outer perimeters – more nodes are strung on the web in a serial manner."[67]

In the sprawling cities of the Third World, then, "periphery" is a highly relative, time-specific term: today's urban edge, abutting fields, forest, or desert, may tomorrow become part of a dense metropolitan core. With the exception of East Asia, where there are significant inventories of peripheral state-built housing (like Beijing's older industrial suburbs of Shijingshan, Fengtai, and Changxiandian), edge development in Third World urban areas takes two principal forms: squatter settlements and – to use the evocative Colombian term –

64 Amy Otchet, "Lagos: The Survival of the Determined." *UNESCO Courier*, 1999.
65 Galal Eldin Eltayeb, "Khartoum, Sudan," UN-HABITAT Case Studies, London 2003, p. 2.
66 Sivaramakrishnan, "Urban Governance," in Cohen, *Preparing for the Urban Future*, p. 229.
67 Çağlar Keyder, "The Housing Market from Informal to Global," in Keyder (ed.), *Istanbul: Between the Global and the Local*, Lanham (Md.) 1999, p. 149.

urbanizaciones piratas. Both generate "shantytown" landscapes with large percentages of self-built, substandard housing with poor infrastructure provision. Although pirate subdivisions are often mislabeled as squatter communities, there are fundamental differences.

Squatting, of course, is the possession of land without sale or title. "No-cost" peripheral land has often been discussed as the magic secret of Third World urbanism: a huge unplanned subsidy to the very poor. Squatting is seldom without up-front costs, however. Squatters very often are coerced to pay considerable bribes to politicians, gangsters, or police to gain access to sites, and they may continue to pay such informal "rents" in money and/or votes for years. In addition, there are the punitive costs of an unserviced location far from an urban center. Indeed, when all the costs are added up – as Erhard Berner points out in his study of Manila – squatting is not necessarily cheaper than buying a plot. Its principal attraction is the "possibility of incremental development and building improvement which leads to a [phased] spreading of the costs."[68]

Squatting can sometimes become front-page political drama. In Latin America from the 1960s to the 1980s, as well as in Egypt, Turkey, and South Africa at different times, squatting took the form of land invasions, often with the support of radical groups or, more rarely, populist national governments (Peru in the 1960s; Nicaragua in the 1980s). Dependent upon public sympathy, land occupiers have traditionally targeted undeveloped public land or the estates of a single large landowner (who sometimes is later compensated). Often squatting becomes a prolonged test of will and endurance against the repressive apparatus of the state. "It is not unusual," wrote a UCLA research team about Caracas in the 1970s, "to hear of a squatter settlement that has been constructed overnight, torn down by the police the next day, constructed again the following night, destroyed again, and reconstructed until the authorities tire of fighting."[69] Similarly, in her novel *Berji Kristin: Tales from the Garbage Hills*, Turkish writer Latife Tekin explains why Istanbul's slums are called *gecekondus* ("set up overnight"): the heroic squatters of "Flower Hill" build and rebuild

68 Berner, *Defending a Place*, pp. 236–37.
69 Kenneth Karst, Murray Schwartz, and Audrey Schwartz, *The Evolution of Law in the Barrios of Caracas*, Los Angeles 1973, pp. 6–7.

every shanty by night, because the authorities tear them down each morning. Only after a Homeric siege of 37 days does the government finally relent and allow the new *gecekondu* to take root on a garbage mountain.[70]

Most squatter communities, however, are the result of what sociologist Asef Bayat, writing about Tehran and Cairo, has called the "quiet encroachment of the ordinary": the small-scale, nonconfrontational infiltration of edge or interstitial sites. Unlike poor peasants' "Brechtian mode of class struggle and resistance" – famously evoked in studies by James Scott – these struggles of the urban poor are "not merely defensive," but, according to Bayat, "surreptitiously offensive" as they ceaselessly aim to expand the survival space and rights of the disenfranchised.[71] Such encroachments, as we shall see in the next chapter, are frequently synchronized to a favorable opportunity for land occupation, such as a tight election, natural disaster, *coup d'état*, or revolution.

Squatting of all varieties probably reached its peak in Latin America, the Middle East, and Southeast Asia during the 1970s. Today squatting, *stricto sensu*, continues primarily in low-value urban land, usually in hazardous or extremely marginal locations such as floodplains, hillsides, swamps, or contaminated brownfields. As the urban economist Eileen Stillwaggon notes: "Essentially, squatters occupy no-rent land, land that has so little worth that no one bothers to have or enforce property right to it."[72] In Buenos Aires, for instance, most of the *villas de emergencia* – often settled by illegal Bolivian and Paraguayan immigrants – are located along the reeking banks of the heavily polluted Río de la Reconquista and Río de la Matanza. "Stagnant water and untreated sewage," writes geographer David Keeling of a visit to a typical *villa* along the Río Reconquista, "created an overpowering stench, and the entire area was overrun with rats, mosquitos, flies, and other insects." The *villas* are tolerated only because such brownfield sites are temporarily worthless in a depressed economy.[73] Likewise, in Caracas precarious

70 Latife Tekin, *Berji Kristin: Tales from the Garbage Hills*, London 1996 (published in Turkey in 1984).

71 Asef Bayat, "Un-civil Society: The Politics of the 'Informal People'," *Third World Quarterly* 18:1 (1997), pp. 56–57.

72 Eileen Stillwaggon, *Stunted Lives, Stagnant Economies: Poverty, Disease and Underdevelopment*, New Brunswick (NJ) 1998, p. 67.

73 Keeling, *Buenos Aires*, pp. 102–05.

squatter *ranchos* continue to inch their way up rugged and landslide-prone mountain slopes that no sane developer would ever consider to be marketable real estate. Squatting has become a wager against inevitable disaster.

But flat peripheral land, even desert, has market value, and today most low-income settlement on the urban edge, although often characterized as squatting, actually operates through an invisible real estate market.[74] This "pirate urbanization" was carefully studied for the first time by the World Bank's Rakesh Mohan and his research team in Bogotá at the end of the 1970s:

> ... these *pirata* subdivision settlements did not result from land invasions: the land has actually changed hands through legal purchases. It is the subdivision itself that is usually illegal. But these settlements are better described as extralegal rather than illegal. Low-, lower-middle-, and middle-income families, having been shut out of the formal housing market, buy lots from entrepreneurs who acquire tracts of undeveloped land and subdivide them without conforming to zoning laws, subdivision regulations, or service provision standards. The lots sold usually provide only a bare minimum of services, often nothing more than some streets and water standposts. Typically, this rudimentary infrastructure is incrementally upgraded after initial settlement has taken place.[75]

Pirate urbanization is, in effect, the privatization of squatting. In an important 1990 study, housing experts Paul Baróss and Jan van der Linden characterized pirate settlements, or "substandard commercial residential subdivisions" (SCRSs), as the new norm in poor people's housing. In contrast to true squatters, the residents of a pirate subdivision have obtained either a legal or *de facto* title to their plot. In the case of a legal title, the subdivider is usually a speculator, a *latifundista* or large farmer, a rural commune (for example, a Mexican *ejido*), or customary entity (such as a Bedouin tribe or village council). The landowners –

74 Paul Baróss, "Sequencing Land Development: The Price Implications of Legal and Illegal Settlement Growth," in Paul Baróss and Jan van der Linden (eds), *The Transformation of Land Supply Systems in Third World Cities*, Aldershot 1990, p. 69.

75 Rakesh Mohan, *Understanding the Developing Metropolis: Lessons from the City Study of Bogotá and Cali, Colombia*, New York 1994, pp. 152–53.

as in the case of an *asentamiento* in suburban Buenos Aires discussed by David Keeling – may even encourage residents to organize themselves as a land invasion in the shrewd expectation that the state will be forced to guarantee eventual compensation as well as infrastructural development.[76]

In the second case of *de facto* tenure, the land is usually state-owned, but settlers have purchased a guarantee of tenure from powerful politicians, tribal leaders, or criminal cartels (for example, the Triads, who are the major informal property developers in Hong Kong).[77] Another notorious example are Karachi's *dalals*, whom Akhtar Hameed Khan, the founder of the famed Orangi Pilot Project, describes as "private entrepreneurs who have learnt the art of collaborating with and manipulating our greedy politicians and bureaucrats. With their costly patronage, the *dalals* secure possession of tracts of [public] land, buy protection against eviction, and obtain water and transport facilities."[78] The *dalals* (the word can mean "pimp" as well as "middleman") dominate the *katchi abadis* – the pirate subdivisions like Orangi – that house almost half of Karachi's population.[79]

Although the actual houses are almost always formally unauthorized by local government, pirate subdivisions, unlike many squatter camps, are generally subdivided into uniform lots with conventional street grids; services are rudimentary or nonexistent, however, and the selling price is based on residents' ability to bootleg or negotiate their own infrastructural improvements. "In short," write Baróss and van der Linden, "planned layouts, low service levels, suburban locations, high-tenure security, non-conformity with urban development plans, and self-help housing are the generic features of SCRSs."[80] With appropriate local wrinkles, this definition characterizes edge development in Mexico City, Bogotá, São Paulo, Cairo, Tunis, Harare, Karachi, Manila, and hundreds of other cities – including, in the Organization for

76 Keeling, *Buenos Aires*, pp. 107–08.

77 On Triads' control of squatting, see Smart, *Making Room*, p. 114.

78 Khan, *Orangi Pilot Project*, p. 72.

79 Urban Resource Center, "Urban Poverty and Transport: A Case Study from Karachi," *Environment and Urbanization* 13:1 (April 2001), p. 224.

80 Paul Baróss and Jan van der Linden, "Introduction," in Baróss and van der Linden, *Transformation of Land Supply Systems in Third World Cities*, pp. 2–7.

Economic Co-operation and Development (OECD) bloc, the *clandestinos* around Lisbon and Naples as well as the recent *colonias* outside El Paso and Palm Springs.

In some countries the commercialization of peripheral slum development has existed for decades. "By the mid-1960s," explains urban planner Ayse Yonder, "squatting in the traditional sense of the term had disappeared in Istanbul. Settlers had to pay local strong men for the right to occupy even public land. In the mid-1970s, entrepreneurs with underground connections started controlling public lands in certain districts of Istanbul, selling land and monopolizing all construction activity."[81] In Nairobi – today a city of rack-rented poor tenants – full-fledged commercialization took off in the early 1970s as wealthy outsiders discovered that squatting was creating a new land market with huge windfalls from legalization. Landowners (often successors to the original Asian owners) began to peddle unauthorized subdivisions. According to poverty researcher Philip Amis, "they in effect invaded their own land, building unauthorized housing according to their own plans … the risk paid off handsomely. No demolition orders were issued and returns on investment were very high."[82]

3. Invisible Renters

As a rule of thumb, both the popular and scholarly literatures on informal housing tend to romanticize squatters while ignoring renters. As World Bank researchers recently acknowledged, "remarkably little research has been done on low-income rental markets."[83] Landlordism is in fact a fundamental and divisive social relation in slum life worldwide. It is the principal way in which urban poor people can monetize their equity (formal or informal), but often in an exploitative relationship to even poorer people. The commodification of informal housing

81 Ayse Yonder, "Implications of Double Standards in Housing Policy: Development of Informal Settlements in Istanbul," in Edésio Fernandes and Ann Varley (eds), *Illegal Cities: Law and Urban Change in Developing Countries*, London 1998, p. 62.

82 Philip Amis, "Commercialized Rental Housing in Nairobi," in Patton, *Spontaneous Shelter*, pp. 240, 242.

83 Marianne Fay and Anna Wellenstein, "Keeping a Roof over One's Head," in Fay (ed.), *The Urban Poor in Latin America*, Washington, D.C. 2005, p. 92.

has included the rapid growth of distinctive rental subsectors: infill developments in older shantytowns, or multifamily constructions in pirate subdivisions. To be sure, most of the urban poor in West Africa have always rented from landlords, as have a majority of residents in Dhaka and some other Asian cities (in Bangkok two-thirds of "squatters" actually rent the land they build their shacks upon).[84] Renting has also become far more common than usually recognized in the peripheries of Latin American, Middle Eastern, and South African cities. In Cairo, for example, the more advantaged poor buy pirated land from farmers, while the less advantaged squat on municipal land; the poorest of the poor, however, rent from the squatters.[85] Likewise, as urban geographer Alan Gilbert observed of Latin America in 1993, the "vast majority of new rental housing is located in the consolidated self-help periphery rather than in the centre of the city."[86]

Mexico City is an important case in point. Despite a Model Law of the *colonias proletarias* which sought to ban absentee ownership, "poaching," and speculation in low-income housing, the Lopez Portillo government (1976–82) allowed slum-dwellers to sell their property at market rates. One result of this reform has been the middle-class gentrification of some formerly poor *colonias* in good locations; another has been the proliferation of petty landlordism. As sociologist Susan Eckstein discovered in her 1987 return to the *colonia* that she had first studied fifteen years earlier, some 25 to 50 percent of the original squatters had built small, 2-to-15-family *vecindades* which they then rented to poorer newcomers. "There is, in essence," she wrote, "a two-tiered housing market, reflecting socioeconomic differences among *colonos*." She also found "a 'downward' socioeconomic leveling of the population since I was last there.... The poorer tenant stratum has increased in size." Although some older residents had thrived as landlords, the newer renters had far less hope of socioeconomic mobility than the earlier generation, and the *colonia* as a whole was no longer a "slum of hope."[87]

84 Rigg, *Southeast Asia*, p. 143.
85 Soliman, *A Possible Way Out*, p. 97.
86 Alan Gilbert et al., *In Search of a Home: Rental and Shared Housing in Latin America*, Tucson 1993, p. 4.
87 Eckstein, pp. 60, 235–38.

Renters, indeed, are usually the most invisible and powerless of slum-dwellers. In the face of redevelopment and eviction, they are typically ineligible for compensation or resettlement. Unlike tenement-dwellers in early-twentieth-century Berlin or New York, moreover, who shared a closeknit solidarity *vis-à-vis* their slumlords, today's slum renters typically lack the power to organize tenants' organizations or mount rent strikes. As two leading housing researchers explain: "Tenants are scattered throughout irregular settlements with a wide range of informal rental arrangements, and they are often unable to organize as a pressure group to protect themselves."[88]

Large peripheral slums, especially in Africa, are usually complex quiltworks of kin networks, tenure systems, and tenant relationships. Diana Lee-Smith, one of the founders of Nairobi's Mazingira Institute, has closely studied Korogocho, a huge slum on the eastern edge of the city. Korogocho includes seven villages offering a menu of different housing and rental types. The most wretched village, Grogan, consists of one-room cardboard shacks and is largely populated by female-headed households evicted from an older shantytown near the city center. Barracks-like Githaa, on the other hand, "is an entirely speculative village, built by entrepreneurs for rent," despite the fact that the land is publicly owned. Nearby Dandora is a sites-and-services scheme where half the owners are now absentee landlords. Lee-Smith emphasizes that petty landlordship and subletting are major wealth strategies of the poor, and that homeowners quickly become exploiters of even more impoverished people. Despite the persistent heroic image of the squatter as self-builder and owner-occupier, the reality in Korogocho and other Nairobi slums is the irresistible increase in tenancy and petty exploitation.[89]

Soweto, having grown from a suburb to a satellite city of almost 2 million, likewise demonstrates a broad spectrum of housing statuses. Two thirds of its residents live either in formal-sector private homes (the professional middle class) or, most commonly, council homes (the traditional working classes); in the backyards of the latter, residents

---

88 Durand-Lasserve and Royston, "International Trends and Country Contexts," p. 7.

89 Diana Lee-Smith, "Squatter Landlords in Nairobi: A Case Study of Korogocho," in Amis and Lloyd, *Housing Africa's Urban Poor*, pp. 176–85.

have illegally constructed shacks that are rented to younger families or single adults. Even poorer people, including rural immigrants, either room in hostels or squat on the outskirts of Soweto. Johannesburg's other famous slum from the high Apartheid era, Alexandra, is more destitute and has fewer formal-sector homes. Most of the population are squatters, renters, or hostel-dwellers.[90]

This diversity of property rights and housing forms in large African and Latin American slums, not surprisingly, generates very different perceptions of interest. As geographer Peter Ward points out in the case of Mexico City, "one's ideological perspective is likely to be shaped by one's housing status":

> The heterogeneity of irregular settlement ... undermines collective response by dividing settlements on the basis of mode of land acquisition, the "stage" of consolidation, the servicing priorities of residents, community leadership structures, social classes, and above all tenure relations (owners versus sharers versus renters). These tenure splits multiply still further the constituencies into which people fall or may be divided. ... Renters, harassed squatters, displaced downtown tenants are likely to be more radical and disposed to anti-government demonstrations than are those who have, in effect, been bought off by the government through successive housing policies.[91]

4. The Pariah Edge

The further analysis moves away from the center of the Third World city, the thicker the epistemological fog. As historian Ellen Brennan stresses, "Most [Third World] cities lack accurate, current data on land conversion patterns, number of housing units (informal and formal) built during the past year, infrastructural deployment patterns, subdivision patterns and so forth."[92] And governments know least about their

90 Jo Beall, Owen Crankshaw, and Susan Parnell, "Local Government, Poverty Reduction and Inequality in Johannesburg," *Environment and Urbanization* 12:1 (April 2000), pp. 112–13.

91 Peter Ward, *Mexico City: The Production and Reproduction of an Urban Environment*, London 1990, p. 193.

92 Ellen Brennan, "Urban Land and Housing Issues Facing the Third World," in Kasarda and Parnell, *Third World Cities*, p. 80.

peri-urban borders, those strange limbos where ruralized cities transition into urbanized countrysides.[93]

The urban edge is the societal impact zone where the centrifugal forces of the city collide with the implosion of the countryside. Thus Dakar's huge impoverished suburb, Pikine, according to researcher Mohamadou Abdoul, is the product of the convergence of "two large-scale demographic influxes beginning in the 1970s: the arrival of populations that had been forced out – often by the military – of Dakar's working-class neighborhoods and shantytowns, and the arrival of people caught up in the rural exodus."[94] Likewise, the two million poor people in Bangalore's rapidly growing slum periphery include both slum-dwellers expelled from the center and farm laborers driven off the land. On the edges of Mexico City, Buenos Aires, and other Latin American cities, it is common to find shantytowns of new rural migrants next to walled suburbs of middle-class commuters fleeing crime and insecurity in the city center.[95]

A migrant stream of polluting, toxic, and often illegal industries also seeks the permissive obscurity of the periphery. Geographer Hans Schenk observes that the urban fringe in Asia is a regulatory vacuum, a true frontier where "Darwin beats Keynes" and piratical entrepreneurs and corrupt politicians are largely unfettered by law or public scrutiny. Most of Beijing's small garment sweatshops, for example, are hidden away in an archipelago of still partly agricultural villages and shantytowns on the city's southern edge. Likewise in Bangalore, the urban fringe is where entrepreneurs can most profitably mine cheap labor with minimal oversight by the state.[96] Millions of temporary workers and desperate peasants also hover around the edges of such world capitals of super-exploitation as Surat and Shenzhen. These labor nomads lack secure footing in either city or countryside, and often spend their lifetimes in a kind of desperate Brownian motion

93 See Seabrook, *In the Cities of the South*, p. 187.

94 Mohamadou Abdoul, "The Production of the City and Urban Informalities," in Enwezor et al., *Under Siege*, p. 342

95 Guy Thuillier, "Gated Communities in the Metropolitan Area of Buenos Aires," *Housing Studies* 20:2 (March 2005), p. 255.

96 Hans Schenk, "Urban Fringes in Asia: Markets versus Plans," in I. S. A. Baud and J. Post (eds), *Realigning Actors in an Urbanizing World: Governance and Institutions from a Development Perspective*, Aldershot 2002, pp. 121–22, 131.

between the two. In Latin America, meanwhile, an inverse logic operates: labor contractors increasingly hire urban shantytown-dwellers for seasonal or temporary work in the countryside.[97]

But the principal function of the Third World urban edge remains as a human dump. In some cases, urban waste and unwanted immigrants end up together, as in such infamous "garbage slums" as the aptly named Quarantina outside Beirut, Hillat Kusha outside Khartoum, Santa Cruz Meyehualco in Mexico City, the former Smoky Mountain in Manila, or the huge Dhapa dump and slum on the fringe of Kolkata. Equally common are the desolate government camps and crude site-and-service settlements that warehouse populations expelled in the course of municipal wars against slums. Outside of Penang and Kuala Lumpur, for example, slum evictees are marooned in minimalist transit camps. As housing activists explain:

> The term "long house" (*rumah panjang* in Bahasa Malay) conjures up comfortable images of some long-ago form of Malay vernacular housing, but the reality of these transit camps is quite different. These long houses are bleak lines of flimsy plywood and asbestos shacks, attached at the sides and facing across unpaved and treeless lanes onto more shacks opposite, with spotty basic services, if any. And these long houses have turned out to be not so temporary after all. Many evictees are still there, twenty years later, still waiting for the government to realize its promise of low-income housing....[98]

Anthropologist Monique Skidmore risked arrest to visit some of the dismal peri-urban townships – so-called "New Fields" – outside Rangoon where the military dictatorship forcibly relocated hundreds of thousands of urbanites whose former slums stood in the way of the tourist-themepark rebuilding of the city center. "Residents speak of the sorrow and pain of loss of former neighborhoods ... alcohol shops, rubbish piles, stagnant water, and mud infused with untreated sewage surround most homes." On the other hand, things are even worse in Mandalay's peripheral shantytowns. There, Skidmore explains,

97 Cristóbal Kay, "Latin America's Agrarian Transformation: Peasantization and Proletarianization," in Bryceson, Kay and Mooij, *Disappearing Peasantries?*, p. 131.
98 Asian Coalition for Housing Rights, "Special Issue on How Poor People Deal with Eviction," *Housing by People in Asia* 15 (October 2003), p. 19.

"township residents must walk to the foothills of the Shan mountains looking for firewood, and there are no industrial zones, garment factories, and other sweatshops to underemploy laborers as there are in some of Rangoon's relocated townships."[99]

International refugees and internally displaced people (IDPs) are often more harshly treated even than urban evictees – and some of the Third World's huge refugee camps have evolved into edge cities in their own right. Thus Gaza – considered by some to be the world's largest slum – is essentially an urbanized agglomeration of refugee camps (750,000 refugees) with two thirds of the population subsisting on less than $2 per day.[100] Dadaad, just inside the Kenyan border, houses 125,000 Somalis, just as Goma in Zaire during the mid-1990s was a pitiful refuge for an estimated 700,000 Rwandans, many of whom died of cholera due to the appalling sanitation conditions. Khartoum's desert periphery includes four huge camps (Mayo Farms, Jebel Aulia, Dar el Salaam and Wad al-Bashir) warehousing 400,000 victims of drought, famine and civil war. Another 1.5 million internally displaced people – mainly Southerners – live in scores of large squatter settlements around the Sudanese metropolis.[101]

Likewise, hundreds of thousands of war victims and returned refugees from Iran and Pakistan squat without water or sanitation in scores of hillside slums above Kabul. "In the Karte Ariana district," reported the *Washington Post* in August 2002, "hundreds of families who fled combat between Taliban and opposition forces in rural northern Afghanistan are now squeezed into a maze of vertical slums without kitchens or bathrooms, sleeping 15 and 20 to a hut." There has been little rain for years and many wells have stopped working; children in these slums suffer from continual sore throats and various diseases from contaminated water. Life expectancy is among the lowest in the world.[102]

Two of the world's largest populations of IDPs are in Angola and Colombia. Angola was forcibly urbanized by more than a quarter-century of civil war (1975 to 2002) – spurred on by the machinations of

---

99 Monique Skidmore, *Karaoke Fascism: Burma and the Politics of Fear*, Philadelphia 2004, pp. 150–51, 156.

100 Fact sheet, Al-Dameer Association for Human Rights Gaza, 2002.

101 Eltayeb, "Khartoum, Sudan," p. 2.

102 *Washington Post*, 26 August 2002.

Pretoria and the White House – which displaced 30 percent of the population. Many refugees never returned to their former homes in the ruined and dangerous countryside, but squatted instead in the bleak *musseques* (shantytowns) that surround Luanda, Lobito, Cabinda, and other cities. As a result, Angola, only 14 percent urban in 1970, is now a majority urban nation. Most of its city-dwellers are both desperately poor and almost totally ignored by the state, which in 1998 was estimated to spend only 1 percent of its budget on public education and welfare.[103]

The unending civil wars in Colombia likewise have added more than 400,000 IDPs to Bogotá's urban poverty belt, which includes the huge informal settlements of Sumapaz, Ciudad Bolívar, Usme, and Soacha. "Most displaced," explains an aid NGO, "are social outcasts, excluded from formal life and employment. Currently, 653,800 Bogotanos (2002) have no employment in the city and, even more shocking, half of them are under the age of 29." Without urban skills and frequently without access to schools, these young peasants and their children are ideal recruits for street gangs and paramilitaries. Local businessmen vandalized by urchins, in turn, form *grupos de limpieza* with links to rightwing death squads, and the bodies of murdered children are dumped at the edge of town.[104]

The same nightmare prevails on the outskirts of Cali, where anthropologist Michael Taussig invokes Dante's *Inferno* to describe the struggle for survival in two "stupendously dangerous" peripheral slums. Navarro is a notorious "garbage mountain" where hungry women and children pick through waste while youthful gunmen (*malo de malo*) are either hired or exterminated by local rightwing paramilitaries. The other settlement, Carlos Alfredo Díaz, is full of "kids running around with homemade shotguns and grenades." "It dawns on me," writes Taussig, "that just as the guerilla have their most important base in the endless forests of the Caquetá, at the end of nowhere on the edge of the Amazon basin, so the gang world of youth gone wild has its sacred grove, too, right here on the urban edge, where the slums hit the cane fields at Carlos Alfredo Díaz."[105]

103 Tony Hodges, *Angola*, 2nd ed., Oxford 2004, p. 22.
104 Project Counseling Services, "Deteriorating Bogotá: Displacement and War in Urban Centres", *Colombia Regional Report: Bogotá* (December 2002), pp. 3–4.
105 Michael Taussig, *Law in a Lawless Land: Diary of a Limpreza in Colombia*, New York 2003, pp. 114–15.

3

The Treason of the State

> If unmitigated capitalism has a mainly unacceptable
> face, a corrupt state acting on behalf of the rich is
> still worse. In such circumstances, little is to be
> gained by even trying to improve the system.
>
> *Alan Gilbert and Peter Ward*[1]

"Astonishingly," two geographers recently complained, "no writer has traced the changing geography of low-income settlement in any third-world city over the whole postwar period."[2] Nor, of course, has anyone yet attempted a modern historical overview of the global pattern of informal settlement. So many national histories and urban specificities make such a synthesis a daunting task; nonetheless, it is possible to venture a rough periodization that emphasizes principal trends and watersheds in the urbanization of world poverty.

But before considering why Third World cities and their slums grew so fast in the second half of the twentieth century, it is first necessary to understand why they grew so *slowly* in the first half. Although there are some exceptions, most of today's megacities of the South share a

---

1 Alan Gilbert and Peter Ward, *Housing, the State and the Poor: Policy and Practice in Three Latin American Cities*, Cambridge 1985, p. 254.
2 Richard Harris and Malak Wahba, "The Urban Geography of Low-Income Housing: Cairo (1947–96) Exemplifies a Model," *International Journal of Urban and Regional Research* 26:1 (March 2002), p. 59.

common trajectory: a regime of relatively slow, even retarded growth, then abrupt acceleration to fast growth in the 1950s and 1960s, with rural in-migrants increasingly sheltered in peripheral slums. Earlier in the twentieth century, the massive transfer of rural poverty to cities was prevented by the economic and political equivalents of city walls – both urban entry and, even more importantly, substantive urban citizenship were systematically withheld from large parts of the agrarian population.

Keeping the Peasants Out

A principal barrier, of course, was European colonialism which, in its most extreme form in the British colonial cities of eastern and southern Africa, denied native populations the rights of urban land ownership and permanent residence. The British, always the ideologues of divide and rule, feared that city life would "detribalize" Africans and foster anticolonial solidarities.[3] Urban migration was controlled by pass laws, while vagrancy ordinances penalized informal labor. Until 1954, for instance, Africans were considered only temporary sojourners in racially zoned Nairobi and were unable to own leasehold property.[4] Likewise Africans in Dar-es-Salaam, according to researcher Karin Nuru, "were only tolerated as a temporary labour force and had to return to the countryside."[5] In Rhodesia (Zimbabwe) Africans had to wait until the eve of independence to acquire the legal right to own urban homes, while in Lusaka – designed as "a highly ordered city segmented by race, class and gender" – African residents were considered to be "more or less temporary urbanites whose only purpose in town was service to the administration's personnel."[6]

Apartheid, of course, took this system to its dystopian extreme. Building on a foundation of colonial racism, postwar South African legislation not only criminalized urban migration, but also provided for the uprooting, with enormous brutality, of historical inner-city

3 Garth Myers, "Colonial and Postcolonial Modernities in Two African Cities," *Canadian Journal of African Studies* 37:2–3 (2003), pp. 338–39.

4 Amis, "Commercialized Rental Housing in Nairobi," p. 238.

5 Karin Nuru, "Tanzania," in Kosta Mathéy, *Housing Policies in the Socialist Third World*, Munich 1990, p. 183.

6 Myers, "Colonial and Postcolonial Modernities in Two African Cities," p. 334.

communities of color. Almost one million people of color were evicted from supposed "white" areas, and as a result, net urbanization hardly increased between 1950 (43 percent) and 1990 (48 percent); indeed, in the 1960s there was a net outflow of Africans from urban areas.[7] Ultimately, however, this ideal of "white cities, black home-lands" collided with the labor-market needs of big capital as well as the heroic resistance of its victims.

In the subcontinent, the British also segregated and policed the influx from the countryside. In her brilliant study of the cities of Uttar Pradesh during the interwar years, Nandini Gooptu chronicles the unceasing efforts of colonial officials and newly enfranchised native elites to push the poor to the cities' edges and beyond. The new-fangled Town Improvement Trusts, in particular, were highly effective in clearing slums and removing so-called "plague spots" from the inter-stices of better residential and commercial areas, and preserving spatial zoning around colonial and native middle-class areas. Vigorously enforced "encroachment laws," meanwhile, outlawed both squatting and street vending.[8] At the same time, urban economic growth under the prewar Raj was fitful at best – even Bombay, with its famed entre-preneurial elites and textile factories, grew slowly, not even doubling its population in the half-century from 1891 to 1941.

Despite their antipathy to large native urban settlements, the British were arguably the greatest slum-builders of all time. Their policies in Africa forced the local labor force to live in precarious shantytowns on the fringes of segregated and restricted cities. In India, Burma, and Ceylon, their refusal to improve sanitation or provide even the most minimal infrastructure to native neighborhoods ensured huge death tolls from early-twentieth-century epidemics (plague, cholera, influenza) and created immense problems of urban squalor that were inherited by national elites after independence.

The other empires, with greater or lesser success, also attempted to restrict and discipline rural migration. With few exceptions, very little manufacturing or processing value-added was left in colonial ports or

7 Michel Garenne, *Urbanization, Poverty and Child Mortality in Sub-Saharan Africa*, Paris 2003, table 1, p. 22.

8 See chapter 3, Gooptu, *The Politics of the Urban Poor in Early Twentieth-Century India*.

transport hubs to generate formal employment and urban growth. Everywhere native labor was consigned to slums and shantytowns. In Congolese cities, according to a recent history, the colonial state "maintained relatively effective urban influx controls and a tentacular regulatory net around the towns, choking off both petty trade outside prescribed channels and 'anarchic' housing construction."[9]

Historian Jean Suret-Canale, meanwhile, reminds us that in tropical Africa, the French tightly regulated the movements of rural labor while consigning African town-dwellers to grim peripheries. In colonial slums like Medina (Dakar), Treichville (Abidjan) and Poto-Poto (Brazzaville), streets "were nothing but sand or mud alleyways .... instead of drainage there were only a few sewers, usually open or crudely covered with flag-stones; there was little or no water, with a few public pumps where queues waited from early in the morning. Public lighting was reserved for the European quarters. Overcrowding created a great hazard to health."[10] Indeed, this almost universal refusal to provide even minimal sanitary infrastructures for the "native quarters" until the 1950s was more than stinginess: it pointedly symbolized the lack of any native "right to the city."

But European colonialism was not the only international system of urban growth control. Although raised to power by peasant revolt, Asian Stalinism also tried to staunch the influx from the countryside. Initially the 1949 Chinese Revolution opened city gates to returning refugees and job-hungry peasant ex-soldiers. The result was an uncontrolled inundation of the cities: some 14 million people arrived in just four years.[11] Finally, in 1953 the new regime dammed the rural flood with stringent controls over internal migration. Maoism simultaneously privileged the urban proletariat – beneficiaries of the "iron rice bowl" and cradle-to-grave welfare – and tightly constrained urban population growth through the adoption of a household registration system (*hukou*) that tied social citizenship to sedentary membership in a work unit.

9 Crawford Young and Thomas Turner, *The Rise and Decline of the Zairian State*, Madison (WI) 1985, p. 87.
10 Jean Suret-Canale, *French Colonialism in Tropical Africa, 1900–1945*, New York 1971, p. 417.
11 On-Kwok Lai, "The Logic of Urban Development and Slum Settlements," in Aldrich and Sandhu, *Housing the Urban Poor*, p. 284.

Having rehoused the homeless and abolished most urban shanty-towns by 1960, Beijing continued to exercise extraordinary vigilance over informal rural emigration. City and countryside were conceived as separate worlds that intersected only under conditions carefully defined by the party-state. If urban residents sometimes obtained official permission to move to another city, it was almost unheard of for peasants to win approval to leave their commune. In the early 1960s, moreover, huge numbers of unregistered urban immigrants – some estimates are as high as 50 million – were deported back to their villages.[12] As a result, according to Guilhem Fabre, a Sinologist at the University of Le Havre, the urban percentage of the population fell from a height of almost 20 percent in 1960 to 12.5 percent in 1971.[13] Similar controls over rural–urban migration were introduced during the 1950s in North Korea, Albania, and, more mildly, North Vietnam (the *ho khau* system), although the climax of ideological antiurbanism was certainly Pol Pot's brutal 1975 deportation of Phnom Penh's citizenry.

In Latin America there were also formidable, if less systematic, obstacles to urban migration. Before the Second World War, most poor urban Latin Americans lived in inner-city rental housing, but in the late 1940s import-substitution industrialization spurred a dramatic wave of squatter invasion on the outskirts of Mexico City and other Latin American cities. In response to the burgeoning of shantytowns, authorities in several countries, ardently supported by the urban middle classes, launched massive crackdowns on informal settlement. Since many of the new urban immigrants were *indigenistas* or descendants of slaves, there was often a racial dimension to this "war on squatting."

The postwar dictator of Venezuela, Marcos Pérez Jiménez, was a particularly notorious enemy of informal housing. According to three UCLA authors: "[His] government's solution to the *barrios* was the bull-dozer. On a given morning, policemen and trucks would arrive at the *barrio*; an official would direct the loading of the residents' belongings onto the truck; policemen would deal with any objections; when the belongings and the residents had been removed to the new apartments,

12 Dorothy Solinger, *Contesting Citizenship in Urban China: Peasant Migrants, the State and the Logic of the Market*, Berkeley 1999, pp. 2, 41.
13 Table 1, Fabre, "La Chine," p. 196.

the houses were demolished." Squatters were deported to the outskirts of Caracas, where they were rehoused in *superbloques*, monstrous fifteen-story dormitories universally despised by their residents.[14]

In Mexico City the traditional middle classes lionized Ernesto Uruchurtu, who throughout his long tenure as mayor (1952–58, 1964–66) fought the tide of rural poor being swept toward the city by the PRI's "DF-centric" model of national economic growth. When he took office in 1952, thousands of rural people from Central Mexico were "parachuting" into the city's periphery each month. Squatter settlements, called *colonias populares*, which had housed only a negligible 2.3 percent of the population in 1947, had in five years become the residences of nearly a quarter of Mexico City's citizens.[15] Uruchurtu determined to stop the peasant influx by evicting *paracaidistas*, driving informal vendors off the streets, and opposing tenure rights and services for existing *colonias*. As sociologist Diane Davis points out, Uruchurtu's strategy of controlled growth reflected the underlying racial bias of his political base: "Like many of the city's residents, Uruchurtu blamed the streaming masses of poor educated migrants – many of them of Indian heritage – for the physical and social destruction of the city."[16]

The Deluge

Institutional roadblocks to fast urban growth were removed by paradoxical combinations of colonial counterinsurgency and national independence in Africa and Asia, and by the overthrow of dictatorships and slow-growth regimes in Latin America. Driven toward the cities by brutal and irresistible forces, the poor eagerly asserted their "right to the city," even if that meant only a hovel on its periphery. Even more than famine and debt, civil war and counterinsurgency were the most ruthlessly efficient levers of informal urbanization in the 1950s and 1960s.

Thus in the case of the subcontinent, Partition and its ethnoreligious aftershocks drove millions into slums. Bombay, Delhi, Calcutta, Karachi, Lahore, and Dhaka were all forced to absorb floods of refugees

14 Karst, Schwartz, and Schwartz, *The Evolution of Law in the Barrios of Caracas*, p. 7.
15 Pezzoli, in Aldrich and Sandhu, *Housing the Urban Poor*, p. 147.
16 Diane Davis, *Urban Leviathan: Mexico City in the Twentieth Century*, Philadelphia 1994, pp. 132–35, 155.

in the violent aftermaths of 1948 (Partition), 1964 (Indo–Pakistani War), and 1971 (secession of Bangladesh).[17] Bombay's population – growing at less than 2 percent per annum during the last decades of the Raj – almost doubled in the late 1940s and early 1950s with the influx of pauperized refugees from Pakistan and the concomitant (although slower) expansion of the textile industry.[18] Half of the 1950s populations of Karachi and Hyderabad, meanwhile, were "Muhajirs", Muslim refugees from the eastern Punjab. They were joined later in the 1970s by hundreds of thousands of impoverished Biharis: Muslim peasants and "double migrants" who fled first to East Pakistan, then, after the secession of Bangladesh, to Pakistan.[19] From the beginning, these slum-based refugee populations were heavily dependent upon political benefactors and corrupt party machines. In both India and Pakistan, as a result, slum development became famously synchronized to election cycles: in Karachi land invasions and pirate subdivisions typically increase in election years, while in India elections provide squatters with leverage to seek legalization or improvement of their *bustees*.[20]

In South Vietnam, forced urbanization (described with unconscious Orwellian irony as "modernization") was an integral part of US military strategy. Since the Vietcong, according to war strategist Samuel Huntington, constituted "a powerful force which cannot be dislodged from its constituency so long as the constituency continues to exist," he and other hawks argued for abolishing the "constituency." American terror bombing provided the force "on such a massive scale as to produce a massive migration from countryside to city [so that] the basic assumptions underlying the Maoist doctrine of revolutionary war no longer operates [*sic*]. The Maoist inspired rural revolution is undercut by the American-sponsored urban revolution."[21] Over the course of

17 Frederic Thomas, *Calcutta Poor: Elegies on a City Above Pretense*, Armonk (NY) 1997, p. 41.

18 Sujata Patel, "Bombay's Urban Predicament," in Patel and Alice Thorner (eds), *Bombay: Metaphor for Modern India*, Delhi 1996, p. xvi.

19 Oskar Verkaaik, *Migrants and Militants: Fun and Urban Violence in Pakistan*, Princeton 2004, p. 64.

20 Robert-Jan Baken and Jan van der Linden, *Land Delivery for Low Income Groups in Third World Cities*, Aldershot 1992, p. 31.

21 Samuel Huntington, "The Bases of Accommodation," *Foreign Affairs* 46:4 (July 1968), pp. 650–53.

the war, as historian Marilyn Young points out, the urban share of South Vietnam's population soared from 15 percent to 65 percent, with five million displaced peasants turned into slum-dwellers or inhabitants of refugee camps.[22]

Seven years of ruthless colonial warfare in Algeria (1954–61) likewise displaced half of the rural population. After independence in 1962, this uprooted mass poured into the cities. Algiers tripled its population in less than two years as poor immigrants crowded into corrugated *bidonvilles* or, preferentially, occupied the apartments left vacant by the flight of 900,000 *colons*. The new regime's initial emphasis on Soviet-bloc-style heavy industrialization and its relative neglect of subsistence agriculture reinforced the exodus from the countryside. Very quickly Algiers became acutely overcrowded, with much of the population crammed into dangerously deteriorated older housing. Scores of ancient houses in the *qasbah* simply collapsed, often killing the residents. Meanwhile, "socialist" *bidonvilles* continued to expand on the urban outskirts and along the principal highways.[23]

In postwar Turkey, meanwhile, migration to the cities was stimulated by Marshall Plan aid, the modernization of agriculture, and the growth of import-substitution manufacture. But the Kemalist state, as the Marxist sociologist Çağlar Keyder observes, was prepared neither to build public housing nor to alienate state land to private-sector development – instead "the vast inertia of populist clientelism prevailed." Anatolian migrants were forced to construct their own shanty cities on the outskirts of Ankara and Istanbul in negotiation with local officials, and so the decade 1955–65 became the heroic age of squatting, as the *gecekondu* population soared from 5 percent (250,000 people) to 23 percent (2.2 million) of the total urban population (a percentage that has not shifted significantly since).[24] At least in this early period, the *gecekondus* synergistically abetted the political system that had made them the primary mode of popular housing. "Politicians," continues Keyder, "generally preferred to retain the privilege of arbitrary allocation to

22 Marilyn Young, *The Vietnam Wars: 1945–1990*, New York 1991, p. 177.
23 Djaffar Lesbet, "Algeria," in Mathéy, *Housing Policies in the Socialist Third World*, pp. 252–63.
24 Keyder, *Istanbul*, p. 147; H. Tarik Şengul, "On the Trajectory of Urbanization in Turkey," *International Development Planning Review* 25:2 (2003), p. 160.

create and maintain popular support and thus strengthen their own positions. The existence of such clientelistic relations was predicated on informal appropriation of land."[25]

In the rest of the Middle East, the biggest upsurge in informal urbanization occurred a decade or two later, during the OPEC boom of the early 1970s. Ahmed Soliman believes that the "heyday of urban residential informality" in Cairo was from 1974 to 1990, as immigrant workers' earnings flowed back from Saudi Arabia to fill some of the gap left by the demise of Nasserite welfarism.[26] Likewise, hundreds of thousands of landless laborers and artisans moved to Tehran in the early 1970s looking for work in brickyards and on construction sites, only to face unemployment after 1976. Their disillusionment and anger soon became the raw material of Islamic revolution.[27] The revolution, in turn, created a unique space for slum growth. "When the revolutionaries were marching in the streets of big cities," explains Asef Bayat, "the very poor were busy extending their hold over their communities and in bringing more urban land under (mal)development." After the flight of the Shah, moreover, "poor families took advantage of the collapse of police control to take over hundreds of vacant homes and half-finished apartment blocks, refurbishing them as their own properties." To the chagrin of traditional merchants, the new poor also set up thousands of stalls, kiosks, and pushcarts, converting "the street sidewalks into vibrant and colorful shopping places."[28]

In sub-Saharan Africa the countryside began pouring into the cities soon after independence. In most countries, South Africa aside, urban growth rates from the 1960s were double the rate of natural population increase. Until the 1980s city growth in most countries was subsidized by coercive policies that forced peasants to deliver farm products at below-market-value prices and taxed rural people at disproportionate rates. In Zaire, for example, President Mobutu regularly denounced "the dangers of hypertrophic urban development, and the attendant

25 Keyder, "The Housing Market from Informal to Global," p. 147.

26 Soliman, *A Possible Way Out*, p. 51.

27 Farhad Kazemi, *Poverty and Revolution in Iran: The Migrant Poor, Urban Marginality, and Politics*, New York 1980, p. 114.

28 Asef Bayat, "Un-civil Society," p. 53.

evils of unemployment and crime" while continuing to squeeze the countryside so ruthlessly that peasants had few options but to flee to the urban areas.[29] But the so-called "urban bias" in African development hardly worked to the advantage of the new urban masses – indeed, as postcolonial elites and armed forces battened off the countryside, infrastructural provision and public services in the cities rapidly deteriorated.[30]

In Latin America, meanwhile, the overthrow of dictatorships created temporary opportunities for land invasion and squatting, even as strong partisan rivalries and the implied threat of revolution gave urban immigrants episodic opportunities to trade votes for land and infrastructure. In Venezuela, according to a recent study, "the crucial dates in the formation of the Caracas *barrios* are 1958–60." After the ouster of Pérez Jiménez and before the election of Rómulo Betancourt, the governing provisional junta suspended evictions in the *barrios* and offered public relief to the unemployed; as a result, 400,000 mostly poor people moved to Caracas in little more than a year. Afterward, the intense competition for votes between the two major political parties, the center-left Acción Democrática and the center-right COPEI, opened the floodgates (which Pérez Jiménez had tried to close) to the explosive expansion of informal *barrios* in the hills around the city. Caracas and other Venezuelan cities consequently grew at African velocity: during the 1960s, the country went from being 30 percent urban to 30 percent rural.[31]

In Mexico City, Uruchurtu's anti-slum, controlled-growth strategy proved ultimately incompatible with the needs of industrialists and foreign investors for cheap labor, as well as workers' demands for cheap housing. Powerful real-estate developers likewise felt stymied by the mayor's conservative Comisión de Planificación. The last straw was Uruchurtu's opposition to the construction of the city's subway. After a final defiance – the bulldozing of Colonia Santa Ursula in Ajusco in

29   Young and Turner, *The Rise and Decline of the Zairian State*, p. 98; Deborah Posel, "Curbing African Urbanization in the 1950s and 1960s," in Mark Swilling, Richard Humphries, and Khehla Shubane (eds), *Apartheid City in Transition*, Cape Town 1991, pp. 29–30.

30   Carole Rakodi, "Global Forces, Urban Change, and Urban Management in Africa," in Rakodi, *The Urban Challenge in Africa*, pp. 32–39.

31   Urban Planning Studio, Columbia University, *Disaster-Resistant Caracas*, New York 2001, p. 25.

September 1966 – he was deposed by President Gustavo Díaz Ordaz, a politician notorious for his many ties to foreign capital and land speculators. A fast-growth agenda that included tolerance for pirate urbanization on the periphery in return for urban renewal in the center became the PRI policy in La Capital.[32]

A generation after the removal of barriers to influx and informal urbanization elsewhere, China began to relax its controls on urban growth in the early 1980s. With a huge reservoir of redundant peasant labor (including more than half of the labor force of Sichuan, according to the *People's Daily*) the loosening of the bureaucratic dike produced a literal "peasant flood."[33] Officially sanctioned migration was overshadowed by a huge stream of unauthorized immigrants or "floaters." Without the official citizenship in the city provided by a valid household registration card, this immense mass of poor peasants (currently estimated at 100 million) had no legal entitlement to social services or housing. Instead they became super-cheap human fuel for the export sweatshops of the Pearl River Delta and the building sites of Shanghai and Beijing, while housing themselves in makeshift shacks and overcrowded rooms at the edges of the cities. The return of capitalism to China brought with it the squalid urban shantytown.

Finally, in the late 1980s South Africa's rulers, faced with the most significant shantytown uprising in world history (the "civics" movement in the black townships), were forced to dismantle the totalitarian system of controls – first, the Pass Law in 1986, then the Group Areas Act in 1991 – that had restricted African urban migration and residence. Writer Rian Malan described the resulting impact in metropolitan Cape Town, where the black African population more then tripled between 1982 and 1992:

> After ... the hated pass laws were scrapped, it was if a distant dam had broken, allowing a mass of desperate and hopeful humanity to come flooding over the mountains and spread out across the Cape Flats. They came at the rate of eighty, ninety families a day, and built homes with their bare hands, using wooden poles, tin sheeting, bits and pieces of trash

32 Davis, *Urban Leviathan*, pp. 135, 177–80.
33 Solinger, *Contesting Citizenship in Urban China*, p. 155.

rescued from landfills and plastic garbage bags to keep out the rain. Within two years, the sand dunes had vanished under an enormous sea of shacks and shanties, as densely packed as a mediaeval city, and populated by fantastic characters – bootleggers, gangsters, prophets, Rastafarians, gun dealers and marijuana czars, plus almost a million ordinary working people.[34]

Broken Promises and Stolen Dreams

The slum was not the inevitable urban future. In early 1960, for example, Cuba's new National Institute of Savings and Housing, led by the legendary Pastorita Núñez, began to replace Havana's notorious shantytowns (Las Yaguas, Llega y Pon, La Cueva del Humo, and so on) with prefabricated homes erected by the residents themselves. Seven years earlier, during his trial for the Moncada barracks attack, Fidel Castro had promised Cubans a revolution that would enforce the progressive 1940 Constitution's guarantee of decent housing. In 1958 almost a third of Cubans lived in slums or squatter settlements. Accordingly, in the first golden years of the revolution, there was a huge national effort to rehouse the poor, even if many of the projects, in retrospect, were drab adaptations of modernism.[35]

Although revolutionary Cuba's commitment to a "new urbanism" was avant-garde, the ideal of a popular entitlement to housing was not unique in the contemporary Third World in the late 1950s and early 1960s: Nasser, Nehru, and Sukarno also promised to rebuild slums and create immense quanitities of new housing. In addition to subsidized housing and rent control, Nasser's "contract with Egypt" guaranteed public-sector jobs to every secondary-school graduate. Revolutionary Algeria legislated free universal healthcare and education, together with rent subsidies for poor city-dwellers. "Socialist" African states, beginning with Tanzania in the early 1960s, all started off with ambitious programs to relocate urban slum-dwellers into new low-cost housing. Mexico City in the Uruchurtu years enlisted the services of stellar émigré architects, such as the Bauhaus's Hannes Meyer, to design highrise

34 Rian Malan quoted in Westen, p. xxii.
35 Joseph Scarpaci, Roberto Segre, and Mario Coyula, *Havana: Two Faces of the Antillean Metropolis*, Chapel Hill 2002, pp. 199–203.

housing for unionized workers and state employees which compared favorably to northern European models. In Brazil, meanwhile, President Jão Goulart and radical Rio Grande do Sul governor Leonel Brizola were winning broad support for their vision of an urban New Deal. And later in the decade, the left-leaning military dictator of Peru, Juan Velasco Alvarado, would steal a step on *Fidelismo* by sponsoring mass urban land invasions and establishing an ambitious state program to upgrade *barriadas* (which he optimistically renamed *pueblos jovenes*).

Almost a half-century later, Cuba's progressive shelter program has now been slowed to a snail's pace by the austerities of the "Special Period" following the collapse of the USSR, and housing provision lags far behind the country's more impressive achievements in health and education. Apart from the special cases of Hong Kong and Singapore, the Chinese state alone in the developing world during the 1980s and 1990s managed to construct vast quantities of decent mass housing (although even this "unsung revolution," as urban expert Richard Kirkby calls it, fell far short of the needs of the tens of millions of peasants moving to the cities).[36]

In the rest of the Third World, the idea of an interventionist state strongly committed to social housing and job development seems either a hallucination or a bad joke, because governments long ago abdicated any serious effort to combat slums and redress urban marginality. In too many poor cities, citizens' relationship to their government is similar to what a Nairobi slum-dweller recently described to a *Guardian* reporter: "The state does nothing here. It provides no water, no schools, no sanitation, no roads, no hospitals." Indeed, the journalist found out that residents bought water from private dealers and relied on vigilante groups for security – the police visited only to collect bribes.[37]

The minimalist role of national governments in housing supply has been reinforced by current neo-liberal economic orthodoxy as defined by the IMF and the World Bank. The Structural Adjustment Programs (SAPs) imposed upon debtor nations in the late 1970s and 1980s required a shrinkage of government programs and, often, the

36 Richard Kirkby, "China," in Kosta Mathéy (ed.), *Beyond Self-Help Housing*, London 1992, pp. 298–99.

37 Andrew Harding, "Nairobi Slum Life," (series), *Guardian*, 4, 8, 10 and 15, October 2002.

privatization of housing markets. However, the social state in the Third World was already withering away even before SAPs sounded the death knell for welfarism. Because so many experts working for the "Washington Consensus" have deemed government provision of urban housing to be an inevitable disaster, it is important to review some case histories, beginning with what, at first sight, seem to be the major exceptions to the rule of state failure.

The two tropical cities where large-scale public housing has provided an alternative to slums are Singapore and Hong Kong. As a city-state with tight migration policies, the former doesn't have to face the usual demographic pressures of a poor agrarian hinterland. "Much of the problem," Erhard Berner explains, "is exported to Johor Baru," Singapore's Tijuana.[38] Hong Kong, on the other hand, has had to absorb millions of refugees, and now, migrants from the Mainland. But the former Crown Colony's success in rehousing squatters, tenement-dwellers, and civil war refugees in new public apartment blocks is not quite the humanitarian miracle often depicted.

As Alan Smart has shown, housing policy in Hong Kong has been a shrewd triangulation of the separate interests of property developers, manufacturing capital, and popular resistance, with potential PRC intervention looming in the background. The challenge was to reconcile a continuing supply of cheap labor with soaring land values, and the preferred solution was not high rents – which would have forced up wages – but peripheralization and overcrowding By 1971, writes Smart, one million squatters had been resettled "on land equivalent to only 34 percent of the land previously occupied, and on peripheral land of much lower value." Likewise hundreds of thousands of poor tenants had been relocated from their former rent-controlled housing in the central area. Space allocation in public housing in the early 1960s was a minuscule 24 square feet per adult, with toilets and kitchens shared by an entire floor. Although conditions improved in projects built later, Hong Kong maintained the highest formal residential densities in the world: the price for freeing up the maximum surface area for highrise offices and expensive market-price apartments.[39]

38 Berner, "Learning from Informal Markets," p. 244.
39 Smart, *Making Room*, pp. 1, 33, 36, 52, 55.

In their restructuring of Hong Kong's spatial economy, planners seldom paid attention to actual livelihood strategies of the urban poor, including their frequent use of their homes as workshops or their need to be located close to central markets or factories. The incompatibility of peripheral, highrise housing with the social structures and informal economies of poor communities is, of course, ancient history: it's an original sin repeated over decades by urban reformers and city czars everywhere. Indeed, back in the 1850s Baron Haussmann's Second Empire showcase of workers' housing, the Cité Napoléon in Paris, was rejected by its intended residents because of its uniformity and "barracks-like" quality. According to historian Ann-Louise Shapiro: "They complained that philanthropists and building societies were beginning to relegate the labouring population to special quarters as in the Middle Ages, and urged instead that the government tax vacant apartments to force down the rental price and make available a greater number of lodgings in the mixed housing of the city centre." In the end, Haussmann's famed project "housed only bourgeois tenants."[40]

The Cité Napoléon has many modern Third World descendants. In Jakarta, for example, public housing is unattractive to the huge informal labor force because it provides no space for home workshops; as a result, most tenants are military personnel and civil servants.[41] In Beijing, where highrise construction has led to real quantitative improvements in residential space, tower-dwellers nonetheless bemoan the loss of community. In surveys residents report dramatic declines in social visits, intercourse with neighbors, and frequency of children's play, as well as the increased isolation and loneliness of old people.[42] Likewise in Bangkok, according to a survey by two European researchers, the poor actively prefer their old slums to the new towerblocks.

40 Ann-Louise Shapiro, "Paris," in M. J. Daunton (ed.), *Housing the Workers, 1850–1914: A Comparative Perspective*, London 1990, pp. 40–41.
41 Hans-Dieter Evers and Rüdiger Korff, *Southeast Asian Urbanism: The Meaning and Power of Social Space*, New York 2000, p. 168.
42 Victor Sit, *Beijing: The Nature and Planning of a Chinese Capital City*, Chichester 1995, pp. 218–19.

The agencies who plan slum eviction see an alternative for the people in the cheap highrise flats: the people in the slums know that eviction and life in these flats would reduce their means of reproduction and the possibilities for subsistence production. Furthermore access to work is more difficult due to the location of these flats. This is the simple reason why the slumdwellers prefer to stay in the slum and are starting to fight against eviction. For them the slum is the place where production under deteriorating circumstances is still possible. For the urban planner, it is a mere cancer in the city.[43]

Meanwhile, middle-class "poaching" – as housing experts call it – of public or state-subsidized housing has become a quasi-universal phenomenon. Algeria in the early 1980s, for example, began to subdivide urban land reserves into plots, ostensibly for development by housing cooperatives; building materials were furnished at subsidized prices. As architect Djaffar Lesbet observes, however, this theoretically elegant balance between state aid and local initiative did not democratize access to housing: "The building plots have allowed those whom the system privileged to hold onto their lead, to achieve their own housing. They have also helped to reduce the dramatic and political tone of the housing crisis, by transforming this national issue into an individual problem."[44] As a result, civil servants and others have acquired subsidized detached homes and villas, while the truly poor have ended up in illegal shacks in *bidonvilles*. Although lacking the revolutionary *élan* of Algeria, Tunisia also developed substantial state-subsidized housing, but 75 percent of it was unaffordable by the poor, who instead crowded into Tunis's sprawling slums such as Ettadhamen, Mellassine, and Djebel Lahmar.[45]

India illustrates the same trend in several different guises. In the 1970s, for example, municipal and state authorities launched a hugely ambitious scheme to create a modern twin city on the mainland, opposite the Bombay peninsula. The urban poor were promised new homes and jobs in glittering New Bombay (now Navi Mumbai), but

43 Evers and Korff, *Southeast Asian Urbanism*, p. 168.

44 Lesbet, "Algeria," pp. 264–65.

45 Frej Stambouli, "Tunis: Crise du Logement et Réhabilitation Urbaine," in Amis and Lloyd, *Housing Africa's Urban Poor*, p. 155.

instead local people on the mainland were displaced with loss of land and livelihood, while the bulk of the new housing went to civil servants and the middle classes.[46] In Delhi, likewise, the Development Agency distributed one half million plots, but "most were grabbed by the well-to-do." Research indicates that only 110,000 houses have actually been built for the poor in a city that is currently evicting 450,000 "illegal" slum-dwellers.[47]

Kolkata, where the Left Front came to power in the late 1970s, should have been a different story, since the Communist Party of India (Marxist) had long campaigned for "liberation" for slum-dwellers. Over time, however, the early promises of rehousing the poor have yielded to the electoral cultivation of the more privileged strata. "Lip service," says writer Frederic Thomas, "is still paid to the needs of the poor, but the lion's share of the budget is used to meet the needs of middle- and upper-income Calcuttans. Only 10 percent of the Calcutta Metropolitan Development Agency's investment is targeted for *bustee* improvement."[48] In Vietnam, as well, revolutionary housing policies have been manipulated to benefit state elites with little spillover to the actual poor. "Access to state or municipal housing," write researchers Nguyen Duc Nhuan and Kosta Mathéy, "is largely reserved for civil servants and members of the army, who have a statutory right to a two bedroom flat, and who, in order to top up their salaries, tend to sublet these units to others if they do not use them themselves."[49]

Nigeria once boasted that it would use its soaring oil revenues to rehouse its urban poor, but the country's Third and Fourth National Development Plans became travesties of this ambitious promise – less than a fifth of the planned homes were actually constructed, and most went to people other than the poor.[50] Likewise in Kano, low-cost housing for civil servants (the continuation of a colonial tradition) has

46 Alain Jacquemin, *Urban Development and New Towns in the Third World*, pp. 196–97.

47 Neelima Risbud, "Policies for Tenure Security in Delhi," in Durand-Lasserve and Royston, *Holding their Ground*, p. 61.

48 Thomas, *Calcutta Poor*, p. 147.

49 Nguyen Duc Nhuan and Kosta Mathéy, "Vietnam," in Mathéy, *Housing Policies in the Socialist Third World*, p. 282.

50 T. Okoye, "Historical Development of Nigerian Housing Policies,' in Amis and Lloyd, *Housing Africa's Urban Poor*, p. 81.

been appropriated by unentitled but politically powerful individuals with incomes high above the threshold set for eligibility.[51] Jamaica is another country where populist rhetoric has never been matched by deeds. To be sure, the National Housing Trust (NHT) has a relatively large asset base, but – as Thomas Klak and Marlene Smith emphasize – it does virtually everything except build for the poor. "Presently most of the NHT's funds go to meet its own payroll, help fulfill central government reserve requirements, provide interim financing of higher income and even non-NHT housing construction, and finance the mortgages of a relatively few and mostly higher-income contributors."[52]

In Mexico, where during the 1980s the formal home market provided for little more than one-third of demand, housing is heavily subsidized for military families, civil servants, and members of a few powerful unions such as the oil workers, but the very poor receive only a trickle of state aid. Thus FOVI, the government trust fund serving the middle segment of the housing market (up to ten times minimum wage), mobilizes 50 percent of federal housing resources, while FONHAPO, serving the poorest segment, receives a mere 4 percent.[53] John Betancur finds a similiar situation in Bogotá, where middle-income groups receive generous subsidies while the state provides only grudging assistance to the housing needs of the poor.[54] In Lima, likewise, most public or subsidized housing is captured by middle-income groups and state employees.[55]

Urban elites and the middle classes in the Third World have also been extraordinarily successful in evading municipal taxation. "In most developing countries," the International Labour Organization's A. Oberai writes, "the revenue potential of real-estate taxation is not fully utilized. The existing systems tend to suffer from poor assessment

51 H. Main, "Housing Problems and Squatting Solutions in Metropolitan Kano," in Robert Potter and Ademola Salau (eds), *Cities and Development in the Third World*, London 1990, p. 22.

52 Thomas Klak and Marlene Smith, "The Political Economy of Formal Sector Housing Finance in Jamaica," in Datta and Jones, *Housing and Finance in Developing Countries*, p. 72.

53 Pezzoli, "Mexico's Urban Housing Environments," p. 142.

54 John Betancur, "Spontaneous Settlements in Colombia," in Aldrich and Sandhu, *Housing the Urban Poor*, p. 224.

55 John Leonard, "Lima: City Profile," *Cities* 17:6 (2000), p. 437.

administration, substantial erosion of the tax base due to exemptions, and poor performance in terms of tax collection."[56] Oberai is too polite: the urban rich in Africa, south Asia, and much of Latin America are rampantly, even criminally undertaxed by local governments. Moreover, as financially hardpressed cities have come to rely on regressive sales taxes and user charges – these generate 40 percent of revenue in Mexico City, for example – the tax burden has shifted even more one-sidedly from the rich to the poor. In a rare comparative analysis of fiscal administration among ten Third World cities, Nick Devas finds a consistently regressive pattern, with little evidence of any serious effort to assess and collect property taxes from the affluent.[57]

Part of the blame must be assigned to the IMF which, in its role as the Third World's financial watchdog, everywhere advocates regressive user fees and charges for public services but never proposes counterpart efforts to tax wealth, conspicuous consumption, or real estate. Likewise, the World Bank crusades for "good governance" in the cities of the Third World but undermines its likelihood by seldom supporting progressive taxation.[58]

Both "poaching" and fiscal bias, of course, are expressions of the poor majority's lack of political clout throughout most of the Third World; urban democracy is still the exception rather than the rule, especially in Africa. Even where the slum poor have the right to vote, they can seldom wield it to effect significant redistributions of expenditures or tax resources: a variety of structural strategies – including metropolitan political fragmentation, control of budgets by provincial or national authorities, and the establishment of autonomous agencies – have been used to insulate urban decision-making from the popular franchise. In his study of the Mumbai region, Alain Jacquemin emphasizes the confiscation of local power by urban development authorities, whose role is to build modern infrastructures that allow the wealthier parts of poor cities to plug themselves – and themselves alone – into the world cyber-economy. These authorities, he writes, "have further undermined the

56 Oberai, *Population Growth, Employment and Poverty in Third-World Mega-Cities*, p. 169.
57 Nick Devas, "Can City Governments in the South Deliver for the Poor?," *International Development and Planning Review* 25:1 (2003), pp. 6–7.
58 Oberai, *Population Growth, Employment and Poverty in Third-World Mega-Cities*, pp. 165, 171.

tasks and functions of democratically elected municipal governments already weakened by the loss of sectoral responsibilities and financial and human resources to special *ad hoc* authorities. No wonder locally expressed needs at the municipal and neighborhood level remain unheard."[59]

With a handful of exceptions, then, the postcolonial state has comprehensively betrayed its original promises to the urban poor. A consensus of urban scholars agrees that public- and state-assisted housing in the Third World has primarily benefited the urban middle classes and elites, who expect to pay low taxes while receiving high levels of municipal services. In Egypt, Ahmed Soliman concludes that "public investment [for housing] has been largely wasted," with the result that "about twenty million people live today in houses that are detrimental to their health and safety."[60]

Similarly in the case of India, Nandini Gooptu describes the transformation of pro-poor policies of the Gandhi era into their opposites:

> Ultimately, the grand conception of urban transformation was whittled away and domesticated to meet the immediate interests of the propertied classes. Instead of unfolding as idealistic projects of social regeneration, the town planning schemes evolved as avenues to further the interests and aspirations of the propertied and the instrument of the growing marginalization of the poor. The war against slums came dangerously close to being a battle to control the settlement and habitation of the poor, and indeed an offensive against the poor themselves.[61]

59 Jacquemin, *Urban Development and New Towns in the Third World*, pp. 41, 65; see also K. Sivaramakrishnan, "Urban Governance: Changing Realities," pp. 232–33.

60 Soliman, in Ananya Roy and Nezar Al Sayyad (eds), *Urban Informality: Transnational Perspectives from the Middle East, Latin America, and South Asia*, Lanham (Md.) 2004, pp. 171, 202.

61 Gooptu, *The Politics of the Urban Poor in Early Twentieth-Century India*, p. 84.

4

Illusions of Self-Help

It would be foolish to pass from one distortion – that the
slums are places of crime, disease and despair – to the
opposite: that they can be safely left to look after themselves.

Jeremy Seabrook[1]

As Third World governments abdicated the battle against the slum in
the 1970s, the Bretton Woods institutions – with the IMF as "bad cop"
and the World Bank as "good cop" – assumed increasingly command-
ing roles in setting the parameters of urban housing policy. Lending for
urban development by the World Bank increased from a mere 10 million
dollars in 1972 to more than 2 billion dollars in 1988.[2] And between
1972 and 1990 the Bank helped finance a total of 116 sites-and-services
and/or slum-upgrading schemes in 55 nations.[3] In terms of need, of
course, this was a mere drop in the bucket, but it gave the Bank tremen-
dous leverage over national urban policies, as well as direct patronage
relationships to local slum communities and NGOs; it also allowed the
Bank to impose its own theories as worldwide urban policy orthodoxy.

---

1 Seabrook, *In the Cities of the South*, p. 197.
2 S. Sethuraman, "Urban Poverty and the Informal Sector: A Critical
Assessment of Current Strategies," International Labour Organization (ILO) working
paper, Geneva 1997, pp. 2–3.
3 Cedric Pugh, "The Role of the World Bank in Housing," in Aldrich and
Sandhu, *Housing the Urban Poor*, p. 63.

Improving rather than replacing slums became the less ambitious goal of public and private intervention. Instead of the top-down structural reform of urban poverty, as undertaken by postwar social democracy in Europe and advocated by revolutionary-nationalist leaders of the 1950s generation, the new wisdom of the late 1970s and early 1980s mandated that the state ally with international donors and, then, NGOs, to become an "enabler" of the poor. In its first iteration, the new World Bank philosophy, which was influenced by the ideas of the English architect John Turner, stressed a "sites-and-services" (provision of basic "wet" infrastructure and civil engineering) approach to help rationalize and upgrade self-help housing. By the late 1980s, however, the World Bank was championing privatization of housing supply across the board and soon became the most powerful institutional megaphone for the schemas of Hernando de Soto, the Peruvian economist who advocates micro-entrepreneurial solutions to urban poverty.

The Friends of the Poor

The intellectual marriage in the 1970s between World Bank President Robert McNamara and architect John Turner was supremely odd. The former, of course, had been chief planner of the war in Vietnam, while the latter had once been a leading contributor to the English anarchist paper *Freedom*. Turner left England in 1957 to work in Peru, where he was mesmerized by the creative genius he discerned at work in squatter housing. He was not the first architect to enthuse about poor people's capacities for communal self-organization and clever construction: French colonial architects and planners, like the Groupe CIAM Alger, had praised the spontaneous order of the *bidonville* for the "'organic' relationship between the buildings and the site (reminiscent of the *casbah*), the flexibility of spaces to accommodate diverse functions, and the changing needs of the users."[4] Turner, however, in collaboration with sociologist William Mangin, was a singularly effective popularizer and propagandist who proclaimed that slums were less the problem than the solution. Despite its radical provenance, Turner's core program

4 Zeynep Çelik, *Urban Forms and Colonial Confrontations: Algiers under French Rule*, Berkeley 1997, p. 112.

of self-help, incremental construction, and legalization of spontaneous urbanization was exactly the kind of pragmatic, cost-effective approach to the urban crisis that McNamara favored.

By 1976, the year of the first UN-HABITAT conference as well as the publication of Turner's *Housing by People: Towards Autonomy in Building Environments*, this amalgam of anarchism and neoliberalism had become a new orthodoxy that "formulated a radical departure from public housing, favoring sites and services projects and *in situ* slum upgrading." The World Bank's new Urban Development Department was to be the chief sponsor of this strategy. "The intention," continues Cedric Pugh, "was to make housing affordable to low-income households without the payment of subsidies, in contrast to the heavily subsidized public-housing approach."[5] Amidst great ballyhoo about "helping the poor help themselves," little notice was taken publicly of the momentous downsizing of entitlement implicit in the World Bank's canonization of slum housing. Praising the praxis of the poor became a smokescreen for reneging upon historic state commitments to relieve poverty and homelessness. "By demonstrating the ability, the courage, and the capacity for self-help of slum people," Jeremy Seabrook writes, "the way [was] prepared for a withdrawal of state and local government intervention and support."[6]

Moreover, Turner and his World Bank admirers considerably romanticized the costs and results of squatter-type incremental housing. As the research of Kavita Datta and Gareth Jones has shown, the loss of economy of scale in housing construction dictates either very high unit prices for construction materials (purchased in small quantities from nearby retailers) or the substitution of secondhand, poor-quality materials. Datta and Jones argue, moreover, that "self-housing" is partly a myth: "Most self-help is actually constructed with the paid assistance of artisans, and for specialist tasks, skilled labour."[7]

Most importantly, the cost-recovery provisions of World Bank lending, part of a hardening neoliberal dogma, effectively priced the poorest of the poor out of the market for self-help loans. Lisa Peattie,

    5 Pugh, "The Role of the World Bank in Housing," p. 64.
    6 Seabrook, *In the Cities of the South*, pp. 196–97.
    7 Kavita Datta and Gareth Jones, "Preface," in Datta and Jones, *Housing and Finance in Developing Countries*, p. 12.

one of the World Bank's most trenchant critics, estimated in 1987 that the bottom 30 to 60 percent of the population, depending on the specific country, were unable to meet the financial obligations of sites-and-services provision or loans for upgrading.[8] Moreover, even the World Bank's most ambitious and touted projects tended to be poached by the middle classes or non-needy in the same way as had public housing.

The Philippines, a pilot country for the World Bank's new global strategy, was a notorious case in point. Working with the Marcos dictatorship, the Bank staff identified 253 blighted "areas for priority development," beginning with the vast section of slum housing along the Tondo foreshore of metropolitan Manila. But "the investments," claims Erhard Berner, simply "trickled straight up to the land developers and the construction industry." St. Joseph's Village in Pasig, for example, was widely heralded as a model project for poor families, and Imelda Marcos even recruited Pope Paul VI as an official sponsor. Yet within five years, according to Berner, "all the original dwellers had left because their lots had been sold to wealthy families."[9] The failures were so embarrassing that the World Bank retooled the program to focus instead on sites-and-services provision in resettlement areas outside metro Manila. These remote locations discouraged gentrification, but at the same time were hated by the poor because of their distance from jobs and services. At the end of the day, Berner says, the World Bank's heroic exertions in Manila left most of the targeted slums "as congested and dilapidated as ever."[10]

In Mumbai, another highly acclaimed World Bank laboratory, slum upgrading on a massive scale (affecting 3 million people) was promised, but the results were again nugatory. The sanitation program, for example, had aimed to provide 1 toilet seat for every 20 residents, but the achieved ratio was only 1 per 100, and sporadic maintenance of the facilities nullified any public-health advantage. Meanwhile, "by 1989," according to an expert review, "the scheme for slum upgrading had

8 Lisa Peattie, "Affordability," *Habitat International* 11:4 (1987), pp. 69–76.

9 Berner, *Defending a Place*, p. 31.

10 Erhard Berner, "Poverty Alleviation and the Eviction of the Poorest," *International Journal of Urban and Regional Research* 24:3 (September 2000), pp. 558–59.

fallen well short of expectation and only 9 percent of recipients belonged to low-income groups."[11]

The balance sheet of first-generation World Bank urban projects in Africa reveals equally bleak or perverse results. In Dar-es-Salaam after the end of an ambitious World Bank intervention (1974–81), a study found that "a majority of squatters allocated plots in the sites and service program have sold their plots and gone back to squat on virgin land on the periphery of the urban areas." Most of the site-and-service lots ended up in the hands of state employees and the middle class.[12] Planning expert Charles Choguill says this is unsurprising because the minimum savings required by the World Bank to qualify for a construction loan was so high that it automatically excluded most of the squatters.[13] Likewise, in another site-and-service scheme in Lusaka, only one fifth went to the target group, and roughly the same dismal result obtained in Dakar.[14]

Writing in 1993, the ILO's A. Oberai concluded that World Bank slum-upgrading and sites-and-services projects had largely failed to have visible impact on the housing crisis in the Third World: "Despite efforts to make projects replicable, the project approach ties up excessive resources and institutional effort in a few locations and has not been able to achieve the desired level of housing stock. The project approach is therefore unlikely to have a significant impact on solving the problem of shelter in most developing countries."[15] Other critics pointed to the programmatic disassociation of housing provision from employment creation, and the inevitable tendency for sites-and-services schemes to be located in peripheries poorly served, if at all, by public transport.[16]

11   Greg O'Hare, Dina Abbott, and Michael Barke, "A Review of Slum Housing Policies in Mumbai," *Cities* 15:4 (1998), p. 279.

12   A. Mosa, "Squatter and Slum Settlements in Tanzania," in Aldrich and Sandhu, *Housing the Urban Poor*, p. 346; John Campbell, "World Bank Urban Shelter Projects in East Africa," in Amis and Lloyd, *Housing Africa's Urban Poor*, p. 211.

13   Charles Choguill, "The Future of Planned Urban Development in the Third World," in Aldrich and Sandhu, *Housing the Urban Poor*, p. 408.

14   Campbell, "World Bank Urban Shelter Projects in East Africa," *Housing Africa's Urban Poor*, p. 211; Richard Stren, "Urban Housing in Africa," ibid, p. 41.

15   Oberai, *Population Growth, Employment and Poverty in Third-World Mega-Cities*, p. 122

16   "Livelihood and Shelter Have To Be Seen as One Rather than Separate Entities," in Kalpana Sharma, *Rediscovering Dharavi: Stories from Asia's Largest Slum*, New Delhi 2000, p. 202.

Yet the Bank continued to press its incrementalist approach – now refurbished and renamed "whole-sector housing development" – as the best strategy to ameliorate slum conditions.

Soft Imperialism

Since the mid-1990s the World Bank, the United Nations Development Program, and other aid institutions have increasingly bypassed or short-circuited governments to work directly with regional and neighborhood non-governmental organizations (NGOs). Indeed, the NGO revolution – there are now tens of thousands in Third World cities – has reshaped the landscape of urban development aid in much the same way that the War on Poverty in the 1960s transformed relations between Washington, big city political machines, and insurgent inner-city constituencies.[17] As the intermediary role of the state has declined, the big international institutions have acquired their own grassroots presence through dependent NGOs in thousands of slums and poor urban communities. Typically, an international lender-donor like the World Bank, the UK Department for International Development, the Ford Foundation, or the German Friedrich Ebert Foundation will work through a major NGO which, in turn, provides expertise to a local NGO or indigenous recipient. This tiered system of coordination and funding is usually portrayed as the last word in "empowerment," "synergy," and "participatory governance."

On the World Bank side, the increased role of NGOs corresponded to the reorientation of Bank objectives under the presidency of James Wolfensohn, the Australian-born financier and philanthropist whose decade in office began in June 1995. Wolfensohn, according to biographer Sebastian Mallaby, arrived in Washington as a self-proclaimed world-fixer, "seeking to revive the messianic energy of McNamara's Bank" by making poverty reduction and "partnership" the new centerpieces of his agenda. Third World governments were required to involve NGOs and advocacy groups in the preparation of the Poverty Reduction Strategy Papers (PRSP) that the Bank now required as proof that aid would actually reach target groups. In a cooptive McNamaran

17 Datta and Jones, "Preface," p. xviii.

vein, Wolfenshohn also sought to incorporate the upper levels of the NGO world into the Bank's functional networks – and despite the emergence of an anti-globalization movement, he largely succeeded, as Mallaby points out, in "turning the enemies of the [1994] Madrid summit into dinner companions."[18]

Although some former critics have hailed this "participatory turn" at the World Bank, the true beneficiaries seem to be big NGOs rather than local people. In a review of recent studies, including a major report by the London-based Panos Institute, Rita Abrahamsen concludes that "rather than empowering 'civil society,' the PRSP process has entrenched the position of a small, homogeneous 'iron triangle' of transnational professionals based in key government ministries (especially Finance), multilateral and bilateral development agencies and international NGOs."[19] What Nobel laureate Joseph Stiglitz in his brief tenure as chief economist for the Bank described as an emerging "post-Washington Consensus" might be better characterized as "soft imperialism," with the major NGOs captive to the agenda of the international donors, and grassroots groups similarly dependent upon the international NGOs.[20]

For all the glowing rhetoric about democratization, self-help, social capital, and the strengthening of civil society, the actual power relations in this new NGO universe resemble nothing so much as traditional clientelism. Moreover, like the community organizations patronized by the War on Poverty in the 1960s, Third World NGOs have proven brilliant at coopting local leadership as well as hegemonizing the social space traditionally occupied by the Left. Even if there are some celebrated exceptions – such as the militant NGOs so instrumental in creating the World Social Forums – the broad impact of the NGO/ "civil society revolution," as even some World Bank researchers acknowledge, has been to bureaucratize and deradicalize urban social movements.[21]

18   Sebastian Mallaby, *The World's Banker: A Story of Failed States, Financial Crises, and the Wealth and Poverty of Nations*, New York 2004, pp. 89–90, 145.

19   Rita Abrahamsen, "Review Essay: Poverty Reduction or Adjustment by Another Name?," *Review of African Political Economy* 99 (2004), p. 185.

20   Stiglitz's 1998 speech, "More Instruments and Broader Goals: Moving Towards the Post-Washington Consensus," is discussed in John Pender, "From 'Structural Adjustment' to 'Comprehensive Development Framework': Conditionality Transformed?," *Third World Quarterly* 22:3 (2001).

21   Imparato and Ruster, *Slum Upgrading and Participation*, p. 255.

Thus development economist Diana Mitlin, writing about Latin America, describes how, on one hand, NGOs "preempt community-level capacity-building as they take over decision-making and negotiating roles," while, on the other hand, they are constrained by "the difficulties of managing donor finance, with its emphasis on shortterm project funds, on financial accountabilities and on tangible outputs."[22] Similarly in the case of urban Argentina, architect Rubén Gazzoli complains that NGOs monopolize expert knowledge and middleman roles in the same way as traditional political machines.[23] Lea Jellinek, a social historian who has spent more than a quarter-century studying the poor in Jakarta, in turn, recounts how one famed NGO, a neighborhood microbank, "beginning as a small grassroots project driven by needs and capacities of local women," grew Frankenstein-like into a "large, complex, top–down, technically oriented bureaucracy" that was "less accountable to and supportive of" its low-income base.[24]

From a Middle Eastern perspective, Asef Bayat deplores the hyperbole about NGOs, pointing out that "their potential for independent and democratic organization has generally been overestimated. [The] professionalization of NGOs tends to diminish the mobilizational feature of grassroots activism, while it establishes a new form of clientelism."[25] Frederic Thomas, writing about Kolkata, argues that "NGOs, moreover, are inherently conservative. They are staffed by retired civil servants and businessmen at the top and, lower down, by social workers, from among the educated unemployed and by housewives and others without roots in the slums."[26]

Veteran Mumbai housing activist P.K. Das offers an even harsher critique of slum-oriented NGOs:

22 Diana Mitlin, "Civil Society and Urban Poverty – Examining Complexity," *Environment and Urbanization* 13:2 (October 2001), p. 164.

23 Rubén Gazzoli, "The Political and Institutional Context of Popular Organizations in Urban Argentina," *Environment and Urbanization* 8:1 (April 1996), p. 163.

24 Lea Jellinek, "Collapsing under the Weight of Success: An NGO in Jakarta," *Environment and Urbanization* 15:1 (April 2003), p. 171.

25 Bayat in Roy and Al Sayyad (eds), *Urban Informality: Transnational Perspectives from the Middle East, Latin America, and South Asia*, pp. 80–81.

26 Thomas, *Calcutta Poor*, p. 131.

Their constant effort is to subvert, dis-inform and de-idealize people so as to keep them away from class struggles. They adopt and propagate the practice of begging favours on sympathetic and humane grounds rather than making the oppressed conscious of their rights. As a matter of fact these agencies and organizations systematically intervene to oppose the agitational path people take to win their demands. Their effort is constantly to divert people's attention from the larger political evils of imperialism to merely local issues and so confuse people in differentiating enemies from friends.[27]

Das's complaints are amplified in detail in Gita Verma's controversial 2002 book *Slumming India*, a fierce, almost Swiftian attack on the celebrity cult of urban NGOs. A rebel planner and exile from what she calls "The System," Verma characterizes NGOs as "new class" middlemen who, with the benediction of foreign philanthropies, are usurping the authentic voices of the poor. She rails against the World Bank paradigm of slum upgrading that accepts slums as eternal realities, as well as anti-eviction movements that refuse to raise more radical demands. The "right to stay," she says, "is no great privilege. ... It may stop the occasional bulldozer but, for the rest, it does little beyond change the label from 'problem' to 'solution' with some creative jargon in fine print." "Saving the slum," she adds, specifically referring to Delhi, "translates into endorsing the inequity of one-fifth to one-fourth of the city's population living on just 5 percent of the city's land."[28]

Verma's account includes a devastating debunking of two of the most celebrated recent slum improvement projects in India. The UK-sponsored Indore scheme, which won awards at the Istanbul Habitat II conference in 1996 and from the Aga Khan in 1998, supposedly provided the city's slum households with individual water and sewer connections, but Verma says it was "faking success out of a civic disaster." Although neighborhoods now had sewers, residents didn't have enough water to drink, much less to flush waste, so sewage consequently backed up into homes and streets; malaria and cholera spread,

27 P.K. Das, "Manifesto of a Housing Activist," in Patel and Thorner, *Bombay*, pp. 179–80.
28 Gita Verma, *Slumming India: A Chronicle of Slums and Their Saviours*, New Delhi 2002, pp. 150–52.

and residents began to die from contaminated water. Each summer, Verma writes, "brought project beneficiaries (or, perhaps, Project Affected Persons) more water shortages, more choked drains, more diseases, more monsoon mess, and more cause to complain about the shoddy project infrastructure and poor quality ..."[29]

Verma is equally scalding about the award-winning Aranya resettlement project: one of a species of projects that rehouse only a small number of evictees or squatters but confer international celebrity on their "slum saviors." In this case, however, most of the project's achievements were literally on paper.

> The truth about Aranya, however, is that its winning elements simply do not exist on the ground. There is no town centre, no flowing pedestrian greens, and no 40,000 poor people living there. These exist only in the literature on Aranya and for more than a decade we have been celebrating a drawing, a design idea, that we are not sure will work because it has not yet been tested.[30]

Even observers less harsh than Verma agree that while the World Bank/NGO approach to slum upgrading may produce local success stories, it leaves the vast majority of the poor behind. NGOs, observes activist and writer Arundhati Roy, "end up functioning like the whistle on a pressure cooker. They divert and sublimate political rage, and make sure it does not build to a head."[31] Syrupy official assurances about "enablement" and "good governance" sidestep core issues of global inequality and debt, and ultimately they are just language games that cloak the absence of any macro-strategy for alleviating urban poverty. Perhaps this guilty awareness of the gap between promise and need explains some of the fervor with which international lending institutions and NGOs have embraced the ideas of Hernando de Soto, the Peruvian businessman who has become the global guru of neo-liberal populism.

A John Turner for the 1990s, de Soto asserts that Third World cities are not so much starved of investment and jobs as suffering an artificial

29 Ibid., pp. 8–15, 33–35.
30 Ibid., pp. 90–91.
31 Arundhati Roy, *The Checkbook and the Cruise Missile: Conversations with Arundhati Roy*, Boston 2004, p. 82.

shortage of property rights. By waving the magic wand of land-titling, de Soto claims, his Institute for Liberty and Democracy could conjure vast pools of capital out of the slums themselves. The poor, he argues, are actually rich, but they are unable to access their wealth (improved real estate in the informal sector) or turn it into liquid capital because they do not possess formal deeds or property titles. Titling, he claims, would instantly create massive equity with little or no cost to government; part of this new wealth, in turn, would supply capital to credit-starved microentrepreneurs to create new jobs in the slums, and shantytowns would then become "acres of diamonds." He speaks of "trillions of dollars, all ready to put to use if only we can unravel the mystery of how assets are transformed into live capital."[32]

Ironically, de Soto, the Messiah of people's capitalism, proposes little more in practice than what the Latin American Left or the Communist Party of India (Marxist) in Kolkata had long fought for: security of tenure for informal settlers. But titling, as land-tenure expert Geoffrey Payne points out, is a double-edged sword. "For owners it represents their formal incorporation into the official city, and the chance to realize what may be a dramatically increased asset. For tenants, or those unable to pay the additional taxes that usually follow, it may push them off the housing ladder altogether." Titling, in other words, accelerates social differentiation in the slum and does nothing to aid renters, the actual majority of the poor in many cities. Payne warns that it even risks "the creation of a large underclass that is denied access to any form of affordable or acceptable housing."[33]

Peter Ward confirms that titling – or rather, "regularization" – in Mexico City has been a mixed blessing for *colonos*. "It is not simply a means of extending full property titles to the poor, but increasingly a means of incorporating them into the tax base." The benefits of being able to use homes as legal collateral are counterbalanced by a new visibility to tax collectors and municipal utilities. Regularization also undermines solidarity within the *colonias* by individualizing the struggle

---

32 Hernando de Soto, *The Mystery of Capital: Why Capitalism Triumphs in the West and Fails Everywhere Else*, New York 2000, pp. 301–31.

33 Geoffrey Payne, unpublished 1989 report, quoted in Alan Gilbert and Ann Varley, *Landlord and Tenant: Housing the Poor in Urban Mexico*, London 1991, p. 4.

for housing and by giving titled homeowners interests that differ from those of other slum residents. "Renters, harassed squatters, displaced downtown tenants," argues Ward, "are likely to be more radical and disposed to anti-government demonstrations than are those who have, in effect, been bought-off by the government through successive housing policies."[34]

This has even been the case in São Paulo, where Workers' Party (PT) administrations, starting in 1989, have tried to regularize and upgrade the "huge illegal city" of the poor. Although the PT's reforms have produced some admirable results, Suzana Taschner, who has carefully studied the local impact, points to negative repercussions as well: "Unfortunately, with the upgrading, the real estate submarket consolidates in the *favela*. Both land and houses become consumption goods and the price soars." One result is the emergence of what Taschner calls the "slum within the *favela*," as squatters' homes are replaced by shoddy *cortiços* (tenements) renting single rooms to the poorest of the poor.[35] Without decisive public intervention in real-estate markets, in other words, titling by itself is hardly an Archimedean lever to raise the fortunes of the great mass of poor urban dwellers.

However, de Sotoan panaceas remain immensely popular for obvious reasons: the titling strategy promises big social gains with a mere act of the pen and, thus, pumps life back into the World Bank's tired self-help paradigms; it accords perfectly with dominant neoliberal, anti-state ideology, including the Bank's current emphasis on government facilitation of private housing markets and the promotion of broad home ownership; and it is equally attractive to governments because it promises them something – stability, votes, and taxes – for virtually nothing. "The acceptance of unauthorized settlements," Philip Amis points out, "is a relatively painless, and potentially profitable, way to appease the urban poor in the Third World."[36] And, as geographers Alan Gilbert and Ann Varley emphasize in the case of Latin America, it is also a classical conservative reform: "The very nature of the self-help housing process has ... contributed to political placidity.

34 Ward, *Mexico City*, p. 193.
35 Suzana Taschner, "Squatter Settlements and Slums in Brazil," in Aldrich and Sandhu, *Housing the Urban Poor*, pp. 216–19.
36 Amis, "Commercialized Housing in Nairobi," p. 237.

Widespread home ownership has individualized what might otherwise have constituted a more community-wide struggle."[37]

In the same vein, Erhard Berner provides some dismal examples from Manila of how land purchase and title formalization have produced vertical social differentiation and bitter competition within once militant squatter movements. He writes:

> The task of fixing the social value of the land, getting it accepted by the members and, eventually, expelling those who are unable or unwilling to pay for it it is an ordeal for every local association. The times when the K-B [squatter association] could be mistaken for a part of an antisystemic "social movement" are definitely over. Now that they have become landowners K-B leaders regard their alliance with other squatter organizations as obsolete and emphasize their relation to government institutions.[38]

Profits of Poverty

Even as NGOs and development lenders tinker with "good governance" and incremental slum improvement, incomparably more powerful market forces are pushing the majority of the poor further to the margins of urban life. The positive achievements of international philanthropy and residual state intervention are entirely dwarfed by the negative impacts of land inflation and property speculation. Real-estate markets, as we have seen in the case of pirate urbanization, have returned to the slums with a vengeance, and despite the enduring mythology of heroic squatters and free land, the urban poor are increasingly the vassals of landlords and developers.

Slumlordism, of course, is an ancient evil, and its contemporary incarnations invoke comparison with its nineteenth-century forebears. In his analysis of the political economy of London's East End (the Victorian world's greatest slum), historian Gareth Stedman Jones described a vicious circle of housing demolition, rising rents, overcrowding, and disease. "The really high profits," he observed, "were not made from investment in the housing boom in the suburbs, but the

---

37 Gilbert and Varley, *Landlord and Tenant*, p. 11.
38 Berner, *Defending a Place*, p. 179.

rack-renting boom in the inner area."[39] Slums like St. Giles, Whitechapel, and Bethnal Green attracted aristocratic investors whose "expectation of high returns on foreign investment had been disappointed," as well as the frugal middle class for whom inner-city housing was "the most popular and the most accessible means of capital gain." Jones finds that a great cross-section of London society, ranging from mega-slumlords like Thomas Flight (reputed to extract rent from more than 18,000 dwellings) to "small tradesmen, retired builders, and vestrymen owning or farming a few houses each," had a lucrative stake in the immiseration of the East End.[40]

Similarly in the case of *fin-de-siècle* Naples ("Europe's Calcutta"), contemporary observers marveled at the miracle of ever larger rents returned from the ever poorer and more wretched *fondaci* and *locande*. Frank Snowden, in his extraordinary study of the Neopolitan poor, writes:

> By the end of the century, rent had increased fivefold while the inhabitants of the city had grown poorer. Ironically, moreover, the highest rents per square metre were for the most dismal rooms in the slums. Because these rooms cost the least in absolute terms, the demand for them was greatest. Unhappily, the demand for slum accommodation grew with increasing poverty, thus giving further twists to the rent spiral affecting those least able to pay.[41]

The same obscene and paradoxical profits are still mined from urban poverty. For generations, rural landowning elites in the Third World have been transforming themselves into urban slumlords. "Absentee landlordism," write Hans-Dieter Evers and Rüdiger Korff, "is in fact largely an urban phenomenon."[42] The relatively broad base of home ownership or legalized squatting in Latin America contrasts with fantastic concentrations of landownership in many African and Asian cities. In their pathbreaking comparative study, the two German researchers discovered

---

39 Gareth Stedman Jones, *Outcast London: A Study in the Relationship Between Classes in Victorian Society*, London 1971, pp. 209.
40 Ibid., pp. 212–13.
41 Frank Snowden, *Naples in the Time of Cholera, 1884–1911*, Cambridge 1995, p. 39.
42 Evers and Korff, *Southeast Asian Urbanism*, p. 180.

that on average 53 percent of land in 16 Southeast Asian cities was owned by the top 5 percent of landlords as compared to 17 percent of land by the top 5 percent in German cities.[43] Indeed, nearly half of Manila, according to Erhard Berner, is owned by a handful of families.[44]

In India, meanwhile, an estimated three-quarters of urban space is owned by 6 percent of urban households, and just 91 people control the majority of all vacant land in Mumbai.[45] Land speculation, meanwhile, confounds housing reform in Karachi and other large Pakistani cities. As Ellen Brennan explains:

> Karachi's government has attempted to control speculation by limiting the number of plots an individual can own. The law has been easily cir-cumvented by the use of family proxies. Moreover, Karachi's property and capital gains taxes have aided investors in holding plots they never intended to occupy. For example, some 80,000 to 100,000 of the 260,000 plots developed by the Karachi Development Authority during the 1970s were held for investment and lay vacant ten years later.[46]

This trend toward urban *latifundia*, moreover, is perversely rooted in the crisis and decline of the productive economy. Presumably there was once a time when urban land values were synchronized to economic growth and industrial investment. Since the late 1970s, however, that relationship has dissolved as urban real estate has increasingly become a capital trap for national savings. The interlocked debt crisis, galloping inflation, and IMF shock therapy of the late 1970s and 1980s destroyed most incentives for productive investment in home industries and public employment. Structural adjustment programs, in turn, channeled domestic savings from manufacture and welfare into land speculation. "The high rate of inflation and the massive scale of devaluation," writes political economist Kwadwo Konadu-Agyemang of Accra, "have discouraged savings and made investment in undeveloped or

---

43 Ibid. As the authors emphasize, "despite the importance of the topic, data on urban land-ownership are extremely rare. This contrasts sharply with research on land tenure in rural areas." (p. 184)

44 Berner, *Defending a Place*, p. 21.

45 Baken and van der Linden, *Land Delivery for Low Income Groups in Third World Cities*, p. 13.

46 Brennan, "Urban Land and Housing Issues Facing the Third World," p. 78.

partially developed land the safest and most profitable way of holding assets that could also be sold in foreign currency."[47]

The result has been the emergence or persistence of property bubbles amidst otherwise general economic stagnation or even decline. Thus in Istanbul, as Çağlar Keyder notes, "in the inflationary environment of the 1980s, real estate became the highest-profit sector ... where political corruption, capitalist development and international finance intersected."[48] In Ankara smart money flowed into the booming market for converting slums into upscale apartment neighborhoods. The central locations of older *gecekondus*, explains planner Özlem Dündar, made them irresistible targets for renewal and gentrification by large-scale developers who alone "had the political influence and financial power to solve the very confusing ownership problems in the *gecekondu* areas."[49]

In the Arab world, as Janet Abu-Lughod has long stressed, oil revenues and overseas earnings flow not into production "but into land as a capital 'bank.' This has resulted in rampant land speculation (which makes rational city planning impossible), grossly inflated land values, and, in some cases, overbuilding of luxury flats."[50] In the case of Egypt at least, the urban land boom in the 1990s was reinforced by massive public subsidies to the banking sector and to politically favored developers. As geographer Timothy Mitchell explains in his striking study of a Cairo suburb called "Dreamland":

> ... structural adjustment was intended to generate an export boom, not a building boom. Egypt was to prosper by selling fruits and vegetables to Europe and the Gulf, not by paving over its fields to build ring roads. But real estate has now replaced agriculture as Egypt's third largest non-oil investment sector, after manufacturing and tourism. Indeed, it may be the largest non-oil sector, since most tourism investment goes into building tourist villages and vacation homes, another form of real estate.[51]

47 Kwadwo Konadu-Agyemang, *The Political Economy of Housing and Urban Development in Africa: Ghana's Experience from Colonial Times to 1998*, Westport 2001, p. 123.
48 Keyder, "The Housing Market from Informal to Global," p. 153.
49 Özlem Dündar, "Informal Housing in Ankara," *Cities* 18:6 (2001), p. 393.
50 Janet Abu-Lughod, "Urbanization in the Arab World and the International System," in Gugler, *Cities of the Developing World*, p. 196.
51 Timothy Mitchell, "Dreamland: The Neoliberalism of Your Desires," *Middle East Report* (Spring 1999), np (internet archive).

Even as metro Cairo has doubled its area in five years and new suburbs sprawl westward into the desert, the housing crisis remains acute: new housing is too expensive for the poor, and much of it is unoccupied because the owner is away working in Saudia Arabia or the Gulf. "Upwards of a million apartments," writes Jeffrey Nedoroscik, "stand empty ... there is no housing shortage per se. In fact, Cairo is filled with buildings that are half-empty."[52]

"Dhaka, the world's poorest megacity," explains Ellen Brennan, "has seen intensive urban land speculation. An estimated one-third of expatriate remittances have gone for land purchases. Land prices have risen about 40 to 60 percent faster than prices of other goods and services and are now completely out of line with income levels."[53] Another South Asia example is Colombo, where property values increased a thousandfold during the late 1970s and 1980s, pushing large numbers of older, poorer urban residents into peri-urban areas.[54]

Overcrowded, poorly maintained slum dwellings, meanwhile, are often more profitable per square foot than other types of real-estate investment. In Brazil, where much of the middle class serves as landlord to the poor, ownership of a few tenements (*çorticos*) leverages many professionals and middle managers into Copacabana lifestyles. Researchers for UN-HABITAT were surprised to find that "*çortico* rent price per square meter in São Paulo is around 90 percent higher than in the formal market."[55] In Quito wealthy landowners sell off parcels of land in foothills and steep ravines – usually above the 2850-meter city limit, the highest level to which the muncipal system can pump water – through intermediaries (*urbanizadores piratas*) to land-hungry immigrants, letting the residents later fight for city services.[56] Discussing Bogotá's "pirate housing market," land economist Umberto Molina claims that speculators are developing the urban periphery at "monopoly prices" and enormous profits.[57]

52 Nedoroscik, *The City of the Dead*, p. 42.
53 Brennan, "Urban Land and Housing Issues Facing the Third World," p. 76.
54 Dayaratne and Samarawickrama, "Empowering Communities, p. 102.
55 Fix, Arantes, and Tanaka, "São Paulo, Brazil," p. 18.
56 Glasser, "The Growing Housing Crisis in Ecuador," p. 151. For Quito, see also Gerrit Burgwal, *Caciquismo, Paralelismo and Clientelismo: The History of a Quito Squatter Settlement*, Amsterdam 1993.
57 Umberto Molina, "Bogotá: Competition and Substitution Between Urban Land Markets," in Baken and van der Linden, p. 300.

In her book on Lagos, Margaret Peil explains that "there has been much less squatting ... than in eastern Africa or Latin America because the low level of government control over construction meant that legitimate houses could be easily and profitably built: housing the poor was good business ... the safest investment available, producing a quick return on capital."[58] Wealthier Lagos landlords prefer to lease rather than sell land so that they can retain control of profits in a rapidly appreciating land market.[59] As in Kenya, politicians, along with traditional chiefs, have been prominent amongst the larger-scale speculators in slum housing.[60]

Nairobi's slums, meanwhile, are vast rent plantations owned by politicians and the upper middle class. Although most of the private rental development "has no formal legal basis ... property relations and ownership [thanks to a corrupt political system] exist in a de facto sense."[61] In Mathare 4A, where 28,000 people – the poorest of the poor – rent 9-by-12-meter mud-and-wattle hovels, the absentee landlords, according to a researcher for the Ministry of Roads, are "powerful, forceful behind the scenes and are often prominent public figures, those connected to them or very wealthy individuals or firms."[62] "Fifty-seven percent of the dwellings in one Nairobi slum," write UN researchers in another study, "are owned by politicians and civil servants, and the shacks are the most profitable housing in the city. A slumlord who pays $160 for a 100-square-foot shack can recoup the entire investment in months."[63]

Land speculation, as these Nairobi cases illustrate, can thrive even where the land involved is officially in the public domain – Egypt, Pakistan, China and Mali offer other egregious examples. In metro Cairo, writes architect-planner Khaled Adham, "the selling-off of

58 Margaret Peil, *Lagos: The City Is the People*, London 1991, p. 146.
59 Margaret Peil, "Urban Housing and Services in Anglophone West Africa," in Hamish Main and Stephen Williams (eds), *Environment and Housing in Third World Cities*, Chichester 1994, p. 176.
60 Drakakis-Smith, *Third World Cities*, p. 146.
61 Amis, "Commercialized Rental Housing in Nairobi," p. 245.
62 Patrick Wasike, "The Redevelopment of Large Informal Settlements in Nairobi," Ministry of Roads and Public Works, Kenya, nd.
63 Cited in Davan Maharaj, "Living on Pennies," part four, *Los Angeles Times*, 16 July 2004.

some public land accommodated a massive transfer of the desert surrounding Cairo to private ownership." The beneficiaries, he adds, were
"a new class of entrepreneurs that is increasingly linked to both the
state and international corporations." High-ranking members of the
Mubarak regime are presumed to have hidden interests in the firms
developing suburbs in the desert west of the Giza Pyramids.[64]

The periphery of Karachi is public land supposedly controlled by the
Karachi Development Authority. Yet, as the Authority, according to
Peter Nientied and Jan van der Linden, has "totally failed to provide
land for housing low income groups," the fringe has been illegally subdivided, as noted earlier, by syndicates of public officials, corrupt police,
and middlemen known as *dalals*. At the end of the day, slum-dwellers
have done little more than lease patronage. "Since the whole operation
is illegal, demands, by definition, are always for favours, rather than for
rights."[65] Likewise in Hyderabad, studied by Erhard Berner, "land-
grabbers connected with the Board of Revenues" hijacked an ambitious
resettlement scheme for the poor, extorting illegal fees from residents
and stealing tracts of public land. "Establishing a police post," Berner
explains, "worsened the situation as the police took the side of the syn-
dicate and began to harass the residents themselves."[66]

Illegal speculation in peripheral urban land, meanwhile, has become
one of the principal forms of official corruption in China. "In one
village in wealthy Zhejian Province," reports the *New York Times*,
"farmers were given $3,040 per *mu*, only to watch city officials lease the
same plots to developers for $122,000 each." An elderly peasant com-
plained that "officials took the land for development and have been
pocketing all the money for themselves." In a similar incident in
Shaanxi, a woman protester was told by a Communist Party official:
"So you dirt-poor trash think you can oppose the city government?
You don't have a chance in hell."[67]

64 Khaled Adham, "Cairo's Urban Déjà vu," in Yasser Elsheshtawy (ed.), *Planning
Middle Eastern Cities: An Urban Kaleidoscope in a Globalizing World*, London 2004, p. 157.
65 Peter Nientied and Jan van der Linden, "The Role of the Government in the
Supply of Legal and Illegal Land in Karachi," in Baken and van der Linden, *Land
Delivery for Low Income Groups in Third World Cities*, pp. 230, 237–38.
66 Berner, "Learning from Informal Markets," p. 241.
67 "Farmers Being Moved Aside by China's Booming Market in Real Estate," *New
York Times*, 8 December 2004.

In Bamako (Mali), where communal landownership coexists with market land, the city periphery was supposed to be subdivided, as need arose, according to customary law amongst family heads. Instead, as in Karachi, the new bureaucratic caste hijacked the system. "Two-thirds of all allotted plots," finds researcher August van Westen, "were used for speculative resales instead of housing the owner's family. The problem is that the juxtaposition of two conflicting modes of land supply – one a formally egalitarian system of public allotments, the other a purely commercial market of already registered land titles – made it fairly easy to gain substantial profits." Traders and civil servants turned themselves into urban landlords, while a growing share of the population became either renters or the occupants of "illegal settlements ... politically held to ransom by sections of the party establishment."[68]

Finally, even squatting can be a stealth strategy for the elite's manipulation of land values. Writing about Lima in the 1970s, geographer Manuel Castells described how squatters were used by landowners as urban pioneers.

Very often landowners and private developers have manipulated the squatters into forcing portions of the land onto the real estate market, by obtaining from the authorities some urban infrastructure for the squatters, thus enhancing the land value and opening the way for profitable housing construction. In a second stage, the squatters are expelled from the land they have occupied and forced to start all over again on the frontier of a city which has expanded as a result of their efforts.[69]

More recently, Erhard Berner observed the same process of "tolerated invasions" in Manila, where squatters "convert barren hillsides, marginal fields, or swampy marshes into housing land," thus leveraging land values for owners who can then either evict residents or jack up their rents.[70]

68 August van Westen, "Land supply for Low-Income Housing: Bamako," in Baróss and van der Linden, *The Transformation of Land Supply Systems in Third World Cities*, pp. 93, 101–02.
69 Manuel Castells, *The City and the Grassroots: A Cross-Cultural Theory of Urban Social Movements*, New York 1983, p. 191
70 Berner, "Learning from Informal Markets," pp. 234–35.

End of the Urban Frontier?

The squatter is still the major human symbol, whether as victim or hero, of the Third World city. Yet, as we saw in the previous chapter, the golden age of squatting – of free or low-cost occupation of peripheral urban land – was clearly over by 1990. Indeed, as early as 1984, a group of leading housing experts meeting in Bangkok warned that the "no cost occupation of land is a temporary phenomenon," and that the "options for informal solutions [to the housing crisis] have been already reduced and will rapidly become more so" as "powerful and integrated private organizations" take control of urbanization at the periphery. "In their view, the formalization of transferable land titles (as distinct from security of tenure) was actually accelerating the process by which entrepreneurs who "circumvented or corrupted" the planning process were able to privatize squatting.[71]

A few years later, Ellen Brennan repeated the same warning: "Many options previously available to low-income people, such as unused public land, are disappearing rapidly even as access to peripheral land is becoming increasingly restricted. Indeed, vacant land on the urban fringes and elsewhere is being assembled and developed by corporate developers, legally and illegally." Brennan observed that the problem was just as acute where most of the land was in the public domain (Karachi and Delhi) as where the periphery was mostly private property (Manila, Seoul, and Bangkok).[72]

In the same period, Alan Gilbert wrote with increasing pessimism about the future role of squatting and self-help housing as safety valves for the social contradictions of Latin American cities. He predicted that the confluence of pirate urbanization, economic stagnation, and the costs of transportation would make homeownership in peripheral subdivisions or shantytowns less attractive than in the past: "More families will occupy smaller plots, will take longer to consolidate their homes, and will be forced to live longer without services."[73] Although emphasizing that peripheral real-estate markets still provided an important

71 Baróss and Jan van der Linden, "Introduction," in *The Transformation of Land Supply in Third World Cities*, pp. 1, 2, 8.
72 Brennan, "Urban Land and Planning Issues Facing the Third World," pp. 75–76.
73 Gilbert et al., *In Search of a Home*, p. 3.

alternative for middle-class families priced out of their former habitats, Alain Durand-Lasserve, another world authority on land management, agreed with Brennan and Gilbert that commercialization had "foreclosed the informal and virtually free access to the land" that the very poor had previously enjoyed.[74]

Everywhere, the most powerful local interests – big developers, politicians, and military juntas – have positioned themselves to take advantage of peripheral land sales to poor migrants as well as members of the urban salariat. For example, a sampling of landownership on the periphery of Jakarta revealed "that vast tracts of land, especially in the hill country of the Priangan, have changed hands and now belong to Indonesian generals and their families, higher government officials, and other members of the Indonesian upper class."[75] Similarly in Mexico City, where most slum housing is now being subdivided from *ejidos*, Keith Pezzoli found that "*ejidatarios* lose out in the process of urbanization," as "developers and speculators are consolidating control over unbuilt land."[76] In Bogotá, as big developers implant middle-class housing estates on the periphery, urban-edge land values soar out of the reach of the poor, while in Brazil speculation grips every category of land, with an estimated one third of building space left vacant in anticipation of future increases.[77]

In China the urban edge – as noted earlier – has become the arena of a vast, one-sided social struggle between city governments and poor farmers. In the face of development authorities' inexhaustible appetite for new land for economic zones and suburbs, peasants are pushed aside with minimal consideration or compensation; likewise, traditional working-class neighborhoods and villages are routinely razed for more upscale developments, often to the advantage of corrupt officials and party leaders. When locals protest, they end up being confronted by paramilitary police and often face prison terms.[78]

---

74 Alain Durand-Lasserve, "Articulation between Formal and Informal Land Markets in Cities in Developing Countries: Issues and Trends," in Baróss and van der Linden, *The Transformation of Land Supply in Third World Cities*, p. 50.

75 Evers and Korff, *Southeast Asian Urbanism*, p. 176.

76 Pezzoli, *Human Settlements*, p. 15.

77 Gilbert and Varley, *Landlord and Tenant*, pp. 3, 5.

78 See the fifth installment in Jim Yardley's outstanding series on rural/urban inequality in China in the *New York Times*, 8 December 2004.

Poor Manilenos, meanwhile, have been driven further into illegality by berserk land values that preclude formal housing for a large minority of the population. "In the 1980s," reports urban-environmental historian Greg Bankoff, "land prices rose 35 to 40 times in Quezon City, 50 to 80 times in Makati, 250 to 400 times in Diliman and a staggering 2000 times in Escolta. In 1996, the CBD was registering an annual increase of 50 percent and even the value of land in peripheral areas rose by 25 percent."[79] Formal housing, as a result, became inaccessible to hundreds of thousands of poor people. With land inflation raging even on the distant urban edge, the only choices seemingly left to the poorest Manilenos are either to risk death in the flood-prone metropolis by squatting in the beds of *esteros* or along the precarious banks of rivers, or to occupy the interstices of wealthier *barangays* where violent eviction is an imminent threat.

Throughout the Third World, then, the (John) Turnerian frontier of free land for poor squatters has ended: the "slums of hope" have been replaced by urban *latifundia* and crony capitalism. The constriction or closure of opportunities for non-market settlement at the edge, in turn, has immense repercussions for the stability of poor cities. In lockstep with the increasing percentage of renters, the most dramatic consequence in the short run has been soaring population density in Third World slums – land inflation in the context of stagnant or declining formal employment has been the piston driving this compression of people. Modern mega-slums like Kibera (Nairobi) and Cité-Soleil (Port-au-Prince) have achieved densities comparable to cattle feedlots: crowding more residents per acre into low-rise housing than there were in famous congested tenement districts such as the Lower East Side in the 1900s or in contemporary highrise cores such as central Tokyo and Manhattan. Indeed, Asia's largest contemporary slum, Dharavi in Mumbai, has a maximum density more than twice that of the nineteenth-century New York and Bombay streets that Roy Lubove believed were the "most crowded spots on earth" in late-Victorian times.[80]

---

79 Greg Bankoff, "Constructing Vulnerability: The Historical, Natural and Social Generation of Flooding in Metropolitan Manila," *Disasters* 27:3 (2003), p. 232.

80 "A certain district of the eleventh ward had 243,641 people per square kilometer, and Koombarwara in Bombay, 187,722." Roy Lubove, *The Progressives and the Slums: Tenement House Reform in New York City, 1890–1917*, Pittsburgh 1962, p. 94.

This urban population implosion via relentless infill and overcrowding almost defies credulity. In Kolkata's *bustees*, for example, an average of 13.4 people are somehow shoehorned into each occupied room. If municipal statistics can be believed, Dharavi compacts an incredible 18,000 people per acre into 10-by-15-foot rooms stacked on top of one another.[81] Manshiyet Nasr, at the foot of the Muqattam Hills east of the Nile, is only slightly less congested: more than one-half million people share a mere 350 hectares. (At its southern edge, "in conditions of Dantesque degradation" according to the *Financial Times*, the famous Zaballeen pick through rubbish for their subsistence.)[82] Rio's *favelas*, meanwhile, are being rapidly Manhattanized in response to a lack of squattable land and thus a burgeoning demand for rental rooms. "We can see side by side with the peripheralization of Rio *favelas*," writes Suzana Taschner, "a verticalization of the oldest ones, where buildings with four to six stories appear, often for rent."[83]

Thanks to the commercialization of edge development, densification has become almost as ubiquitous on the periphery as in the urban core. In Caracas, for example, *barrios* are densifying at the rate of almost 2 percent per year: much of this is vertical growth up the mountainsides. Columbia University scientists, researching the city's landslide hazard, were amazed by the mountaineering challenge of being poor in the Venezuelan metropolis. "Indeed some residents are required to climb up the equivalent of 25 stories to reach their *rancho* houses and the average *barrio* dweller needs almost 30 minutes on foot to reach public transportation."[84] In Bogotá the southward expansion of the zone of poverty has preserved high density despite increasing household size toward the periphery.[85]

Lagos's greatest slum, Ajegunle, exemplifies the worst of worlds: overcrowding coupled with extreme peripherality. In 1972, Ajegunle contained 90,000 people on 8 square kilometers of swampy land; today 1.5 million people reside on an only slightly larger surface area, and

81 Sharma, *Rediscovering Dharavi*, pp. xx, xxvii, 18.
82 James Drummond, "Providing Collateral for a Better Future," *Financial Times*, 18 October 2001.
83 Suzana Taschner, "Squatter Settlements and Slums in Brazil," pp. 196, 219.
84 Urban Planning Studio, *Disaster Resistant Caracas*, p. 27.
85 Mohan, *Understanding the Developing Metropolis*, p. 55.

they spend a hellish average of three hours each day commuting to their workplaces.[86] Likewise in supercrowded Kibera in Nairobi, where more than 800,000 people struggle for dignity amidst mud and sewage, slum-dwellers are caught in the vise of soaring rents (for chicken-coop-like shacks) and rising transport costs. Rasna Warah, writing for UN-Habitat, cites the case of a typical Kibera resident, a vegetable hawker, who spends almost half her monthly income of $21 on transportation to and from the city market.[87]

The commodification of housing and next-generation urban land in a demographically dynamic but job-poor metropolis is a theoretical recipe for exactly the vicious circles of spiraling rents and overcrowding that were previously described in late-Victorian London and Naples. The very market forces, in other words, that the World Bank currently hails as the solution to the Third World urban housing crisis are the classical instigators of that same crisis. But the market rarely acts alone. In the next chapter, we'll consider the class struggle over urban space in cities of the South, and the role of state violence in the commodification of land. "To date," Erhard Berner sourly but accurately observes, "states have been far more effective in the destruction of mass housing than in its construction."[88]

86 Peil, *Lagos*, p. 178; and Peil, "Urban Housing and Services in Anglophone West Africa," p. 180.

87 Rasna Warah, "Nairobi's Slums: Where Life for Women Is Nasty, Brutish and Short," *Habitat Debate* 8:3 (September 2002), np.

88 Berner, "Learning from Informal Markets," p. 230.

5

Haussmann in the Tropics

> The root cause of urban slumming seems to
> lie not in urban poverty but in urban wealth.
>
> *Gita Verma*[1]

Urban inequality in the Third World is visible even from space: satellite reconnaissance of Nairobi reveals that more than half of the population lives on just 18 percent of the city area.[2] This implies, of course, colossal contrasts in population density. "The gulf between rich and poor in Nairobi, one of the world's most unequal cities," writes journalist Jeevan Vasagar in the *Guardian*, "is starkly illustrated by its neighborhoods. In the leafy suburb of Karen there are fewer than 360 inhabitants per square kilometer, according to the 1999 census; parts of Kibera have more than 80,000 people in the same sized area."[3] But Nairobi is scarcely unique in forcing the poor to live in slums of anthill-like density while the wealthy enjoy their gardens and open spaces. In Dhaka 70 percent of the population is estimated to be concentrated into only 20 percent of the surface

1 Gita Verma, *Slumming India*, p. xix.
2 G. Sartori, G. Nembrini, and F. Stauffer, "Monitoring of Urban Growth of Informal Settlements and Population Estimation from Aerial Photography and Satellite Imagining," Occasional Paper #6, Geneva Foundation, June 2002, np.
3 Jeevan Vasagar, "Bulldozers Go in To Clear Kenya's Slum City," *Guardian*, 20 April 2004.

area.[4] Likewise in Santo Domingo, two thirds of the population, living
in tenements and squatter settlements, uses only one fifth of urban
space, with the poorest eighth in the central city slum crowded into
1.6 percent of the city's area.[5] Bombay, according to some urban
geographers, may be the extreme: "While the rich have 90 percent of
the land and live in comfort with many open areas, the poor live
crushed together on 10 percent of the land."[6]

These polarized patterns of land use and population density recapitulate older logics of imperial control and racial dominance.
Throughout the Third World, postcolonial elites have inherited and
greedily reproduced the physical footprints of segregated colonial
cities. Despite rhetorics of national liberation and social justice, they
have aggressively adapted the racial zoning of the colonial period to
defend their own class privileges and spatial exclusivity.

Sub-Saharan Africa, not surprisingly, is the extreme case. In Accra,
writes Kwadwo Konadu-Agyemang, the "indigenous elite [after inde-
pendence] took over the 'European posts' and all the benefits attached
thereto, and have not only maintained the status quo, but have, through
zoning and other planning mechanisms, created several other upper
class residential areas where income, position and clout determine
access."[7] Likewise in Lusaka, the colonial template provided a basis for
the almost total segregation of state officials and African professionals
from their poorer compatriots. In Harare, as politicians and civil
servants moved into white suburbs and garden cities after 1980, they
acquired a growing stake in the maintenance of the *ancien régime*'s spatial

4 Shihabuddin Mahmud and Umut Duyar-Kienast, "Spontaneous Settlements in
Turkey and Bangladesh: Preconditions of Emergence and Environmental Quality of
Gecekondu Settlements and Bustees," *Cities* 18:4 (2001), p. 272.

5 Edmundo Morel and Manuel Mejía, "The Dominican Republic," in Antonio
Azuela, Emilio Duhau, and Enrique Ortiz (eds), *Evictions and the Right to Housing:
Experience from Canada, Chile, The Dominican Republic, South Africa, and South Korea*,
Ottawa 1998, p. 90; Fay and Wellenstein, "Keeping a Roof Over One's Head,"
p. 97.

6 O'Hare, Abbott, and Barke, "A Review of Slum Housing Policies in Mumbai,"
p. 276. Arjun Appadurai gives the figure of 6 million poor people on only 8 percent
of the city's land area. ("Deep Democracy: Urban Governmentality and the Horizon
of Politics," *Environment and Urbanization* 13:2 [October 2001], p. 27.)

7 Konadu-Agyemang, *The Political Economy of Housing and Urban Development in
Africa*, p. 73.

barriers and residential privileges.[8] "The movement of these blacks," writes Cape Town geographer Neil Dewar, "provided a demonstration effect that further militated against eventual implementation of a socialist housing delivery system."[9]

In Kinshasa, meanwhile, "Zaireanization" under the Mobutu dictatorship did nothing to bridge the vast gulf between La Ville of the *blancs* (inherited by the new kleptocrats) and La Cité of the *noirs*. Lilongwe, on the other hand, is a new city purpose-built to showcase Malawi's independence; yet it adheres unswervingly to a colonial model of urban control. According to Allen Howard, "President Hastings Kamuzu Banda supervised its construction and put white South Africans and other Europeans in charge of planning. The result was apartheid-like patterns of segregation, 'containerized' residential areas, and buffer zones."[10] Meanwhile, Luanda is more than ever polarized between the "asphalt" city, ceded by the Portuguese to the *novos ricos*, and the vast dusty periphery of poor *barrios* and *musseques*. Even Addis Ababa, one of the relatively few sub-Saharan cities with an autochthonous origin, has preserved the racist imprint of its brief Italian occupation from 1936 to 1941 – now in the form of economic segregation.

In India independence did little to alter the exclusionary geography of the Raj. Kalpana Sharma, in her book about Asia's largest slum, *Rediscovering Dharavi*, emphasizes that "the inequalities that defined Bombay as a colonial port town have continued. ... Investment is always available to beautify the already well-endowed parts of the city. But there is no money to provide even basic services to the poorer areas."[11] For urban India as a whole, Nandini Gooptu has shown how the "socialist" Congress Party middle classes – who during the 1930s and 1940s extolled the *garib janata* (the poor common people) in the abstract – ended up after independence as enthusiastic custodians of

8 Alison Brown, "Cities for the Urban Poor in Zimbabwe: Urban Space as a Resource for Sustainable Development," in Westendorff and Eade, *Development in Cities*, p. 269; Chalo Mwimba, "The Colonial Legacy of Town Planning in Zambia," paper, Planning Africa 2002 Conference, Durban, September 2002, p. 6.

9 Neil Dewar, "Harare: A Window on the Future for the South African City?," in Anthony Lemon (ed.), *Homes Apart: South Africa's Segregated Cities*, Cape Town 1991, p. 198.

10 Allen Howard, "Cities in Africa, Past and Present," *Canadian Journal of African Studies* 37:2/3 (2003), p. 206.

11 Sharma, *Rediscovering Dharavi*, p. 8.

the colonial design of urban exclusion and social separation. Gooptu writes: "Implicitly or explicitly, the poor were denied a place in civic life and urban culture, and were seen as an impediment to progress and betterment of society."[12]

Removing "Human Encumberments"

Urban segregation is not a frozen status quo, but rather a ceaseless social war in which the state intervenes regularly in the name of "progress," "beautification," and even "social justice for the poor" to redraw spatial boundaries to the advantage of landowners, foreign investors, elite homeowners, and middle-class commuters. As in 1860s Paris under the fanatical reign of Baron Haussmann, urban redevelopment still strives to simultaneously maximize private profit and social control. The contemporary scale of population removal is immense: every year hundreds of thousands, sometimes millions, of poor people – legal tenants as well as squatters – are forcibly evicted from Third World neighborhoods. The urban poor, as a result, are nomads, "transients in a perpetual state of relocation" (as planner Tunde Agbola characterizes their plight in his native Lagos).[13] And like the *sans-culottes* driven from their ancient *quartiers* by Haussmann – to whom Blanqui apostrophized a famous complaint – they "are weary of grandiose homicidal acts ... this vast shifting of stones by the hand of despotism."[14] They are also exasperated with the ancient language of modernization that defines them as "human encumberments" (to quote the Dakar authorities who cleared 90,000 residents from central *bidonvilles* in the 1970s).[15]

The most intense class conflicts over urban space, of course, take place in downtowns and major urban nodes. In an exemplary study, Erhard Berner discusses the case of Manila, where globalized property values collide with the desperate need of the poor to be near central sources of income.

12   Gooptu, *The Politics of the Urban Poor in Twentieth-Century India*, p. 421.
13   Tunde Agbola, *Architecture of Fear*, Ibadan 1997, p. 51.
14   Auguste Blanqui "Capital et travail" (1885), quoted in Walter Benjamin, *The Arcades Project*, Cambridge 2002, p. 144
15   Richard Stren, "Urban Housing in Africa," p. 38.

Metro Manila [is] one of the most densely populated areas in the world. The price of one square meter anywhere near the commercial centers far exceeds the annual income of any jeepney driver or security guard. Yet, the very nature of the income-generating possibilities requires one to stay close to where the action is, because distance from place of work means prohibitive costs in time and money. ... The logical result is wide-spread squatting. Virtually all the gaps left open by city development are immediately filled with makeshift settlements that beat every record in population density.[16]

Street vendors and other informal entrepreneurs also crowd Manila's central plazas, street corners, and parks. Berner describes the failure of market mechanisms or even private security to turn back this invasion of poor people who, after all, are only behaving like rational economic actors – in the end, landowners are dependent upon state repression to keep squatters and vendors at bay, as well as to help evict residual populations of working-class renters and tenement-dwellers.

Regardless of their political complexions and their different levels of tolerance for squatting and informal settlement on their peripheries, most Third World city governments are permanently locked in conflict with the poor in core areas. In some cities – Rio is a famous case – slum clearance has been going on for generations, but it gained irresistible momentum in the 1970s as land values exploded. Some metropolitan governments – Cairo, Mumbai, Delhi, and Mexico City, to name a few – built satellite cities to induce poor residents to relocate to the periphery, but in most cases the new towns simply sucked more population from the adjacent countryside (or, in the case of New Bombay, middle-class commuters) while the traditional urban poor clung desperately to neighborhoods closer to centrally located jobs and services. As a result, squatters and renters, sometimes even small landlords, are routinely evicted with little ceremony, compensation or right of appeal. In big Third World cities, the coercive Panoptican role of "Haussmann" is typically played by special-purpose development agencies; financed by offshore lenders like the World Bank and immune to local vetoes, their mandate is to clear, build, and defend islands of cyber-modernity amidst unmet urban needs and general underdevelopment.

16 Berner, *Defending a Place*, p. xv.

Urbanist Solomon Benjamin has studied the example of Bangalore, where the Agenda Task Force, which directs overall strategic decision-making, is firmly in the hands of the chief minister and major corporate interests, with negligible accountability to local elected representatives. "The zeal of the political elite to turn Bangalore into a Singapore has resulted in extensive evictions and demolitions of settlements, especially small business clusters in productive urban locations. The demolished land is reallocated by master planning to higher income interest groups, including corporations."[17]

Similarly in Delhi – where Banashree Chatterjimitra finds that the government has utterly "subverted the objectives of supplying land for low income housing" by allowing it to be poached by the middle classes – the development authority has targeted nearly half a million squatters for eviction or "voluntary relocation."[18] The Indian capital offers brutal confirmation of Jeremy Seabrook's contention that "the word 'infra-structure' is the new code word for the unceremonious clearance of the fragile shelters of the poor."[19] Sprawling along the banks of Delhi's Yamuna River, Yamuna Pushta is a large and very poor *jhuggi* (squatter town) of 150,000, housing mainly Bengali Muslim refugees. Despite protests and riots, clearance of the area began in 2004 in order to make way for a river promenade and tourist amenities. While the government basks in international praise for its new "green plan," residents are being trucked away some 20 kilometers to a new peripheral slum, despite official evidence, according to the *Hindustan Times*, that "revealed that shifting *jhuggi* dwellers of the Capital has decreased the average income of the relocated families by about 50 percent."[20] "We have to spend at least half of what we earn commuting to our places of work in the city," evictees complained to another newspaper reporter.[21]

17 Solomon Benjamin, "Globalization's Impact on Local Government," *UN-HABITAT Debate* 7:4 (December 2001), p. 25.
18 Banashree Chatterjimitra, "Land Supply for Low-Income Housing in Delhi," in Baken and van der Linden, *Land Delivery for Low Income Groups in Third World Cities*, pp. 218–29; Neelima Risbud, "Policies for Tenure Security in Delhi," p. 61.
19 Seabrook, *In the Cities of the South*, p. 267.
20 Varun Soni, "Slumming It," *Hindustan Times*, 24 October 2003.
21 Ranjit Devraj, "No Way but Down for India's Slum Dwellers," *Asia Times*, 20 July 2000.

Urban Africa, of course, has been the scene of repeated forced exoduses to clear the way for highways and luxury compounds. One of the most notorious and heartbreaking – rivaling Apartheid's demolitions of Sofiatown and Crossroads – was the destruction of Maroko in Lagos in 1990. A former fishing village at the swampy end of Lekki Peninsula, Maroko was colonized by poor people displaced in the late 1950s "so that Victoria Island and Ikoyi could be drained and developed for Europeans and wealthy Africans." Although impoverished, Maroko became famous for its populist *joie de vivre*, dark humor and spectacular music. By the early 1980s, the once marginal Lekki Peninsula itself was considered a prime site for the extension of high-income residences. The 1990 bulldozing of Maroko left 300,000 homeless.[22] "Few Nigerians alive," writes the poet Odia Ofeimun, "can forget the sense of betrayal and the trauma of severance that was occasioned when it happened under military jackboots. It was memorialized across Nigerian literature in poetry, drama and prose."[23]

Under the regime of Daniel Arap Moi, Nairobi's political bosses and influential slumlords were allowed to build rental tenements on public land earmarked for roads, including a 60-meter strip through the heart of Kibera. Now the post-Moi government of President Mwai Kibaki wants to "restore order" to planning by clearing out more than one-third million tenants and squatters.[24] During recent demolitions, residents – many of whom had been conned into investing their lives' savings into buying plots already dedicated to roads – were told by heavily armed police that they had a scant two hours to evacuate their homes.[25]

When it comes to the reclamation of high-value land, ideological symbols and promises made to the poor mean very little to the bureaucrats in power. In Communist-governed Kolkata, for example, squatters have been evicted from the center to the edge, then evicted

22 Margaret Peil, "Urban Housing and Services in Anglophone West Africa," p. 178.
23 Odia Ofeimun, "Invisible Chapters and Daring Visions," *This Day*, 31 July 2003. Some examples: Ogaga Ifowodo, *Red Rain* (originally, *Maroko's Blood*); Maik Nwosu, *Invisible Chapters*; J.P. Clark, "Maroko" (in *A Lot From Paradise*); and Chris Abani's deliriously wonderful *Graceland*.
24 Vasagar, "Bulldozers Go in to Clear Kenya's Slum City."
25 See articles in *The East African Standard* (Nairobi), 8–9 February 2004.

Figure 10[26]

Some Famous Slum Evictions

Year(s)	City	Number evicted
1950	Hong Kong	107,000
1965–74	Rio de Janeiro	139,000
1972–76	Dakar	90,000
1976	Mumbai	70,000
1986–92	Santo Domingo	180,000
1988	Seoul	800,000
1990	Lagos	300,000
1990	Nairobi	40,000
1995–96	Rangoon	1,000,000
1995	Beijing	100,000
2001–03	Jakarta	500,000
2005	Harare	750,000+

again when necessary to create space for middle-class subdivisions. As planner Ananya Roy notes, "the territorial frontier of the Calcutta region has come to be marked by unrelenting cycles of settlement, eviction and resettlement."[27] Likewise, the formerly "Marxist" MPLA regime in Angola doesn't blink an eye when it drives thousands of poor Luandans out of their shanties. As Tony Hodges of the *Economist* Intelligence Unit explains, "between 80 and 90 percent of urban residents live in settlements or buildings that have no clearly defined legal status. ... The problem is yet more serious for the residents of the slum settlements in the peri-urban areas, where the majority of urban-dwellers now live. In these informal settlements, huge numbers of squatters, many of them *deslocados* or migrants from the rural areas, have no legal documents and thus no security of tenure. As a result, they live in permanent fear of evictions. ..." The fear is well founded:

26 Diverse newspaper sources too numerous to cite.
27 Ananya Roy, "The Gentleman's City: Urban Informality in the Calcutta of New Communism," in Roy and Al Sayyad, *Urban Informality*, p. 159.

in July 2001, the provincial governments sent armed police and bulldozers to clear more than 10,000 families from the Boavista slum on
Luanda Bay to make way for a luxury housing development. Two
residents were shot dead; the rest were trucked out to the countryside,
40 kilometers from their old homes, and left to fend for themselves.[28]

The most extraordinary contradictions between residual ideology
and current practice, however, are enacted in China, where the still
putatively "socialist" state allows urban growth machines to displace
millions of history's former heroes. In a thought-provoking article
comparing recent inner-city redevelopment in the PRC to urban
renewal in the United States in the late 1950s and early 1960s, Yan
Zhang and Ke Fang claim that Shanghai forced the relocation of more
than 1.5 million citizens between 1991 and 1997 to make way for skyscrapers, luxury apartments, malls, and new infrastructure; in the same
period nearly 1 million residents of Beijing's old city were pushed into
the outskirts.[29]

In the beginning, urban redevelopment in Deng Xiaoping's China,
as in Harry Truman's America, consisted of pilot housing projects that
seemed to pose little threat to the traditional urban fabric.

When localities scaled up these experiments and accelerated the pace of
housing redevelopment, however, there was not a provision in the
programs to limit market-rate housing and nonresidential uses.
Therefore, moderate and low-income housing quickly lost favor: developers have exploited the loophole to build as many luxury apartments
and commercial developments as possible. In some cases, such as the
Hubeikou project [Beijing], none of the original residents could afford
to return. In others such as the New Oriental Plaza, no housing units
have been built; the largest commercial complex in Asia sprang up there
instead.[30]

28 Hodges, *Angola*, pp. 30–31.
29 Yan Zhang and Ke Fang, "Is History Repeating Itself? From Urban Renewal
in the United States to Inner-City Redevelopment in China," *Journal of Planning
Education and Research* 23 (2004), pp. 286–89.
30 Ibid.

The City Beautiful

In the urban Third World, poor people dread high-profile international events – conferences, dignitary visits, sporting events, beauty contests, and international festivals – that prompt authorities to launch crusades to clean up the city: slum-dwellers know that they are the "dirt" or "blight" that their governments prefer the world not to see. During the Nigerian Independence celebration in 1960, for example, one of the first acts of the new government was to fence the route from the airport so that Queen's Elizabeth's representative, Princess Alexandria, would not see Lagos's slums.[31] These days governments are more likely to improve the view by razing the slums and driving the residents out of the city.

Manilenos have a particular horror of such "beautification campaigns." During Imelda Marcos's domination of city government, shanty-dwellers were successively cleared from the parade routes of the 1974 Miss Universe Pageant, the visit of President Gerald Ford in 1975, and the IMF–World Bank meeting in 1976.[32] Altogether 160,000 squatters were moved out of the media's field of vision, many of them dumped on Manila's outskirts, 30 kilometers or more from their former homes.[33] The subsequent "People's Power" of Corazon Aquino was even more ruthless: some 600,000 squatters were evicted during the Aquino presidency, usually without relocation sites.[34] Despite campaign promises to preserve housing for the urban poor, Aquino's successor, Joseph Estrada, continued the mass evictions: 22,000 shanties were destroyed in the first half of 1999 alone.[35] Then, in preparation for the Association of Southeast Asian Nations (ASEAN) Summit, demolition crews in November 1999 attacked the slum of Dabu-Dabu in Pasay. When 2000 residents formed a human wall, a SWAT team armed with M16s was called in, killing 4 people and wounding 20. Homes and their contents were burnt to the ground, and Dabu-Dabu's miserable

31 Ben Omiyi, *The City of Lagos: Ten Short Essays*, New York 1995, p. 48.

32 Erhard Berner, "Poverty Alleviation and the Eviction of the Poorest," *International Journal of Urban and Regional Research* 24:3 (September 2000), p. 559.

33 Drakakis-Smith, *Third World Cities*, p. 28.

34 Berner, *Defending a Place*, p. 188.

35 Task Force Detainees of the Philippines (TFDP-AMRSP), "Urban Poor, Demolition and the Right to Adequate Housing," briefing paper, Manila 2000.

inhabitants were relocated to a site along the banks of a sewer where their children promptly caught deadly gastrointestinal infections.[36]

As president upon a throne built by US Marines in 1965, the Dominican Republic's Juan Balaguer was notorious as "the Great Evictor." Returning to power in 1986, the elderly autocrat decided to rebuild Santo Domingo in preparation for the quincentenary of Columbus's discovery of the New World and the visit of the Pope. With support from European governments and foundations, he launched a series of over-scaled projects without precedent in Dominican history: the Columbus Lighthouse, Plaza de Armas, and an archipelago of new middle-class subdivisions. In addition to monu-mentalizing himself, Balaguer also aimed to Haussmannize the traditional hearths of urban resistance. His principal target was the huge low-income upper town area of Sabana Perdida, northeast of the city center. "The plan," write researchers working in Sabana Perdida, "was to get rid of troublesome elements in the working-class *barrios* of the upper town by shunting them to the outskirts. Memories of the 1965 revolts and the riots of 1984 suggested it would be wise to elim-inate this centre of political protest and opposition."[37]

After massive protests by the *barrio* rights *coordinadora* supported by the UN Commission on Human Rights, the upper city was saved, but massive demolitions, often involving the army, were carried out in the center, southwest, and southeast of Santo Domingo. Between 1986 and 1992, 40 *barrios* were bulldozed and 180,000 residents were evicted. In an important report on the neighborhood demolitions, Edmundo Morel and Manuel Mejía described the campaign of government terror against the poor.

> Houses were demolished while their inhabitants were still inside, or
> when the owners were away; paramilitary shock troops were used to
> intimidate and terrorize people and force them to abandon their
> homes; household goods were vandalized or stolen; notice of eviction
> was given only on the very day a family was to be thrown out; people

36 Helen Basili, "Demolition the Scourge of the Urban Poor," *Transitions* (newsletter of Service for the Treatment and Rehabilitation of Torture and Trauma Survivors [STARTTS]), #6 (May 2000).

37 Morel and Mejía, "The Dominican Republic," p. 85.

were kidnapped; pregnant women and children were subjected to physical violence; public services to the *barrios* were cut off – a pressure tactic; families were insulted and threatened; and the police acted as judges.[38]

The modern Olympics have an especially dark but little-known history. In preparation for the 1936 Olympics, the Nazis ruthlessly purged homeless people and slum-dwellers from areas of Berlin likely to be seen by international visitors. While subsequent Olympics – including those in Mexico City, Athens, and Barcelona – were accompanied by urban renewal and evictions, the 1988 Seoul games were truly unprecedented in the scale of the official crackdown on poor homeowners, squatters, and tenants: as many as 720,000 people were relocated in Seoul and Injon, leading a Catholic NGO to claim that South Korea vied with South Africa as "the country in which eviction by force is most brutal and inhuman."[39]

Beijing seems to be following the Seoul precedent in its preparations for the 2008 Games: "350,000 people will be resettled to make way for stadium construction alone."[40] Human Rights Watch has drawn attention to extensive collusion between official planners and developers, who manipulate the patriotic excitement inherent to the Olympics in order to justify mass evictions and selfish landgrabs in the heart of Beijing.[41] Anne-Marie Broudehoux, in her brilliant book, *The Making and Selling of Post-Mao Beijing* (2004), claims that in state-capitalist China the current preference is to hide poverty behind "Potemkin-like" façades, not substantively ameliorate it. She predicts that Olympic planning will repeat the traumatic (and for the working classes, darkly ironic) experience of the fiftieth anniversary celebration of the Chinese Revolution.

38 Ibid., pp. 95–97.

39 Catholic Institute for International Relations, *Disposable People: Forced Evictions in South Korea*, London 1988, p. 56

40 Asian Coalition for Housing Rights, *Housing by People in Asia* (newsletter), 15 October 2003, p. 12.

41 See Human Rights Watch, current news reports, and "Demolished: Forced Evictions and the Tenants' Rights Movement in China" at hrw.org/reports/2004/china.

For more than two years, Beijingers had endured the disruption caused by the diverse beautification campaigns initated to camouflage the city's social and physical blight. Hundreds of houses had been demolished, thousands of people expelled, and billions of taxpayers' yuans spent to build a façade of order and progress. To ensure that the carefully planned ceremonies were carried out smoothly, the capital had been brought to a standstill for the duration of the week-long festivities. Beijing residents were ordered to stay home and follow the festivities on television as they had been during the opening ceremony for the Asian Games.[42]

The most Orwellian "urban beautification" program in Asia in recent times, however, was undoubtedly the preparations for "Visit Myanmar Year 1996" undertaken by the heroin-financed Burmese military dictatorship in Rangoon and Mandalay. One-and-a-half million residents – an incredible 16 percent of the total urban population – were removed from their homes (frequently by state-sponsored arson) between 1989 and 1994 and shipped out to hastily constructed bamboo-and-thatch huts in the urban periphery, now creepily renamed the "New Fields." No one knew when their turn might come, and even the dead were evicted from the cemeteries. In her book *Karaoke Fascism*, Monique Skidmore describes brutal scenes in Rangoon and Mandalay reminiscent of Pol Pot's infamous depopulation of Phnom Penh. "Whole city blocks disappear in a matter of days, the population loaded onto trucks and forcibly relocated to the new townships that the government has established on rice fields outside the major cities." Urban neighborhoods were replaced by projects like the new Rangoon Golf Course, aimed at Western tourists and Japanese businessmen. "The generals moved a community that had been on the site for 40 years. Those who resisted were either arrested or forcibly removed to a settlement 15 miles away."[43]

Skidmore argues that this constant spatial dislocation has become the foundation of the regime's "politics of fear." "Through the

42 Anne-Marie Broudehoux, *The Making and Selling of Post-Mao Beijing*, New York 2004, p. 162.

43 Skidmore, *Karaoke Fascism*, Philadelphia 2002, p. 88. See also the file on Burma at www.idpproject.org.

renaming, rebuilding, and relocating of familiar landmarks and the
heavy presence of the army and weaponry, the military council
imposes a new spatial configuration on Rangoon ... suppressing
potential democratic neighborhoods, demolishing the inner city, and
creating new urban centers that immortalize the principle of authori-
tarianism." In place of traditional neighborhoods and historic
buildings, laundered drug money finances glass-and-concrete highrises
("narco-architecture"), hard-currency tourist hotels, and garish pagoda
complexes. Rangoon has become a nightmare combination of a
"Buddhist tourist wonderland," a giant barracks, and a graveyard: it is
"a landscape glorifying the control and authoritarian vision of its
leaders."[44]

Criminalizing the Slum

The urban cleansing strategy of the Burmese generals, of course, has
sinister precedents in the Western hemisphere. In the 1960s and 1970s,
for example, the Southern Cone military dictatorships declared war on
favelas and *campamientos* which they perceived to be potential centers of
resistance, or simply obstacles to urban bourgeoisification. Thus,
writing about Brazil after 1964, Suzana Taschner says: "the beginning
of the military period was characterized by an authoritarian attitude,
removing squatter settlements compulsorily and with the aid of the
public security forces." Evoking the threat of a tiny urban *foco* of
Marxist guerrillas, the military razed 80 *favelas* and evicted almost
140,000 poor people from the hills overlooking Rio.[45] With financial
support from USAID, other *favelas* were later demolished to clear the
way for industrial expansion or to "beautify" the borders of upper-
income areas. Although the authorities failed in their goal of
eliminating all "slums within Rio within a decade," the dictatorship
ignited conflicts between bourgeois neighborhoods and the *favelas*, and
between the police and slum youth, which continue to rage three
decades later.[46]

44 Skidmore, *Karaoke Fascism*, pp. 84–85, 89, 159–60.
45 Taschner, "Squatter Settlements and Slums in Brazil," p. 205.
46 Michael Barke, Tony Escasany and Greg O'Hare, "Samba: A Metaphor for
Rio's Favelas," *Cities* 18:4 (2001), p. 263.

Meanwhile, in Santiago in 1973, one of the first acts of the Pinochet dictatorship – after murdering the leadership of the popular Left – was to reestablish middle-class hegemony in the central city by expelling squatters (some 35,000 families) from the shanty *poblaciónes* and *callampas* that the Allende government had tolerated.[47] "The openly stated objective," says community-organization researcher Hans Harms, "was to create 'homogeneous socio-economic areas in the city.' ... A climate of isolation and fear was created with the disbanding of all neighbourhood organizations under 30 years of Pinochet's military dictatorship."[48] Following a revival of political activism in 1984, the regime again unleashed the wrecking crews against the *pobladores* in another round of "eradications"; the cumulative result, as Cathy Schneider explains in her important history of neighborhood resistance to the dictatorship, was to force evictees and young families to double up with friends or relatives. "The percentage of families living as *allegados* (with more than three persons per bedroom) grew from 25 percent in 1965 to 41 percent in 1985."[49]

A counterinsurgency-driven strategy of slum removal was first adopted in Argentina during the military junta of 1967–70. As Cecilia Zanetta has emphasized, the government's "Plan de Erradicacíon de Villas de Emergencia" was targeted specifically at radicalized self-government in the shantytowns, and the evictees were forced to undergo a phase of "social adjustment" before being resettled in the periphery. However, this first military attempt to roll back informal settlement was only partly successful, and with the restoration of civilian rule in the early 1970s, the slums again became hotbeds of radical Peronist and socialist agitation. When the generals came back into power in March 1976, they were determined to destroy the *villas miserias* once and for all; during the terrible years of *el Proceso*, rent control was repealed, 94 percent of the "illegal" settlements in Gran Buenos Aires were razed, and 270,000 poor people were rendered homeless. Rank-and-file organizers, including lay Catholics as well as leftists, were systematically "disappeared." As in Chile, the liquidation of slum-based

47 Alfredo Rodriguez and Ana Maria Icaza, "Chile," in Azuela, Duhau, and Ortiz, *Evictions and the Right to Housing*, p. 51.

48 Harms, "To Live in the City Centre," p. 198.

49 Cathy Schneider, *Shantytown Protest in Pinochet's Chile*, Philadelphia 1995, p. 101.

social resistance went hand in hand with the speculative recycling of the newly conquered urban lands, and so eradications were especially concentrated, according to one study, "in the capital city and in the north of the Buenos Aires metropolitan area, where land values were higher."[50]

In Egypt, the decade of the 1970s was also an era of fierce state repression directed against "subversive" urban neighborhoods.[51] A famous example was the aftermath of the January 1977 IMF riots in Cairo. The failed neoliberal policies of Sadat's *Infitah* had produced a huge deficit that both Jimmy Carter and the IMF pressed the Egyptian president to correct. "To close this gap," writes journalist Geneive Abdo, "Sadat was forced either to end the subsidies or bleed the well-to-do by imposing high taxes on personal income. The bourgeoisie, a key constituency, was too important to Sadat, so the state opted to cut in half subsidies [for staple foods of the poor]."[52] Furious Cairenes, in turn, attacked such in-their-face symbols of the *Infitah*'s luxury lifestyles as five-star hotels, casinos, nightclubs, and department stores, as well as police stations. Eighty people were killed during the uprising and almost 1000 injured.

After filling the jails with Leftists (a repression that had the side effect of benefiting the rise of Egypt's radical Islamists), Sadat focused his rage on the Ishash al-Turguman slum in the Bulaq district, close to Cairo's center, as the fount of what he denounced as a "Communist-led uprising of thieves." He told foreign journalists that the area was a literal nest of subversion, where Communists hid "where it was impossible to reach them, since narrow streets prevented the use of police cars."[53] Anthropologist Farha Ghannam says that Sadat, like Napoleon III in his day, wanted "the city center to be replanned to allow more effective control and policing." The stigmatized inhabitants of Ishash al-Turguman were divided into two groups and expelled to different

50 Cecilia Zanetta, *The Influence of the World Bank on National Housing and Urban Policies: The Case of Mexico and Argentina in the 1990s*, Aldershot 2004, pp. 194–96.

51 Harris and Wahba, "The Urban Geography of Low-Income Housing," p. 68.

52 Geneive Abdo, *No God but God: Egypt and the Triumph of Islam*, Oxford 2000, pp. 129–30.

53 Farha Ghannam, *Remaking the Modern: Space, Relocation, and the Politics of Identity in a Global Cairo*, Berkeley 2002, p. 38.

parts of the periphery, while their old neighborhood became a parking lot. Ghannam argues that the purge of Bulaq was the first step in a hugely ambitious vision – which Sadat had neither time nor resources to actually implement – of rebuilding Cairo "using Los Angeles and Houston as models."[54]

Since the 1970s it has become commonplace for governments everywhere to justify slum clearance as an indispensable means of fighting crime. Slums, moreover, are frequently seen as threats simply because they are invisible to state surveillance and, effectively, "off-Panopticon." Thus in 1986, when Zambian president Kenneth Kaunda ordered demolitions and evictions throughout Lusaka, he claimed it was because "the majority of crime perpetrators find refuge in unauthorized townships because by virtue of their existence, they lack proper monitoring systems."[55]

Colonial-era law is also frequently used to justify expulsions. In the West Bank, for example, the Israeli army routinely invokes British or even Ottoman statutes when it evicts families and blows up the homes of "terrorists." Likewise, Kuala Lumpur, in pursuit of its goal of becoming "slum free" by 2005, has used police powers derived from the Emergency of the 1950s, when the British bulldozed Chinese squatter communities alleged to be Communist strongholds. Now anti-subversion laws serve what has been described by Kuala Lumpur activists as a "massive and corrupt landgrab" by politicians and developers: "by 1998 half the city's squatters [had] been evicted, leaving 129,000 people living in squalor and fear in 220 settlements."[56] Dhaka's government, meanwhile, used the gang murder of a policeman in 1999 as a pretext to bulldoze 19 "criminal slums" and evict 50,000 people into the streets.[57]

Beijing's "security," of course, was one of the pretexts for the 1989 massacre in Tiananmen Square; six years later it became the official excuse for the brutal dispersal of Zhejiang Village, a sprawling slum on the capital's southern edge. ("Traditionally," notes writer Michael

54 Ibid., p. 135.
55 Mpanjilwa Mulwanda and Emmanuel Mutale, "Never Mind the People, the Shanties Must Go," *Cities* 11:5 (1994), pp. 303, 311.
56 Asian Coalition for Housing Rights, *Housing by People in Asia*, pp. 18–19.
57 BBC News, 8 and 23 August 1999.

Dutton, "the southern part of the city was for the poor, as summed up in the old Beijing adage, 'In the east are the wealthy, in the west live the aristocrats and bureaucrats, while in the south there is only poverty.'"[58]) Most of the slum's 100,000 or so residents came from the Wenzhou district of Zhejiang: an area famous for both the business acumen of its inhabitants and the shortage of arable land. A majority were young, poorly educated *mangliu*, or "floaters," without official residence papers who leased shacks from local farmers and worked in sweatshops, organized by clan-based gangs, where Beijing's cheap winter garments and leather goods are made.[59] Political scientist Dorothy Solinger describes how everywhere in Zhejiang Village, "it was common to find four or five sewing machines, four or five adults, at least one infant, and only two or three beds within one ten-square-meter room."[60]

The demolition of the slum, which began in early November 1995 and went on for two months, was a protracted military operation that involved 5000 armed police and party cadres, and was coordinated by members of the Party Central Committee and State Council. Although Zhejiang Village had long been stigmatized for its alleged gangs, drugs, crime, and high incidences of venereal disease, its destruction – Solinger says – was "decided at the very highest level by Premier [Li] Peng himself ... as a warning to all others who ventured into cities illegally." In the end, 9917 homes were destroyed, 1645 "illegal" businesses (ranging from pedicabs to medical clinics) were shut down, and 18,621 "illegal" residents deported.[61] (As Solinger notes, "within a few months of this dramatic destruction, however, many of the transients were back in place."[62])

Large-scale slum clearance – as exemplified by the destruction of Zhejiang Village – is frequently coordinated with the repression of street vendors and informal workers. General Sutiyoso, the powerful governor of Jakarta, is probably second only to the Burmese generals

58 Dutton, *Streetlife China*, p. 149.
59 Liu Xiaoli and Liang Wei, "Zhejiangcun: Social and Spatial Implications of Informal Urbanization on the Periphery of Beijing," *Cities* 14:2 (1997), pp. 95–98.
60 Solinger, *Contesting Citizenship in Urban China*, p. 233.
61 Dutton (quoting from official documents), *Streetlife China*, pp. 152–59.
62 Solinger, *Contesting Citizenship in Urban China*, p. 69.

in his abuse of the human rights of the poor in Asia. Notorious for his persecution of dissent under the Suharto dictatorship, Sutiyoso has since 2001 "made it his personal crusade to clear Jakarta of informal *kampungs*, as well as its vendors, street musicians, homeless people, and pedicabs." With support from big business, mega-developers, and, more recently, President Megawati herself, the governor has evicted more than 50,000 slum-dwellers, thrown 34,000 pedicab drivers out of work, demolished the stalls of 21,000 street vendors, and arrested hundreds of street musicians. His ostensible aim is to make Jakarta (population 12 million) into a "second Singapore," but grassroots opponents, such as the Urban Poor Consortium, have charged that he is simply clearing slums for future development by his influential backers and political cronies.[63]

If some slum-dwellers commit the "crime" of being in the path of progress, others err by daring to practice democracy. In the aftermath of the corruption-tainted 2005 Zimbabwe elections, President Robert Mugabe turned his wrath against the street markets and shantytowns of Harare and Bulawayo, where the poor had voted in large numbers for the opposition Movement for Democratic Change (MDC). The first stage of sinisterly titled Operation Murambasvina ("Drive Out Trash") in early May was a police assault on the city's 34 flea markets. One police official reportedly urged his men: "From tomorrow, I need reports on my desk saying that we have shot people. The President has given his full support for this operation so there is nothing to fear. You should treat this operation as war."[64]

And the police did. Stalls and inventories were systematically burned or looted, and more than 17,000 traders and jitney drivers were arrested. A week later, the police began to bulldoze shacks in MDC strongholds as well as in pro-Mugabe slums (Chimoi and Nyadzonio, for instance) that were located in areas coveted for redevelopment. In one case, Hatcliffe Extension west of Harare, the police evicted

63 Asian Coalition for Housing Rights, "Housing by People in Asia," as well as press releases from the Asian Human Rights Commission and Urban Poor Consortium (see Urban Poor website: www.urbanpoor.or.id).

64 Munyaradzi Gwisai, "Mass Action Can Stop Operation Murambasvina," International Socialist Organisation (Zimbabwe), 30 May 2005; BBC News, 27 May 2005; *Guardian*, 28 May 2005; *Los Angeles Times*, 29 May 2005.

thousands of residents from a shantytown to which they had been moved in the early 1990s after an earlier "clean-up" campaign before a state visit by Queen Elizabeth II. By mid-July, more than 700,000 slum-dwellers – human "trash" in official terminology – had been expelled, while those who tried to protest were punctually shot, beaten, or arrested.[65] United Nations investigators found that the "scale of suffering is immense, particularly among widows, single mothers, children, orphans, the elderly and disabled people," and Secretary-General Kofi Annan denounced Operation Murambasvina as a "catastrophic injustice."[66]

A socialist opponent of the regime, Brian Raftopoulos from the University of Zimbabwe, compared Mugabe's ethnic cleansing of the urban poor to the despised policies of the colonial and Ian Smith eras.

> As in the colonial past the current regime has used the arguments of criminality and urban squalor to "restore order" to the cities, and as with past attempts this one will not solve the problems.... For the basis of this urban poverty is the crisis of the reproduction of labour, and the continued failure of current economic policy to stabilize the livelihoods of urban workers. In fact labour is now more vulnerable in livelihood terms than it was in 1980, having had to endure the eroding effects of falling real wages, increased food prices and the massive cutbacks of the social wage. ... At no time in the post-1980 period, and perhaps even before that, has the capital city been so badly run with so little regard for the majority of its residents.[67]

Off Worlds

In contrast to Second Empire Paris, contemporary Haussmannization often reclaims the center for ungrateful upper classes whose bags are already packed for the suburbs. If the poor bitterly resist eviction from the urban core, the well-heeled are voluntarily trading their old

65 BBC News, 8 June 2005; and *Mail & Guardian* online (www.mg.co.za), 21 July 2005.

66 BBC News, 22 July 2005.

67 Brian Raftopoulos, "The Battle for the Cities," a contribution to an ongoing Internet debate on Zimbabwe (http://lists.kabissa.org/mailman/listsinfo/debate).

neighborhoods for fantasy-themed walled subdivisions on the periphery. Certainly the old gold coasts remain – like Zamalek in Cairo, Riviera in Abidjan, Victoria Island in Lagos, and so on – but the novel global trend since the early 1990s has been the explosive growth of exclusive, closed suburbs on the peripheries of Third World cities. Even (or especially) in China, the gated community has been called the "most significant development in recent urban planning and design."[68]

These "off worlds" – to use the terminology of *Blade Runner* – are often imagineered as replica Southern Californias. Thus, "Beverly Hills" does not exist only in the 90210 zip code; it is also, with Utopia and Dreamland, a suburb of Cairo, an affluent private city "whose inhabitants can keep their distance from the sight and severity of poverty and the violence and political Islam which is seemingly permeating the localities."[69] Likewise, "Orange County" is a gated estate of sprawling million-dollar California-style homes, designed by a Newport Beach architect and with Martha Stewart décor, on the northern outskirts of Beijing. (As the suburb's developer explained to an American reporter: "People in the United States may think of Orange County as a place, but in China, people feel Orange County is a brand name, something like Giorgio Armani."[70]) Long Beach – which the *New York Times* designated as "the epicenter of *faux* L.A. in China" – is also north of Beijing, astride a new six-lane super-highway.[71] Palm Springs, meanwhile, is a heavily guarded enclave in Hong Kong where affluent residents can "play tennis and stroll through the theme park, where Disney comic strip characters are surrounded by mock Greek columns and neo-classical pavilions." Urban theorist Laura Ruggeri contrasts the expansive imported California lifestyles of residents in their large semi-detached homes with the living conditions of their Filipino maids, who sleep in chicken-coop-like sheds on the rooftops.[72]

68 Pu Miao, "Deserted Streets in a Jammed Town: The Gated Community in Chinese Cities and Its Solution," *Journal of Urban Design* 8:1 (2003), p. 45.

69 Asef Bayat and Eric Denis, "Who Is Afraid of *Ashwaiyat*?," *Environment and Urbanization* 17:2 (October 2000), p. 199.

70 *Orange County Register*, 14 April 2002.

71 *New York Times*, 3 Feburary 2003.

72 Laura Ruggeri, "Palm Springs: Imagineering California in Hong Kong," 1991/94, author website (www.spacing.org). Another "Palm Springs" is a elegant condominium complex in Beijing.

Bangalore, of course, is famous for re-creating Palo Alto and Sunnyvale lifestyles, complete with Starbucks and multiplexes, in its southern suburbs. According to planner Solomon Benjamin, the wealthy expats (officially "non-resident Indians") live as they might in California in "exclusive 'farmhouse' clusters and apartment blocks with their own swimming pools and health clubs, walled-in private security, 24-hour electrical power backup and exclusive club facilities."[73] Lippo Karawaci in the Tangerang district, west of Jakarta, doesn't have an American name but is otherwise also a copy of a West Coast suburb, boasting a more or less self-sufficient infrastructure with hospital, shopping mall, cinemas, sport and golf club, restaurants, and a university. It also contains internally gated areas known locally as "totally protected zones."[74]

The quests for security and social insulation are obsessive and universal. In both central and suburban districts of Manila, wealthy homeowners' associations barricade public streets and crusade for slum demolition. Erhard Berner describes the exclusive Loyola Heights district:

> An elaborate system of iron gates, roadblocks and checkpoints demarcates the boundaries of the area and cuts it off from the rest of the city, at least at nighttime. The threats to life, limb, and property are the overwhelming common concern of the wealthy residents. Houses are turned into virtual fortresses by surrounding them with high walls topped by glass shards, barbed wire, and heavy iron bars on all windows.[75]

This "architecture of fear," as Tunde Agbola describes fortified lifestyles in Lagos, is commonplace in the Third World and some parts of the First, but it reaches a global extreme in large urban societies with the greatest socio-economic inequalities: South Africa, Brazil, Venezuela, and the United States.[76] In Johannesburg, even before the

---

73 Solomon Benjamin, "Governance, Economic Settings and Poverty in Bangalore," *Environment and Urbanization* 12:1 (April 2000), p. 39.

74 Harald Leisch, "Gated Communities in Indonesia," *Cities* 19:5 (2002), pp. 341, 344–45.

75 Berner, *Defending a Place*, p. 163.

76 For a description of Lagos's fortress homes, see Agbola, *Architecture of Fear*, pp. 68–69.

election of Nelson Mandela, big downtown businesses and affluent white residents fled the urban core for northern suburbs (Sandton, Randburg, Rosebank, and so on) which were transformed into high-security analogues of American "edge cities." Within these sprawling suburban *laagers* with their ubiquitous gates, housing clusters, and barricaded public streets, anthropologist Andre Czegledy finds that security has become a culture of the absurd.

> The high perimeter walls are often topped by metal spikes, razor wire, and more recently, electrified wiring connected to emergency alarms. In conjunction with portable "panic button" devices, the house alarms are electronically connected to "armed response" security companies. The surreal nature of such implicit violence was highlighted in my mind one day when walking with a colleague in Westdene, one of the more middle-class neighborhoods of the Northern suburbs. On the streets was parked a minivan from a local security company that boasted in large letters on the vehicle's side panel that they respond with "firearms and explosives." Explosives?[77]

However, in Somerset West, Cape Town's tony suburban belt, the post-Apartheid fortress house is being replaced by more innocent homes without elaborate security hardware. The secret of these gentle residences is the state-of-the-art electric fence surrounding the entire subdivision or, as they are locally known, "security village." Ten-thousand-volt fences, originally developed to keep lions away from livestock, deliver a huge, pulsating shock that is supposed to disable, without actually killing, any intruder. With burgeoning global demand for such residential security technologies, South Africa's electric fencing firms hope to exploit the export market for suburban security.[78]

Brazil's most famous walled and Americanized edge city is Alphaville, in the northwest quadrant of greater São Paulo. Named (perversely) after the dark new world in Godard's dystopian 1965 film,

77 Andre Czegledy, "Villas of the Highveld: A Cultural Perspective on Johannesburg and Its Northern Suburbs," in Richard Tomlinson et al. (eds), *Emerging Johannesburg: Perspectives on the Postapartheid City*, New York 2003, p. 36.

78 Murray Williams, "Gated Villages Catch on among City's Super-Rich," *Cape Argus* (Cape Town), 6 January 2004. For details on suburban electric fence technology, see www.electerrific.co.za.

Alphaville is a complete private city with a large office complex, an up-scale mall, and walled residential areas – all defended by more than 800 private guards. In *City of Walls* (2000), her justly celebrated study of the militarization of urban space in Brazil, Teresa Caldeira writes that "security is one of the main elements in its advertising and an obses-sion of all involved with it." In practice, this has meant vigilante justice for criminal or vagrant intruders, while Alphaville's own gilded youth are allowed to run amuck; one resident quoted by Caldeira affirms: "there is a law for the mortal people, but not for Alphaville residents."[79]

The Johannesburg and São Paulo edge cities (as well as those in Bangalore and Jakarta) are self-sufficient "off worlds" because they incorporate large employment bases as well as most of the retail and cultural apparatus of traditional urban cores. In the cases of more purely residential enclaves, the construction of high-speed highways – as in North America – has been the *sine qua non* for the suburbanization of affluence. As the Latin Americanist Dennis Rodgers argues in the case of Managua elites, "It is the interconnection of these privately protected spaces that constitutes them as a viable 'system,' and it can be contested that the most critical element that has permitted the emer-gence of this 'fortified network' has been the development of a strategic set of well-maintained, well-lit, and fast-moving roads in Managua during the past half decade."[80]

Rodgers goes on to discuss the "Nueva Managua" project of con-servative mayor (and in 1996, president) Arnoldo Alemán who, in addition to destroying revolutionary murals and harassing peddlers and squatters, built the new road system with meticulous attention to the security of wealthier drivers in their SUVs:

> The proliferation of roundabouts … can be linked to the fact that they reduce the risk of carjacking (since cars do not have to stop), while the primary purpose of the bypass seems to have been to allow drivers to avoid a part of Managua reputed for its high levels of crime…. Not only

79 Teresa Caldeira, *City of Walls: Crime, Segregation, and Citizenship in São Paulo*, Berkeley 2000, pp. 253, 262, 278.
80 Dennis Rodgers, "'Disembedding' the City: Crime, Insecurity and Spatial Organization in Managua," *Environment and Urbanization* 16:2 (October 2004), pp. 120–21.

do the road works seem predominantly to connect locations associated with the lives of the urban elites, but there has been simultaneously an almost complete neglect of roads in parts of the city that are unequivocally not associated with the urban elites [read: pro-Sandinista].[81]

In a similar fashion, privately built motorways in Buenos Aires now allow the rich to live full time in their "countries" (country club homes) in distant Pilar and commute to their offices in the core. (Gran Buenos Aires also has an ambitious edge city or *megaempredimiento*, called Nordelta, whose financial viability is uncertain.)[82] In Lagos, likewise, a vast corridor was cleared through densely populated slums to create an expressway for the managers and state officials who live in the wealthy suburb of Ajah. Examples of such networks are numerous, and Rodgers emphasizes that the "ripping out [of] large swaths of the metropolis for the sole use of the urban elites ... encroaches on the public space of the city in a much more extensive way than fortified enclaves do."[83]

It is important to grasp that we are dealing here with a fundamental reorganization of metropolitan space, involving a drastic diminution of the intersections between the lives of the rich and the poor, which transcends traditional social segregation and urban fragmentation. Some Brazilian writers have recently talked about "the return to the medieval city," but the implications of middle-class secession from public space – as well as from any vestige of a shared civic life with the poor – are more radical.[84] Rodgers, following Anthony Giddens, conceptualizes the core process as a "disembedding" of elite activities from local territorial contexts, a quasi-utopian attempt to disengage from a suffocating matrix of poverty and social violence.[85] Laura Ruggeri (discussing Hong Kong's Palm Springs) stresses as well the contemporary

81 Ibid.

82 Guy Thuillier, "Gated Communities in the Metropolitan Area of Buenos Aires," pp. 258–59.

83 Rodgers, "'Disembedding' the City," p. 123.

84 Amália Geraiges de Lemos, Francisco Scarlato, and Reinaldo Machado, "O Retorno a Cidade Medieval: Os Condominios Fechados da Metropole Paulistana," in Luis Felipe Cabrales Barajas (ed.), *Latinoamérica: Países Abiertos, Ciudades Cerradas*, Guadalajara 2000, pp. 217–36.

85 Rodgers, "'Disembedding' the City," p. 123.

quest of deracinated Third World elites for a "real imitation life," modeled on television images of a mythified Southern California, that "to succeed must be bounded – [i.e.], isolated from the ordinary landscape."[86]

Fortified, fantasy-themed enclaves and edge cities, disembedded from their own social landscapes but integrated into globalization's cyber-California floating in the digital ether – this brings us full circle to Philip K. Dick. In this "gilded captivity," Jeremy Seabrook adds, the Third World urban bourgeoisie "cease to be citizens of their own country and become nomads belonging to, and owing allegiance to, a superterrestrial topography of money; they become patriots of wealth, nationalists of an elusive and golden nowhere."[87]

Back in the local world, meanwhile, the urban poor are desperately mired in the ecology of the slum.

86 Ruggeri, "Palm Springs."
87 Seabrook, *In the Cities of the South*, p. 211.

6

Slum Ecology

Those who went to the metropolis have fallen into a desert.

Pepe Kalle

A *villa miseria* outside Buenos Aires may have the world's worst *feng shui*: it is built "over a former lake, a toxic dump, and a cemetery and in a flood zone."[1] But then a hazardous, health-threatening location is the geographical definition of the typical squatters' settlement: whether it is a *barrio* perched precariously on stilts over the excrement-clogged Pasig River in Manila, or the *bustee* in Vijayawada where "residents have door numbers written on pieces of furniture because the houses, along with the doors, [are] washed away by floods every year."[2] Squatters trade physical safety and public health for a few square meters of land and some security against eviction. They are the pioneer settlers of swamps, floodplains, volcano slopes, unstable hillsides, rubbish mountains, chemical dumps, railroad sidings, and desert fringes. Visiting Dhaka, Jeremy Seabrook describes a small slum – "a refuge for people displaced by erosion, cyclones, floods, famine, or that more recent generator of insecurity, development" – that has found a Faustian bargain in a precarious ledge of land between a toxic factory and a poisoned lake. Precisely because the site is so hazardous and unattractive, it offers "protection from rising land values in the city."[3] Such sites are poverty's

---

1 Stillwaggon, *Stunted Lives, Stagnant Economies*, p. 67.
2 Verma, *Slumming India*, p. 69.
3 Seabrook, *In the Cities of the South*, p. 177.

niche in the ecology of the city, and very poor people have little choice but to live with disaster.

Unnatural Hazards

Slums begin with bad geology. Johannesburg's shantytown periphery, for example, conforms unerringly to a belt of dangerous, unstable dolomitic soil contaminated by generations of mining. At least half of the region's non-white population lives in informal settlements in areas of toxic waste and chronic ground collapse.[4] Likewise, the highly weathered lateritic soils underlying hillside *favelas* in Belo Horizonte and other Brazilian cities are catastrophically prone to slope failure and landslides.[5] Geomorphological surveys in 1990 revealed that one quarter of São Paulo's *favelas* were located on dangerously eroded sites, and all the rest, on steep hillsides or erodable river banks. Sixteen percent of squatters were under imminent to medium-term "life risk and/or loss of their property."[6] Rio de Janeiro's more famous *favelas* are built on equally unstable soils atop denuded granite domes and hillsides which frequently give way with truly deadly results: 2000 killed in debris flows in 1966–67, 200 in 1988, and 70 at Christmas 2001.[7] The worst natural disaster in the postwar United States, meanwhile, was the avalanche following heavy rains that killed some 500 people in the shantytown of Mamayes, built on a precarious hillside above Ponce, Puerto Rico.

Caracas (2005 population, 5.2 million), however, is the soil geologist's "perfect storm": slums housing almost two thirds of the urban population are built on unstable hillsides and in deep gorges surrounding the seismically active Caracas Valley. Originally, vegetation held the friable, highly-weathered schist in place, but brush clearance and cut-and-fill construction have destabilized the densely inhabited hillsides, and the

4 Malcolm Lupton and Tony Wolfson, "Low-Income Housing, the Environment and Mining on the Witwatersrand," in Main and Williams, *Environment and Housing in Third World Cities*, pp. 115, 120.

5 Claudia Viana and Terezinha Galvão, "Erosion Hazards Index for Lateritic Soils," *Natural Hazards Review* 4:2 (May 2003), pp. 82–89.

6 Taschner, "Squatter Settlements and Slums in Brazil," p. 218.

7 Richard Pike, David Howell, and Russell Graymer, "Landslides and Cities: An Unwanted Partnership," in Grant Heiken, Robert Fakundiny, and John Sutter (eds), *Earth Science in the City: A Reader*, Washington, D.C. 2003, p. 199.

result has been a radical increase in major landslides and slope failures, from less than one per decade before 1950 to the current average of two or more per month.[8] Increasing soil instability, however, has failed to prevent squatters from colonizing precarious perches on the hillsides, on the slopes of alluvial fans, or in the mouths of regularly flooded canyons.

In mid-December 1999, northern Venezuela, especially the El Avila massif, was clobbered by an extraordinary storm. A year's average rain fell in a few days upon already saturated soil; indeed, rainfall in some areas was reckoned to be "a once in a 1000 year" event.[9] Flash floods and debris flows in Caracas – and especially along the Caribbean coast on the other side of the Avila mountains – killed an estimated 32,000 people and left 140,000 homeless and another 200,000 jobless. The coastal resort of Caraballeda was devastated by the onrush of 1.8 million tons of debris, including boulders as big as houses.[10] A Catholic prelate implied that it was divine retribution for the recent election of the leftist government of Hugo Chávez, but foreign minister Jose Vincente Rangel responded: "It would be a harsh God who took out his vengeance on the poorest section of the community."[11]

What the Caracas region is to landslides, metropolitan Manila is to frequent flooding. Situated in a semi-alluvial plain bordered by three rivers and subject to torrential rains and typhoons, Manila is a natural flood basin. After 1898 American colonial authorities dug canals, dredged tidal channels (*esteros*), and built pumping stations to drain storm waters and protect the central parts of the city. Improvements in the system over recent years, however, have been counteracted by vast volumes of waste dumped into drains and *esteros* (the bottom of the Pasig River is supposedly a 12-foot-deep deposit of refuse);[12] subsidence due to overextraction of ground water; the deforestation of the Marikina and Montalban watersheds; and, most of all, by the ceaseless

8 Virginia Jimenez-Diaz, "The Incidence and Causes of Slope Failure in the Barrios of Carracas," in Main and Williams, *Environment and Housing in Third World Cities*, pp. 127–29.

9 Gerald F. Wieczorek et al., "Debris-Flow and Flooding Hazards Associated with the December 1999 Storm in Coastal Venezuela and Strategies for Mitigation," US Geological Survey, Open File Report 01-0144, Washington, D.C. 2000, p. 2.

10 Pike, Howell, and Graymer, "Landslides and Cities," p. 200.

11 Quoted in Richard Gott, *In the Shadow of the Liberator: Hugo Chávez and the Transformation of Venezuela*, London 2001, p. 3.

12 Berner, *Defending a Place*, p. xiv.

encroachment of shanty housing into wetlands. The housing crisis, in other words, has transformed both the character and magnitude of the flood problem, with the poorest fifth of the population exposed to regular danger and property loss. In November 1998, for example, flooding damaged or destroyed the homes of more than 300,000 people, and on another occasion, the squatter colony of Tatlon was drowned under more than 6 meters of water. In July 2000, moreover, a typhoon deluge caused the collapse of a notorious "garbage mountain" in Quezon City's Payatas slum, burying 500 shacks and killing at least 1000 people. (Payatas has been the subject of several remarkable documentaries by Japanese filmmaker Hiroshi Shinomiya.)[13]

The Caracas and Manila examples illustrate how poverty magnifies local geological and climatic hazards. Urban environmental vulnerability, or *risk*, is sometimes calculated as the product of *hazard* (frequency and magnitude of natural event) times *assets* (population and shelter exposed to hazard) times *fragility* (physical characteristics of built environment): risk = hazard × assets × fragility. Informal urbanization has everywhere multiplied – sometimes by a decimal order of magnitude or more – the inherent natural hazards of urban environments. A textbook example was the August 1988 rainstorms and Nile flood that displaced 800,000 poor residents of Khartoum: scientists point out that while the flood highwater mark was lower than the 1946 peak, it did *ten times* as much damage, largely due to the increased sprawl of slums without drainage in the floodplain.[14]

Wealthy cities in hazardous sites such as Los Angeles or Tokyo can reduce geological or meteorological risk through massive public works and "hard engineering": stabilizing landslides with geotextile nets, gunnite, and rock bolts; terracing and regrading oversteep hillsides; drilling deep drainage wells and pumping water out of saturated soils; intercepting debris flows with small dams and basins; and channeling storm runoff into vast systems of concrete channels and sewers. National flood insurance programs, together with cross-subsidization

13 Bankoff, "Constructing Vulnerability," pp. 224–36; *Asian Economic News*, 31 December 2001 (about the film on the Payatas disaster).
14 Hamish Main and Stephen Williams, "Marginal Urban Environments as Havens for Low-Income Housing," in Main and Williams, *Environment and Housing in Third World Cities*, p. 159.

of fire and earthquake insurance, guarantee residential repair and rebuilding in the event of extensive damage. In the Third World, by contrast, slums that lack potable water and latrines are unlikely to be defended by expensive public works or covered by disaster insurance. Researchers emphasize that foreign debt and subsequent "structural adjustment" drive sinister "trade-offs between production, competition and efficiency, and adverse environmental consequences in terms of potentially disaster-vulnerable settlements."[15] "Fragility" is simply a synonym for systematic government neglect of environmental safety, often in the face of foreign financial pressures.

Yet state intervention itself can be a risk multiplier. In November 2001 the poor districts of Bab el-Oued, Frais Vallon, and Beaux Fraisier in Algiers were struck by devastating floods and mudslides. For 36 hours torrential rain washed fragile shacks from hillsides and flooded low-lying tenement neighborhoods, and at least 900 people were killed. In the face of laggardly official response, rescue efforts were mounted instead by local people, particularly the youth. Three days afterwards, when President Abdelaziz Bouteflika finally made an appearance, angry residents shouted anti-government slogans. Bouteflika told the victims that "the disaster was simply the will of God. Nothing, he said, could be done about that."[16]

Locals knew that this was nonsense. As civil engineers immediately pointed out, the hillside dwellings were a disaster waiting to happen: "These were weak structures vulnerable to heavy rain. Across the country, these kinds of housing constructions have suffered much damage from rain because of degradation, inadequate repair, aging and neglect."[17] Even more to the point, much of the destruction was a direct consequence of the government's war against Islamist guerrillas – to deny insurgents hiding places and escape routes, the authorities had deforested the hills above Bab el-Oued and sealed the sewers. "The blocked drains," writes social scientist Azzedine Layachi, "left rain waters with nowhere to go. Corrupt authorities also gave permits for

15 Mohamed Hamza and Roger Zetter, "Structural Adjustment, Urban Systems, and Disaster Vulnerability in Developing Countries," *Cities* 15:4 (1998), p. 291.

16 Azzedine Layachi, "Algeria: Flooding and Muddled State–Society Relations," *The Middle East Research and Information Project (MERIP) Online*, 11 December 2001.

17 "Flood and Mudslides in Algeria," *Geotimes* (January 2002).

shoddy housing and other construction in the riverbed, enriching individual contractors at the expense of public safety."[18]

Even more than landslides and floods, earthquakes make precise
audits of the urban housing crisis. Although some long-wavelength
quakes, like the 1985 Mexico City disaster, single out tall buildings,
seismic destruction usually maps with uncanny accuracy to poor-quality
brick, mud, or concrete residential housing, especially when associated
with slope failure and soil liquefaction. Seismic hazard is the fine print
in the devil's bargain of informal housing. "Relaxed attitudes to
planning regulations and standards," emphasizes Geoffrey Payne, "has
enabled the urban poor in Turkey to obtain relatively easy access to
land and services for many decades, yet a similar attitude to the
enforcement of building regulations led to a heavy death toll and
massive destruction when earthquakes struck in 1999."[19]

Earthquakes, hazard geographer Kenneth Hewitt claims, destroyed
more than 100 million homes during the twentieth century, mostly in
slums, tenement districts, or poor rural villages. Seismic risk is so
unevenly distributed in most cities, Hewitt explains, that the term
"classquake" was coined to characterize the biased pattern of
destruction.

> The problem was, perhaps, most starkly evident in the February 1978
> Guatemala catastrophe in which almost 1.2 million people lost their
> homes. In Guatemala City, nearly all of some 59,000 destroyed homes
> were in urban slums built in ravines, above and below steep, unstable
> bluffs, or on poorly consolidated young fluvio-volcanic sediments.
> Losses to the rest of the city, and among more expensive homes, were
> negligible, since they occupied much more stable sites.[20]

With the majority of the world's urban population now concentrated on or near active tectonic plate margins, especially along Indian
and Pacific Ocean littorals, several billion people are at risk from earth-

18 Layachi, "Algeria."
19 Geoffrey Payne, "Lowering the Ladder: Regulatory Frameworks for
Sustainable Development," in Westendorff and Eade, *Development and Cities*, p. 259.
20 Kenneth Hewitt, *Regions of Risk: A Geographical Introduction to Disasters*, Harlow
1997, pp. 217–18.

quakes, volcanoes, and tsunamis, as well as from storm surges and typhoons. If the December 2004 Sumatra mega-earthquake and tsunami were relatively rare events, others are virtually inevitable within the next century. Istanbul *gecekondus*, for example, are the ultimate bull's-eye for the earthquakes creeping inexorably westward along the "opening zipper" of the North Anatolia transform fault system. Likewise, Lima authorities predict that at least 100,000 structures – mostly in the *turgurios* and *barriadas* – will collapse during the major earthquake expected sometime in the next generation.[21]

But the urban poor do not lose much sleep at night worrying about earthquakes or even floods. Their chief anxiety is a more frequent and omnipresent threat: fire. Slums, not Mediterranean brush or Australian eucalypti as claimed in some textbooks, are the world's premier fire ecology. Their mixture of inflammable dwellings, extraordinary density, and dependence upon open fires for heat and cooking is a superlative recipe for spontaneous combustion. A simple accident with cooking gas or kerosene can quickly become a mega-fire that destroys hundreds or even thousands of dwellings. Fire spreads through shanties at extraordinary velocity, and fire-fighting vehicles, if they respond, are often unable to negotiate narrow slum lanes.

Slum fires, however, are often anything but accidents: rather than bear the expense of court procedures or endure the wait for an official demolition order, landlords and developers frequently prefer the simplicity of arson. Manila has an especially notorious reputation for suspicious slum fires. "Between February and April 1993," explains Jeremy Seabrook, "there were eight major burnings in the slums, including arson attacks on Smoky Mountain, Aroma Beach and Navotas. The most threatened area is close to the docks where the container terminal is to be extended."[22] Erhard Berner adds that a favorite method for what Filipino landlords prefer to call "hot demolition" is to chase a "kerosene-drenched burning live rat or cat – dogs die too fast – into an annoying settlement … a fire started this way is hard to fight as the unlucky animal can set plenty of shanties aflame before it dies."[23]

21 Leonard, "Lima", p. 439.
22 Seabrook, *In the Cities of the South*, p. 271.
23 Berner, *Defending a Place*, p. 144.

Figure 11

Combustible Poverty

	City	Homes destroyed	Population homeless
2004			
January	Manila (Tondo)	2500	22,000
February	Nairobi		30,000
March	Lagos		5000
April	Bangkok	5000	30,000
November	Dhaka	150	
2005			
January	Khulna City		7000
	Nairobi	414	1500
February	Delhi		3000
	Hyderabad	4000	30,000

In India's Cinderella city of Bangalore, where land values are soaring and the poor are frequently in the wrong place, arson is also employed as *ad hoc* urban renewal. "Partly these fires, " Hans Schenk writes, "are said to be organized by slum leaders who can cash (part of) the government compensation money; partly by some political party-affiliated gangs to clear 'unwelcome' categories of the urban poor; partly by private landowners who want their land cleared in an easy way from (illegal) squatters and have it 'developed.'"[24]

Pathologies of Urban Form

If natural hazards are magnified by urban poverty, new and entirely artificial hazards are created by poverty's interactions with toxic industries, anarchic traffic, and collapsing infrastructures. The chaotic form of so many Third World cities — "urban mandelbrots," according to urban theorist Matthew Gandy — annuls much of the environmental

24 Hans Schenk, "Living in Bangalore's Slums," in Schenk (ed.), *Living in India's Slums: A Case Study of Bangalore*, Delhi 2001, p. 34.

efficiency of city life and breeds the small disasters that constantly terrorize metropolises like Mexico City, Cairo, Dhaka, and Lagos. ("Lagos," explains Gandy, "does not really exist as a city in a conventional sense: its boundaries are unclear; many of its constituent elements appear to function independently of one another....")[25] All the classical principles of urban planning, including the preservation of open space and the separation of noxious land uses from residences, are stood on their heads in poor cities. A kind of infernal zoning ordinance seems to surround dangerous industrial activities and transport infrastructures with dense thickets of shanty housing. Almost every large Third World city (or at least those with some industrial base) has a Dantesque district of slums shrouded in pollution and located next to pipelines, chemical plants, and refineries: Mexico's Iztapalapa, São Paulo's Cubatäo, Rio's Belford Roxo, Jakarta's Cibubur, Tunis's southern fringe, southwestern Alexandria, and so on.

In his book about the poor cities of the South, Jeremy Seabrook chronicles the relentless calendar of disaster in Klong Toey, Bangkok's port slum sandwiched between docks, chemical factories, and expressways. In 1989 a chemical explosion poisoned hundreds of residents; two years later a chemical warehouse exploded and left 5500 residents homeless, many of whom would later die from mysterious illnesses. Fire destroyed 63 homes in 1992, 460 homes in 1993 (also the year of another chemical explosion), and several hundred more in 1994.[26] Thousands of other slums, including some in rich countries, have similar histories to Klong Toey. They suffer from what Gita Verma calls the "garbage dump syndrome": a concentration of toxic industrial activities such as metal plating, dyeing, rendering, tanning, battery recycling, casting, vehicle repair, chemical manufacture, and so on, which middle classes would never tolerate in their own districts.[27] Very little research has been conducted on environmental health in such settings, especially the risks that arise from synergies of multiple toxins and pollutants in the same location.

---

25 Matthew Gandy, "Amorphous Urbanism: Chaos and Complexity in Metropolitan Lagos," manuscript, November 2004 (published in *New Left Review* 33 [May/June 2005]), pp. 1–2.
26 Seabrook, *In the Cities of the South*, p. 192.
27 Verma, *Slumming India*, p. 16.

The world usually pays attention to such fatal admixtures of poverty and toxic industry only when they explode with mass casualties – 1984 was the *annus horribilis*. In February a gasoline pipeline blew up in Cubatão, São Paulo's "Pollution Valley," and burned more than 500 people to death in an adjacent *favela*. Eight months later, a Pemex liquefied natural gas plant exploded like an atomic bomb in Mexico City's San Juanico district, killing as many as 2000 poor residents (no accurate count of mortality was ever established).

> Hundreds never woke up. They were killed even before they realized what had happened. Enormous flames leapt from the nearby gas storage plant and shot a mile into the air. Bodies simply disappeared in the fireball, snatched from the earth without a trace. People ran through the street, some with their clothes and hair on fire, all screaming in fear. The sun had not yet come up, but the light from the flames lit up the scene as if it were noon.[28]

Less than three weeks later, the Union Carbide plant in Bhopal, the capital of Madhya Pradesh, released its infamous cloud of deadly methyl isocyanate; according to a 2004 study by Amnesty International, 7000 to 10,000 people perished immediately and another 15,000 died in subsequent years from related illnesses and cancers. The victims were the poorest of the poor, mainly Muslims. The pesticide packaging plant – "a relatively simple and safe activity" – had been constructed on a site already long occupied by squatters. As the plant expanded and changed over to the more dangerous production of pesticides, *bustees* burgeoned around its periphery. Up to the moment when they found their children dying in the streets, poor squatters had no idea of what was produced in the plant or the apocalyptic hazard posed by massive quantities of methyl isocyanate.[29]

Slum-dwellers, on the other hand, are acutely aware of the dangers posed by the wild traffic that gridlocks the streets of most Third World

28   Joel Simon, *Endangered Mexico: An Environment on the Edge*, San Francisco 1997, p. 157.
29   Amnesty International, *Clouds of Injustice: The Bhopal Disaster 20 Years On*, London 2004, pp. 12, 19; Gordon Walker, "Industrial Hazards, Vulnerability and Planning," in Main and Williams, *Environment and Housing in Third World Cities*, pp. 50–53.

cities. Sprawling urban growth without counterpart social investment in mass transit or grade-separated highways has made traffic a public-health catastrophe. In spite of nightmarish congestion, motor vehicle use in developing cities is soaring (see Figure 12). In 1980 the Third World accounted for only 18 percent of global vehicle ownership; by 2020, about half of the world's projected 1.3 billion cars, trucks, and buses – along with several hundred million motorbikes and scooters – will clog the streets and alleys of poorer countries.[30]

The automobile population explosion is driven by powerful forces of inequality. As Daniel Sperling and Eileen Clausen explain, transportation policy in most cities is a vicious circle in which the declining quality of public transport reinforces private auto use and vice versa:

Public transport is heavily subsidized in almost all cities because of its large positive externalities (reduced need for roadways and reduced congestion) but also to ensure access by poor people. Nevertheless, many

Figure 12
Motorization of the Third World[31]

(Millions)

Cairo	1978	0.5	
	1991	2.6	
	2006	7.0	
Bangkok	1984	0.54	(private cars)
	1992	10.5	
Indonesia	1995	12.0	(motorized vehicles of all kinds)
	2001	21.0	

30 M. Pemberton, *Managing the Future – World Vehicle Forecasts and Strategies to 2020, Vol. 1: Changing Patterns of Demand*, 2000; and Daniel Sperling and Eileen Clausen, "The Developing World's Motorization Challenge," *Issues in Science and Technology Online* (Fall 2002), p. 2.

31 M. El Arabi, "Urban Growth and Environment Degradation: The Case of Cairo", *Cities* 19:6 (2002), p. 294; Expressway and Rapid Transit Authority of Bangkok, *Statistical Report*, 1992, Bangkok 1993; US Department of Energy, Energy Information Administration, "Indonesia: Environmental Issues," fact sheet (February 2004).

poor people still cannot afford transit services. Thus cities face pressure to keep fares very low. But in doing so, they sacrifice bus quality and comfort. Middle-class riders react by buying cars as soon as they can. With low cost scooters and motorcycles, the flight of the middle class is hastened, transit revenues diminish, and operators reduce quality further as they serve a poorer clientele. Although the quality of service suffers first, a decrease in quantity of service often follows.[32]

International development agencies encourage destructive transport policies by their preference for financing roads rather than rails, as well as by encouraging the privatization of local transportation. In China – formerly the home of the egalitarian bicycle – planners now give irrational priority to automobiles. Beijing has destroyed vast swaths of traditional courtyard housing for the poor as well as its picturesque *hutong* (back alley) network in order to make room for boulevards and motorways. Simultaneously, bicycle commuters have been penalized by new license fees, restrictions on using arterial roads, and the end of the bicycle subsidies formerly paid by work units.[33]

The result of this collision between urban poverty and traffic congestion is sheer carnage. More than one million people – two-thirds of them pedestrians, cyclists, and passengers – are killed in road accidents in the Third World each year. "People who will never own a car in their life," reports a World Health Organization researcher, "are at the greatest risk."[34] Minibuses and jitneys, often unlicensed and poorly maintained, are particularly dangerous: in Lagos, for example, the buses are known locally as *danfos* and *molues*, "flying coffins" and "moving morgues."[35] Nor does the snail's pace of traffic in most poor cities reduce its lethality. Although cars and buses crawl through Cairo at average speeds of less than 10 kilometers per hour, the Egyptian capital still manages an accident rate of 8 deaths and 60 injuries per 1000

32 Sperling and Clausen, "The Developing World's Motorization Challenge," p. 3.
33 Example of Beijing in Sit, *Beijing*, pp. 288–89.
34 Study by WHO-funded Road Traffic Injuries Research Network, quoted in *Detroit Free Press*, 24 September 2002.
35 Vinand Nantulya and Michael Reich, "The Neglected Epidemic: Road Traffic Injuries in Developing Countries," *British Journal of Medicine* 324 (11 May 2002), pp. 1139–41.

automobiles per year.[36] In Lagos, where the average resident spends an incredible three hours each day marooned in angry gridlock, private commuters and minibus drivers literally go berserk – indeed, so many drivers jump curbs or drive on the wrong side of the road that the Traffic Ministry has recently imposed mandatory psychiatric tests on offenders.[37] In Delhi, meanwhile, the *Hindustan Times* recently complained that middle-class commuters seldom bother to stop after running over homeless ragpickers or poor children.[38]

The overall economic cost of road deaths and injuries, according to the World Health Organization (WHO), is estimated as "almost twice the total development assistance received worldwide by developing countries." The WHO, indeed, considers traffic to be one of the worst health hazards facing the urban poor, and predicts that road accidents by 2020 will be the third leading cause of death.[39] China, where cars are wresting control of urban streets from bicycles and pedestrians, will unfortunately lead the way: almost one-quarter-million Chinese were killed or seriously injured in traffic accidents in the first five months of 2003 alone.[40]

Rampant motorization, of course, is also exacerbating the nightmare of air pollution in Third World cities. Myriad old cars, beat-up buses, and superannuated trucks asphyxiate urban areas with their deadly exhaust, while the dirty two-stroke engines that power small vehicles emit ten times as much fine particulate matter as modern cars. According to a recent study, foul air is most deadly in the sprawling megacities of Mexico (300 bad ozone smog days per year), São Paulo, Delhi, and Beijing.[41] Breathing Mumbai's air, meanwhile, is the

36 El Arabi, "Urban Growth and Environmental Degradation," pp. 392–94; and Oberai, *Population Growth, Employment and Poverty in Third World Mega-Cities*, p. 16 (accident rate).

37 Glenn McKenzie, "Psychiatric Tests Required for Traffic Offenders," *RedNova*, 20 June 2003; and Peil, "Urban Housing and Services in Anglophone West Africa," p. 178.

38 *Hindustan Times*, 1 February 2004.

39 WHO, "Road Safety Is No Accident!" (November 2003); and Road Traffic Injuries Research Network cited in *Detroit Free Press*, 24 September 2002.

40 *People's Daily* (English), 24 June 2003.

41 Asim Khan, "Urban Air Pollution in Megacities of the World," *Green Times* (Spring 1997); published by Penn Environmental Group). See also: "Commentary: Urban Air Pollution," in *Current Science* 77:3 (10 August 1999), p. 334; "World Bank Group Meets to Clean Up Asia's Deadly Air," Associated Press, 22 July 2003.

equivalent of smoking two-and-one-half packs of cigarettes per day, and the Centre for Science and the Environment in Delhi recently warned that Indian cities were becoming "lethal gas chambers."[42]

Encroaching on Environmental Reserves

Cities in the abstract are the solution to the global environmental crisis: urban density can translate into great efficiencies in land, energy, and resource use, while democratic public spaces and cultural institutions likewise provide qualitatively higher standards of enjoyment than individualized consumption and commodified leisure. However, as urban theorists, beginning with Patrick Geddes (the true father of bioregionalism), have long recognized, both environmental efficiency and public affluence require the preservation of a green matrix of intact ecosystems, open spaces, and natural services: cities need an alliance with Nature in order to recycle their waste products into usable inputs for farming, gardening, and energy production. Sustainable urbanism presupposes the preservation of surrounding wetlands and agriculture. Unfortunately, Third World cities – with few exceptions – are systematically polluting, urbanizing, and destroying their crucial environmental support systems.

Urban open space, for example, is typically buried under uncollected waste, creating small utopias for rats and insect vectors like mosquitoes. The chronic shortfalls between the rates of trash generation and disposal are often staggering: the average collection rate in Dar-es-Salaam is barely 25 percent; in Karachi, 40 percent; and in Jakarta, 60 percent.[43] Likewise, the city planning director in Kabul complains that "Kabul is turning into one big reservoir of solid waste ... every 24 hours, 2 million people produce 800 cubic meters of solid waste. If all 40 of our trucks make three trips a day, they can still transport only 200 to 300 cubic meters out of the city."[44] The content of the waste is

42 Suketu Mehta, *Maximum City: Bombay Lost and Found*, New York 2004, p. 29; Karina Constantino-David, "Unsustainable Development: The Philippine Experience," in Westendorff and Eade, *Development and Cities*, p. 163.
43 Vincent Ifeanyi Ogu, "Private Sector Participation and Municipal Waste Management in Benin City," *Environment and Urbanization* 12:2 (October 2000), pp. 103, 105.
44 *Washington Post*, 26 August 2002.

sometimes grisly: in Accra, the *Daily Graphic* recently described "sprawling refuse dumps, full of black plastic bags containing aborted fetal bodies from the wombs of *Kayayee* [female porters] and teenage girls in Accra. According to the Metropolitan Chief Executive, '75 percent of the waste of black polythene bags in the metropolis contains human aborted fetuses.'"[45]

Peripheral greenbelts, meanwhile, are being converted into ecological wastelands. Food security is imperiled throughout Asia and Africa by the needless destruction of farmland by unnecessary urban overspill. In India more than 50,000 hectares of valuable croplands are lost every year to urbanization.[46] At the height of the "peasant flood" in China between 1987 and 1992, nearly 1 million hectares were converted annually from agricultural to urban uses.[47] In Egypt, the most densely settled agricultural nation on earth, sprawl has clearly reached a crisis point: around Cairo, urban development consumes up to 30,000 hectares per year, "a land mass," Florian Steinberg points out, "roughly equivalent to the land gains for agricultural purposes from the massive irrigation projects which were initiated with the inception of the Aswan High Dam."[48]

Peri-urban agriculture that survives development, moreover, is contaminated by the toxics found in human and animal manure. Asian cities, as seen from the air, have been traditionally surrounded by a bright green corona of high-productivity market gardening, extending to the radius of the economic cartage of nightsoil. But modern industrial sewage has become toxic with heavy metals and dangerous pathogens. Outside Hanoi, where farmers and fishermen are constantly uprooted by urban development, urban and industrial effluents are

45 *Daily Graphic* (Accra), 12 August 2000, quoted in H. Wellington, "Kelewle, Kpokpoi, Kpanlogo," in Ralph Mills-Tettey and Korantema Adi-Dako (eds), *Visions of the City: Accra in the Twenty-First Century*, Accra 2002, p. 46.

46 Shahab Fazal, "Urban Expansion and Loss of Agricultural Land – a GIS-Based Study of Saharanpur City, India," *Environmental and Urbanization* 12:2 (October 2000), p. 124.

47 See "Loss of Agricultural Land to Urbanization" at www.infoforhealth.org/pr/m13/m13chap3_3.shtml#top; and "Farmland Fenced off as Industry Makes Inroads," *China Daily*, 18 August 2003.

48 Florian Steinberg, "Cairo: Informal Land Development and the Challenge for the Future," in Baken and van der Linden, *Land Delivery for Low Income Groups in Third World Cities*, p. 131.

now routinely employed as free substitutes for artificial fertilizers. When researchers questioned this noxious practice, they discovered "cynicism among vegetable and fish producers" about the "rich people in cities." "They don't care about us and fool us around with useless compensation [for farm land], so why not take some form of revenge?"[49] Similarly, in Colombo, where slums sprawl into fields, "a unique form of cultivation known as *keera kotu* has emerged, whereby urban waste, including that which is hygienically unsuitable, is used to grow vegetables as fast as possible and wherever possible."[50]

As the housing crisis worsens in most cities, slums are also directly invading vital ecological sanctuaries and protected watersheds. In Mumbai, slum-dwellers have penetrated so far into the Sanjay Gandhi National Park that some are now being routinely eaten by leopards (ten in June 2004 alone): one angry cat even attacked a city bus. In Istanbul *gecekondus* encroach on the crucial watershed of the Omerli forest; in Quito, shantytowns surround the Antisana reservoir; and in São Paulo, *favelas* threaten to further contaminate the water in the Guarapiranga reservoir – already notorious for its unpleasant taste – which accounts for 21 percent of the city's supply. São Paulo, indeed, is waging an uphill struggle, as it is forced to to use 170,000 tons (or 17,000 truck-loads!) of water-treatment chemicals per year to keep the water supply potable. Experts warn that such expedients are an unsustainable solution.

Half of São Paulo's *favelas* are located on the banks of the reservoirs that supply water to the city. This puts public health at risk, since the squatters throw their wastes directly into the reservoir or into the brooks that supply water to it. Systems for quality control of the municipal water network have had numerous problems in the last few years. In addition to increasing water chlorination to prevent enteric diseases, they can hardly control algae proliferation since it grows enormously with the accumulation of organic material.[51]

49 Van den Berg, van Wijk, and Van Hoi, "The Transformation of Agriculture and Rural Life Downsteam of Hanoi," p. 52.
50 Dayaratne and Samarawickrama, "Empowering Communities," p. 102.
51 Taschner, "Squatter Settlements and Slums in Brazil," p. 193; Luis Galvão, "A Water Pollution Crisis in the Americas," *Habitat Debate* (September 2003), p. 10.

Sewage everywhere poisons sources of drinking water. In Kampala, slum runoff contaminates Lake Victoria, while in Monrovia – swollen to 1.3 million residents after years of civil war, but with an infrastructure designed for less than one quarter million – excrement fouls the entire landscape: beaches, streets, yards, and streams.[52] In poorer parts of Nairobi, piped water is no longer potable because of fecal contamination at source.[53] Meanwhile, Mexico City's essential ecological buffer zone, the Ajusco recharge area, is now dangerously polluted by sewage from surrounding *colonias*.[54] Indeed, experts estimate that fully 90 percent of Latin America's sewage is dumped untreated in streams and rivers.[55] From a sanitary viewpoint, poor cities on every continent are little more than clogged, overflowing sewers.

Living in Shit

Excremental surplus, indeed, is the primordial urban contradiction. In the 1830s and early 1840s, with cholera and typhoid rampant in London and the industrial cities of Europe, the anxious British middle class was forced to confront a topic not usually discussed in the parlor. Bourgeois "consciousness," Victorian scholar Steven Marcus explains, "was abruptly disturbed by the realization that millions of English men, women and children were virtually living in shit. The immediate question seems to have been whether they weren't drowning in it."[56] With epidemics believed to originate from the stinking fecal "miasmas" of the slum districts, there was sudden elite interest in conditions like those catalogued by Friedrich Engels in Manchester, where in some streets "over two hundred people shared a single privy," and the once-rustic River Irk was "a coal-black stinking river full of filth and garbage." Marcus, in a Freudian gloss on Engels, ponders the irony that "generations of human beings, out of whose lives the wealth of

52 *The News* (Monrovia), 23 January 2004.
53 Peter Mutevu, "Project Proposal on Health and Hygiene Education to Promote Safe Handling of Drinking Water and Appropriate Use of Sanitation Facilities in Informal Settlements," brief, Nairobi (April 2001).
54 Imparato and Ruster, *Slum Upgrading and Participation*, p. 61; Pezzoli, *Human Settlements*, p. 20.
55 Stillwaggon, *Stunted Lives, Stagnant Economies*, p. 97.
56 Stephen Marcus, *Engels, Manchester and the Working Class*, New York 1974, p. 184.

England was produced, were compelled to live in wealth's symbolic, negative counterpart."[57]

Eight generations after Engels, shit still sickeningly mantles the lives of the urban poor as (to quote Marcus again), "a virtual objectification of their social condition, their place in society."[58] Indeed, one can set Engels's *The Condition of the Working-Class in England in 1844* side by side with a modern African urban novel, such as Meja Mwangi's *Going Down River Road* (1976), and ponder the excremental and existential continuities. "In one of these courts," wrote Engels of Manchester, "right at the entrance where the covered passage ends is a privy without a door. This privy is so dirty that the inhabitants can only enter or leave the court by wading through puddles of stale urine and excrement."[59] Similarly, Mwangi writes of Nairobi in 1974: "Most of the paths crisscrossing the dewy grassland were scattered with human excrement.... The cold wet wind that blew across it carried, in the same medium with the smell of shit and urine, the occasional murmur, the rare expression of misery, uncertainty, and resignation."[60]

The subject, of course, is indelicate, but it is a fundamental problem of city life from which there is surprisingly little escape. For ten thousand years urban societies have struggled against deadly accumulations of their own waste; even the richest cities only flush their excrement downstream or dump it into a nearby ocean. Today's poor megacities – Nairobi, Lagos, Bombay, Dhaka, and so on – are stinking mountains of shit that would appall even the most hardened Victorians. (Except, perhaps, Rudyard Kipling, a connoisseur, who in *The City of Dreadful Night* happily distinguished the "Big Calcutta Stink" from the unique pungencies of Bombay, Peshawar, and Benares.)[61] Constant intimacy with other people's waste, moreover, is one of the most profound of social divides. Like the universal prevalence of parasites in the bodies of the poor, living in shit, as the Victorians knew, truly demarcates two existential humanities.

57 Ibid.
58 Ibid., p. 185.
59 Friedrich Engels, *The Condition of the Working-Class in England in 1844*, Marx–Engels Collected Works, Volume 4, Moscow 1975, p. 351.
60 Meja Mwangi, *Going Down River Road*, Nairobi 1976, p. 6.
61 Kipling, *The City of Dreadful Night*, pp. 10–11.

The global sanitation crisis defies hyperbole. Its origins, as with many Third World urban problems, are rooted in colonialism. The European empires generally refused to provide modern sanitation and water infrastructures in native neighborhoods, preferring instead to use racial zoning and *cordons sanitaires* to segregate garrisons and white suburbs from epidemic disease; postcolonial regimes from Accra to Hanoi thus inherited huge sanitation deficits that few regimes have been prepared to aggressively remedy. (Latin American cities have serious sanitation problems, but nothing to compare with the magnitude of those in Africa or South Asia.)

The megacity of Kinshasa, with a population fast approaching 10 million, has no waterborne sewage system at all. Across the continent in Nairobi, the Laini Saba slum in Kibera in 1998 had exactly ten working pit latrines for 40,000 people, while in Mathare 4A there were two public toilets for 28,000 people. As a result, slum residents rely on "flying toilets" or "scud missiles," as they are also called: "They put the waste in a polythene bag and throw it on to the nearest roof or pathway."[62] The prevalence of excrement, however, does generate some innovative urban livelihoods: in Nairobi, commuters now confront "10-year-olds with plastic solvent bottles wedged between their teeth, brandishing balls of human excrement – ready to thrust them into an open car window – to force the driver to pay up."[63]

Sanitation in South and Southeast Asia is only marginally better than in sub-Saharan Africa. Dhaka, a decade ago, had piped water connections serving a mere 67,000 houses and a sewage disposal system with only 8500 connections. Likewise, less than 10 percent of homes in metro Manila are connected to the sewer systems.[64] Jakarta, despite its glitzy skyscrapers, still depends on open ditches for disposal of most of its wastewater. In contemporary India – where an estimated 700 million people are forced to defecate in the open – only 17 of 3700 cities and large towns have any kind of primary sewage treatment before final disposal. A study of 22 slums in India found 9 with no

62 Katy Salmon, "Nairobi's 'Flying Toilets': Tip of an Iceburg," *Terra Viva* (Johannesburg), 26 August 2002; Mutevu, "Project Proposal on Health and Hygiene Education."

63 Andrew Harding, "Nairobi Slum Life" (series), *Guardian*, 4, 8, 10 and 15 October 2002.

64 Berner, *Defending a Place*, p. xiv.

latrine facilities at all; in another 10, there were just 19 latrines for 102,000 people.[65] The filmmaker Prahlad Kakkar, the auteur of the toilet documentary *Bumbay*, told a startled interviewer that in Bombay "half the population doesn't have a toilet to shit in, so they shit outside. That's five million people. If they shit half a kilo each, that's two and a half million kilos of shit each morning."[66] Similarly, "a 1990 survey of Delhi," reports Susan Chaplin, "showed that the 480,000 families in 1100 slum settlements had access to only 160 toilet seats and 110 mobile toilet vans. The lack of toilet facilities in slum areas has forced slum dwellers to use any open space, such as public parks, and thus has created tensions between them and middle class residents over defecation rights."[67] Indeed, Arundhati Roy tells of three Delhi slum-dwellers who in 1998 were "shot for shitting in public places."[68]

Meanwhile in China, where urban shantytowns reappeared after the market reforms, many in-migrants live without sanitation or running water. "There are reports of people," writes Dorothy Solinger, "squeezed into shacks in Beijing, where one toilet served more than six thousand people; of a shantytown in Shenzhen housing fifty shelters, in which hundreds subsisted without running water; ... [and] a 1995 survey in Shanghai revealed that a mere 11 percent of nearly 4500 migrant households actually possessed a toilet."[69]

Being forced to exercise body functions in public is certainly a humiliation for anyone, but, above all, it is a feminist issue. Poor urban women are terrorized by the Catch-22 situation of being expected to maintain strict standards of modesty while lacking access to any private means of hygiene. "The absence of toilets," writes journalist Asha Krishnakumar, "is devastating for women. It severely affects their

65 UN-HABITAT, *Debate* 8:2 (June 2002), p. 12.

66 Quoted in Mehta, *Maximum City*, p. 127.

67 Susan Chaplin, "Cities, Sewers and Poverty: India's Politics of Sanitation," *Environment and Urbanization* 11:1 (April 1999), p. 152. Such class struggles over the "right to defecate" are a continuation of a chronic conflict in colonial cities. Gooptu, for example, cites the 1932 case of squatters in Kanpur who, after the Municipal Board rebuffed their attempts to acquire potable water and sanitary latrines, invaded a field next to civil service bungalows and used it (in protest) as their communal latrine. The police were promptly called in and a riot ensued (Gooptu, *The Politics of the Urban Poor in Early Twentieth-Century India*, p. 87.)

68 Arundhati Roy, "The Cost of Living," *Frontline* 17:3 (5–8 February 2000).

69 Solinger, *Contesting Citizenship in Urban China*, p. 121.

dignity, health, safety and sense of privacy, and indirectly their literacy and productivity. To defecate, women and girls have to wait until dark, which exposes them to harassment and even sexual assault."[70]

In the slums of Bangalore – the high-tech poster city for "India Shining" – poor women, unable to afford the local pay latrines, must wait until evening to wash or relieve themselves. Researcher Loes Schenk-Sandbergen writes:

> Men can urinate at any time at any place, whereas women can only be seen following the call of nature before sunrise and after sunset. To avoid hazards, women have to go in groups at five o'clock in the morning ... often [to] marshy land where snakes would be hiding, or some deserted dumping ground with rats and other rodents. Women often say that they do not eat during the daytime just to avoid having to go to the open field in the evening.[71]

Similarly, in Bombay women have to relieve themselves "between two and five each morning, because it's the only time they get privacy." The public toilets, explains the writer Suketu Mehta, are rarely a solution for women because they seldom function: "People defecate all around the toilets, because the pits have been clogged for months or years."[72]

The solution to the sanitation crisis – at least as conceived by certain economics professors sitting in comfortable armchairs in Chicago and Boston – has been to make urban defecation a global business. Indeed, one of the great achievements of Washington-sponsored neoliberalism has been to turn public toilets into cash points for paying off foreign debts – pay toilets are a growth industry throughout Third World slums. In Ghana a user fee for public toilets was introduced by the military government in 1981; in the late 1990s toilets were privatized and are now described as a "gold mine" of profitability.[73] In Kumasi, for instance, where members of the Ghanaian Assembly won the lucrative contracts,

70 Asha Krishnakumar, "A Sanitation Emergency," *Focus* 20:24 (22 November–5 December 2003).

71 Loes Schenk-Sandbergen, "Women, Water and Sanitation in the Slums of Bangalore: A Case Study of Action Research," in Schenk, *Living in India's Slums*, p. 198.

72 Mehta, *Maximum City*, p. 128.

73 Deborah Pellow, "And a Toilet for Everyone!," in Mills-Tetley and Adi-Dako, *Visions of the City*, p. 140.

private toilet use for one family, once a day, costs about 10 percent of the basic wage.[74] Likewise, in Kenyan slums such as Mathare it costs 6 cents (US) for every visit to a privatized toilet: this is too expensive for most poor people, who would prefer to defecate in the open and spend their money on water and food.[75] This is also the case in Kampala slums such as Soweto or Kamwokya, where the public toilets cost a daunting one hundred shillings per visit.[76]

Baby Killers

"In Cité-Soleil," says Lovly Josaphat, who lives in Port-au-Prince's largest slum, "I've suffered a lot."

> When it rains, the part of the Cité I live in floods and the water comes in the house. There's always water on the ground, green smelly water, and there are no paths. The mosquitoes bite us. My four-year-old has bronchitis, malaria, and even typhoid now.... The doctor said to give him boiled water, not to give him food with grease, and not to let him walk in the water. But the water's everywhere; he can't set foot outside the house without walking in it. The doctor said that if I don't take care of him, I'll lose him.[77]

Green smelly water everywhere. "Every day, around the world," according to public-health expert Eileen Stillwaggon, "illnesses related to water supply, waste disposal, and garbage kill 30,000 people and constitute 75 percent of the illnesses that afflict humanity."[78] Indeed, digestive-tract diseases arising from poor sanitation and the pollution of drinking water – including diarrhea, enteritis, colitis, typhoid, and paratyphoid fevers – are the leading cause of death in the world,

74 Nick Devas and David Korboe, "City Governance and Poverty: The Case of Kumasi," *Environment and Urbanization* 12:1 (April 2000), pp. 128–30.

75 Salmon, "Nairobi's 'Flying Toilets.'"

76 Halima Abdallah, "Kampala's Soweto," *The Monitor* (Kampala), 19–25 November 2003.

77 Beverly Bell, *Walking on Fire: Haitian Women's Stories of Survival and Resistance*, Ithaca 2001, p. 45.

78 Stillwaggon, *Stunted Lives, Stagnant Economies*, p. 95.

affecting mainly infants and small children.[79] Open sewers and contaminated water are likewise rife with intestinal parasites such as whipworm, roundworm, and hookworm, and so on that infect tens of millions of children in poor cities. Cholera, the scourge of the Victorian city, also continues to thrive off the fecal contamination of urban water supplies, especially in African cities like Antananarivo, Maputo, and Lusaka, where UNICEF estimates that up to 80 percent of deaths from preventable diseases (apart from HIV/AIDS) arise from poor sanitation. The diarrhea associated with AIDS is a grim addition to the problem.[80]

The ubiquitous contamination of drinking water and food by sewage and waste defeats the most desperate efforts of slum residents to practice protective hygiene. In Nairobi's vast Kibera slum, UN-HABITAT's Rasna Warah studied the daily life of a vegetable hawker named Mberita Katela, who walks a quarter mile every morning to buy water. She uses a communal pit latrine just outside her door. It is shared with 100 of her neighbors and her house reeks of the sewage overflow. She constantly frets about contamination of her cooking or washing water – Kibera has been devastated in recent years by cholera and other excrement-associated diseases.[81] In Calcutta likewise, there is little that mothers can do about the infamous service privies they are forced to use. These small brick sheds sit above earthware bowls that are almost never cleaned on a regular schedule, thus ensuring that "the stinking mess around the *bustee*'s privy is washed straight into the ponds and tanks of water in which the people clean themselves and their clothes and their cooking utensils."[82]

Examples of poor people's powerlessness in the face of the sanitation crisis are legion. Mexico City residents, for example, inhale shit: fecal dust blowing off Lake Texcoco during the hot, dry season causes

79 See Pellow, "And a Toilet for Everyone!;" Nikhil Thapar and Ian Sanderson, "Diarrhoea in Children: an Interface Between Developing and Developed Countries," *The Lancet* 363 (21 February 2004), pp. 641–50; and Mills-Tettey and Adi-Dako, *Visions of the City*, p. 138.

80 UN Integrated Regional Information Networks, press release, 19 February 2003.

81 Rasna Warah, "Nairobi's Slums: Where Life for Women is Nasty, Brutish and Short," UN-HABITAT, *Debate* 8:3 (2002).

82 Chaplin, "Cities Sewers, and Poverty," p. 151.

typhoid and hepatitis. In the "New Fields" around Rangoon, where the military regime has brutally moved hundreds of thousands of inner-city residents, Monique Skidmore describes families living in the sanitary equivalent of the mud hell of World War I trench warfare: they cook and defecate in the mud directly in front of the tiny plastic sheets under which they sleep. The "New Fields," not surprisingly, are ravaged by cholera, dysentery, dengue, and malaria.[83] In Baghdad's giant slum of Sadr City, hepatitis and typhoid epidemics rage out of control. American bombing wrecked already overloaded water and sewerage infrastructures, and as a result raw sewage seeps into the household water supply. Two years after the US invasion, the system remains broken, and the naked eye can discern filaments of human excrement in the tap water. In the 115-degree heat of summer there is no other available water supply that poor people can afford.[84]

Sanitation crusades, meanwhile, come and go over the years. The 1980s were the UN's Decade of International Drinking Water and Sanitation, but as World Bank researcher Anqing Shi emphasizes, "At the end of the 1980s, the situation had not improved greatly."[85] Indeed, the WHO concedes that "there will still be about 5 million [preventable] deaths in children younger than five years by 2025 ... mostly caused by infectious diseases, within which diarrhoea will continue to play a prominent part."[86] "At any one time," a 1996 WHO report adds, "close to half of the South's urban population is suffering from one or more of the main diseases associated with inadequate provision for water and sanitation."[87] Although clean water is the cheapest and single most important medicine in the world, public provision of water, like free toilets, often competes with powerful private interests.

Water sales is a lucrative industry in poor cities. Nairobi, as usual, is an egregious example, where politically connected entrepreneurs resell

83 Skidmore, *Karaoke Fascism*, p. 156.

84 *Los Angeles Times*, 4 August 2004.

85 Shi, "How Access to Urban Potable Water and Sewerage Connections Affects Child Mortality," p. 2.

86 Thapar and Sanderson, "Diarrhoea in Children," p. 650.

87 1996 WHO report paraphrased by David Satterthwaite, "The Links Between Poverty and the Environment in Urban Areas of Africa, Asia, and Latin America," *The ANNALS of the American Academy of Political and Social Science* 590 (1993), p. 80.

municipal water (which costs very little to families wealthy enough to afford a tap) in the slums at exorbitant prices. As Mayor Joe Aketch recently complained, "A study shows that the population of Kibera slum pays up to five times for a litre of water more than average American citizens. It is a shame that the rich people of Nairobi can use their wealth to divert services meant for the poor, to their advantage."[88] Unable or unwilling to pay the extortionate price of water from vendors, some Nairobi residents resort to desperate expedients, including, two local researchers write, "the use of sewerage water, skipping bathing and washing, using borehole water and rainwater, and drawing water from broken pipes."[89]

The situation in Luanda is even worse: there, the poorest households are forced to spend 15 percent of their income on water that private companies simply pump from the nearby, sewage-polluted

Figure 13

Water: The Poor Pay More[90]

Water from vendor versus piped water
(price mark-up in percentage)

	%
Faisalabad	6800
Bundun	5000
Manila	4200
Mumbai	4000
Phnom Penh	1800
Hanoi	1300
Karachi	600
Dhaka	500

88 *Intermediate Technology Development Group (ITDG) East Africa Newsletter* (August 2002).

89 Mary Amuyunzu-Nyamongo and Negussie Taffa, "The Triad of Poverty, Environment and Child Health in Nairobi Informal Settlements," *Journal of Health and Population in Developing Countries*, 8 January 2004, p. 7.

90 Figures from UN Economic and Social Commission for Asia and the Pacific, 1997.

Bengo River.[91] "Water is as rare in Kinshasa" – situated on the banks of the world's second greatest river – "as it is in the Sahara." Although piped water is relatively cheap, report geographer Angeline Mwacan and anthropologist Theodore Trefon, the taps are usually dry, so the poor must walk kilometers to draw water from polluted rivers. Charcoal is too expensive to waste boiling water, and as a result 30 percent of medical visits are for water-related diseases such as cholera, typhoid, and shigella.[92] In Dar-es-Salaam, meanwhile, municipal authorities were pressured by the World Bank to turn over the water utility to the private British firm Biwater – the result, according to aid agencies, was a sharp rise in prices despite little increase in service; poor families have had to turn to unsafe water sources. "At a private well in Tabata," reports the *Guardian*, "a 20-litre jerrycan sells for up to 8p, a substantial sum in a city where many people live on less than 50p a day. Families too poor to buy this water dig shallow wells." Government officials, however, have won applause from Washington for their support of privatization.[93]

The Double Burden

The most extreme health differentials are no longer between towns and countrysides, but between the urban middle classes and the urban poor. The mortality rate for children under the age of five (151 per 1000) in Nairobi's slums is two or three times higher than in the city as a whole, and half again as high as in poor rural areas.[94] Likewise in Quito infant mortality is 30 times higher in the slums than in wealthier neighborhoods, while in Cape Town, tuberculosis is 50 times more common amongst poor blacks than amongst affluent whites.[95] Mumbai, as of old, remains a charnel house with slum death rates 50 percent higher than in adjoining rural districts. A staggering 40 percent of total

91 Hodges, *Angola*, p. 30.

92 Angeline Mwacan and Theodore Trefon, "The Tap Is on Strike," in Trefon (ed.), *Reinventing Order in the Congo: How People Respond to State Failure in Kinshasa*, Kampala 2004, pp. 33, 39, 42.

93 Jeevan Vasagar, "Pipes Run Dry in Tanzania," *Guardian* (27 September 2004).

94 Herr and Karl, *Estimating Global Slum Dwellers*, p. 14.

95 Carolyn Stephens, "Healthy Cities or Unhealthy Islands? The Health and Social Implications of Urban Inequality," *Environment and Urbanization* 8:2 (October 1996), pp. 16, 22.

mortality, moreover, is attributed to infections and parasitic diseases arising from water contamination and wretched sanitation.[96] And in Dhaka and Chittagong, according to medical statisticians, "around one-third of the people in slum communities are thought to be ill at any given time" – the equivalent of a pandemic in any other urban context.[97]

Slum-dwellers, health researchers emphasize, carry a double burden of disease. "The urban poor," write a research team, "are the interface between underdevelopment and industrialization, and their disease patterns reflect the problems of both. From the first they carry a heavy burden of infectious diseases and malnutrition, while from the second they suffer the typical spectrum of chronic and social diseases."[98] "Hand in hand with urbanization," adds *Lancet* editor Richard Horton, "have come epidemics of diseases that heretofore were usually confined to rural areas, such as tapeworms, roundworms, schistosomiasis, trypanosomiasis, and dengue."[99] Yet diabetes, cancers, and heart disease also take their greatest toll amongst the urban poor.[100] This double burden, moreover, is usually heaviest, according to UN researchers, in the "smaller and less prosperous cities in lower income countries or in the lower income regions of middle income countries." Politically dominant megacities, it seems, find it relatively easy to export some of their environmental and sanitation problems downstream, using other regions as sinks for waste and pollution.[101]

The neoliberal restructuring of Third World urban economies that has occurred since the late 1970s has had a devastating impact on the public provision of healthcare, particularly for women and children. As the Women's Global Network for Reproductive Rights points out,

96 Jacquemin, *Urban Development and New Towns in the Third World*, pp. 90–91.

97 Abul Barkat, Mati Ur Rahman, and Manik Bose, "Family Planning Choice Behavior in Urban Slums of Bangladesh: An Econometric Approach," *Asia-Pacific Population Journal* 12:1 (March 1997) offprint, p. 1.

98 Edmundo Werna, Ilona Blue, and Trudy Harpham, "The Changing Agenda for Urban Health," in Cohen et al., *Preparing for the Urban Future*, p. 201.

99 Richard Horton, *Health Wars: On the Global Front Lines of Modern Medicine*, New York 2003, p. 79.

100 Thus 11 million of the 17 million deaths from strokes and heart attacks worldwide are in developing countries. See D. Yach *et al.*, "Global Chronic Diseases," *Science* (21 January 2005), p. 317, as well as the exchange of letters (15 July 2005), p. 380.

101 David Satterthwaite, "Environmental Transformations in Cities as They Get Larger, Wealthier and Better Managed," *The Geographical Journal* 163:2 (July 1997), p. 217.

structural adjustment programs (SAPs) – the protocols by which indebted countries surrender their economic independence to the IMF and World Bank – "usually require public spending, including health spending (but not military spending), to be cut."[102] In Latin America and the Caribbean, SAP-enforced austerity during the 1980s reduced public investment in sanitation and potable water, thus eliminating the infant survival advantage previously enjoyed by poor urban residents. In Mexico, following the adoption of a second SAP in 1986, the percentage of births attended by medical personnel fell from 94 percent in 1983 to 45 percent in 1988, while maternal mortality soared from 82 per 100,000 in 1980 to 150 in 1988.[103]

In Ghana, "adjustment" not only led to an 80 percent decrease in spending on health and education between 1975 and 1983, but also caused the exodus of half of the nation's doctors. Similarly, in the Philippines in the early 1980s, per capita health expenditures fell by half.[104] In oil-rich but thoroughly "SAPed" Nigeria, a fifth of the country's children now die before age five.[105] Economist Michel Chossudovsky blames the notorious outbreak of plague in Surat in 1994 upon "a worsening urban sanitation and public health infrastructure which accompanied the compression of national and municipal budgets under the 1991 IMF/World Bank-sponsored structural adjustment programme."[106]

The examples can easily be multiplied: everywhere obedience to international creditors has dictated cutbacks in medical care, the emigration of doctors and nurses, the end of food subsidies, and the switch of agricultural production from subsistence to export crops. As Fantu Cheru, a leading UN expert on debt, emphasizes, the coerced tribute that the Third World pays to the First World has been the literal difference between life and death for millions of poor people.

102 Women's Global Network for Reproductive Rights, *A Decade After Cairo: Women's Health in a Free Market Economy*, Corner House Briefing 30, Sturminister Newton 2004, p. 8.

103 Shi, "How Access to Urban Portable Water and Sewerage Connections Affects Child Mortality," pp. 4–5.

104 Frances Stewart, *Adjustment and Poverty: Options and Choices*, London 1995, pp. 196, 203, 205.

105 World Bank statistic quoted in *Financial Times*, 10 September 2004.

106 Quoted in *A Decade After Cairo*, p. 12.

Over 36 million people in the world today are HIV/AIDS infected. Of these, some 95 percent live in the global south. In particular, sub-Saharan Africa is home to over 25 million people suffering from HIV and AIDS. ... Each day in Africa more than 5000 people die from AIDS. Experts estimated that the world community needs to invest US $7–10 billion every year to fight HIV/AIDS, as well as other diseases like tuberculosis and malaria. In the face of this humanitarian crisis, however, African countries continue annually to pay $13.5 billion in debt service payments to creditor countries and institutions, an amount far in excess of the United Nations' proposed global HIV/AIDS trust fund. This massive transfer of resources from poor African countries to wealthy Northern creditors is one of the factors that has critically weakened health care and education in the countries that are now worst affected by the pandemic.[107]

More recently the World Bank has combined a feminist rhetoric about the reproductive rights of women and gender equity in medicine with relentless pressure (in the name of "reform") on aid recipients to open themselves to global competition from private First World healthcare providers and pharmaceutical companies. The Bank's 1993 *Investing in Health* outlined the new paradigm of market-based healthcare: "Limited public expenditure on a narrowly defined package of services; user fees for public services; and privatized health care and financing."[108] A sterling instance of the new approach was Zimbabwe, where the introduction of user fees in the early 1990s led to a doubling of infant mortality.[109]

But the urban health crisis in the Third World is scarcely the fault of foreign creditors alone. As urban elites move to gated compounds in the suburbs, they worry less about the threat of disease in the slums and more about household security and the construction of high-speed roads. In India, for example, Susan Chaplin sees sanitation reform undermined by corrupt officials and an indifferent middle class:

107 Fantu Cheru, "Debt, Adjustment and the Politics of Effective Response to HIV/AIDS in Africa," *Third World Quarterly*, 23:2 (2002), p. 300.

108 Ibid., p. 9.

109 Deborah Potts and Chris Mutambirwa, "Basics Are Now a Luxury: Perceptions of Structural Adjustment's Impact on Rural and Urban Areas in Zimbabwe," *Environment and Urbanization* 10:1 (April 1998), p. 75.

The environmental conditions in Indian cities are continuing to deteriorate because the middle class is actively participating in the exclusion of large sections of the population from access to basic urban services. The consequence of such monopolization of state resources and benefits is that whilst an awareness of environmental problems is growing amongst the middle class, to date they have been more concerned about the inconveniences they suffer on congested roads and the resultant air pollution than about the risk of epidemic and endemic disease.[110]

But in the face of plagues like HIV/AIDS that "shake the earth and churn the skies,"[111] urban segregation offers only an illusion of biological protection. Indeed, today's megaslums are unprecedented incubators of new and reemergent diseases that can now travel across the world at the speed of a passenger jet. As I argue in my recent book about the imminent peril of avian influenza (*The Monster at Our Door*, 2005), economic globalization without concomitant investment in a global public-health infrastructure is a certain formula for catastrophe.[112]

110 Chaplin, "Cities, Sewers and Poverty," p. 156.
111 Meja Mwangi, *The Last Plague*, Nairobi 2000, p. 4.
112 Mike Davis, *The Monster at Our Door: The Global Threat of Avian Flu*, New York 2005.

7

SAPing the Third World

After their mysterious laughter, they quickly changed the topic
to other things. How were people back home surviving SAP?

Fidelis Balogun[1]

Slums, however deadly and insecure, have a brilliant future. The countryside will for a short period still contain the majority of the world's
poor, but that dubious distinction will pass to urban slums no later than
2035. At least half of the coming Third World urban population explosion will be credited to the account of informal communities.[2] Two
billion slum-dwellers by 2030 or 2040 is a monstrous, almost incompre-
hensible prospect, but urban poverty overlaps and exceeds slum
populations *per se*. Researchers with the UN Urban Observatory project
warn that by 2020, "urban poverty in the world could reach 45 to 50
percent of the total population living in the cities."[3]

The evolution of this new urban poverty, as we have seen, has been
a nonlinear historical process. The slow accretion of shantytowns to
the shell of the city has been punctuated by storms of poverty and
sudden explosions of slum-building. In his collection of stories entitled

---

1 Fidelis Odun Balogun, *Adjusted Lives: Stories of Structural Adjustments*, Trenton
(NJ) 1995, p. 75

2 Martin Ravallion, *On the Urbanization of Poverty*, World Bank paper, 2001.

3 Eduardo López Moreno, *Slums of the World: The Face of Urban Poverty in the New
Millenium?*, Nairobi 2003, p. 12.

Adjusted Lives, the Nigerian writer Fidelis Balogun describes the coming of the IMF-mandated Structural Adjustment Program (SAP) in the mid-1980s as the equivalent of a great natural disaster, destroying forever the old soul of Lagos and "re-enslaving" urban Nigerians.

> The weird logic of this economic programme seemed to be that to restore life to the dying economy, every juice had first to be SAPed out of the under-privileged majority of the citizens. The middle class rapidly disappeared and the garbage heaps of the increasingly rich few became the food table of the multiplied population of abjectly poor. The brain drain to the oil-rich Arab countries and to the Western world became a flood.[4]

Balogun's complaints about "privatizing in full stream and getting more hungry by the day," as well as his enumeration of SAPs' malevolent consequences, would be instantly familiar not only to survivors of the 30 other African SAPs, but also to hundreds of millions of Asians and Latin Americans. The 1980s – when the IMF and the World Bank used the leverage of debt to restructure the economies of most of the Third World – are the years when slums became an implacable future not just for poor rural migrants, but also for millions of traditional urbanites displaced or immiserated by the violence of "adjustment."

Urban Poverty's Big Bang

In 1974–75, the International Monetary Fund, followed by the World Bank, shifted focus from the developed industrial countries to a Third World reeling under the impact of soaring oil prices. As it increased its lending step by step, the IMF ratcheted up the scope of the coercive "conditionalities" and "structural adjustments" it imposed on client nations. As economist Frances Stewart emphasizes in her important study, the "exogenous developments that necessitated adjustment were not tackled by these institutions – the major ones being falling commodity prices and exorbitant debt servicing," but every domestic policy and public program was fair game for retrenchment.[5] By August 1982,

4 Balogun, *Adjusted Lives*, p. 80.
5 Stewart, *Adjustment and Poverty*, p. 213.

when Mexico threatened to default on its loan repayments, both the IMF and the World Bank, in synchronization with the largest commercial banks, had become explicit instruments of the international capitalist revolution promoted by the Reagan, Thatcher, and Kohl regimes. The 1985 Baker Plan (named after then Secretary of Treasury James Baker but drafted by his deputy secretary, Richard Darman) bluntly required the 15 largest Third World debtors to abandon state-led development strategies in return for new loan facilities and continued membership in the world economy. The Plan also pushed the World Bank to the fore as the longterm manager of the scores of structural adjustment programs that were shaping the brave new world of the so-called "Washington Consensus."

This is, of course, a world in which the claims of foreign banks and creditors always take precedence over the survival needs of the urban and rural poor; it is a world in which it is taken as "normal" that a poor country like Uganda spends twelve times as much per capita on debt relief each year as on healthcare in the midst of the HIV/AIDS crisis.[6] As *The Challenge of Slums* emphasizes, SAPs were "deliberately anti-urban in nature," and designed to reverse any "urban bias" that previously existed in welfare policies, fiscal structure, or government investment. Everywhere the IMF and World Bank – acting as bailiffs for the big banks and backed by the Reagan and George H. W. Bush administrations – offered poor countries the same poisoned chalice of devaluation, privatization, removal of import controls and food subsidies, enforced cost-recovery in health and education, and ruthless downsizing of the public sector. (A notorious telegram from Treasury Secretary George Shultz to overseas USAID officials commanded: "In most cases, public sector firms should be privatized.")[7] At the same time SAPs devastated rural smallholders by eliminating subsidies and pushing them sink or swim into global commodity markets dominated by heavily subsidized First World agribusiness.

Debt – as William Tabb reminds us in his recent history of global economic governance – has been the forcing-house of an epochal

6 Mallaby, *The World's Banker*, p. 110.
7 Quoted in Tony Killick, "Twenty-five Years in Development: The Rise and Impending Decline of Market Solutions," *Development Policy Review* 4 (1986), p. 101.

transfer of power from Third World nations to the Bretton Woods institutions controlled by the United States and other core capitalist countries.
According to Tabb, the Bank's professional staff are the postmodern
equivalent of a colonial civil service, and "like the colonial administrators
they never seem to go away except to be replaced by a fresh adviser team
with the same outlook and powers over the local economy and society."[8]

Although the debt-collectors claim to be in the business of economic
development, they seldom allow poor nations to play by the same rules
that richer countries used to promote growth in the late nineteenth or
early twentieth centuries. Structural adjustment, as economist Ha-Joon
Chang points out in a valuable article, hypocritically "kicked away the
ladder" of protectionist tariffs and subsidies that the OECD nations
had historically employed in their own climb from economies based on
agriculture to those based on urban high-value goods and services.[9]
Stefan Andreasson, looking at the grim results of SAPs in Zimbabwe
and self-imposed neoliberal policies in South Africa, wonders if the
Third World can hope for anything more than "virtual democracy" as
long as its macro-economic policies are dictated from Washington:
"Virtual democracy comes at the expense of inclusive, participatory
democracy and of any possibility of the extension of public welfare
provision that social democratic projects elsewhere have entailed."[10]

The Challenge of Slums makes the same point when it argues that the
"main single cause of increases in poverty and inequality during the
1980s and 1990s was the retreat of the state." In addition to the direct
SAP-enforced reductions in public-sector spending and ownership, the
authors stress the more subtle diminution of state capacity that resulted
from "subsidiarity": defined as the devolution of sovereign power to
lower echelons of government, and especially NGOs, linked directly to
major international aid agencies.

The whole, apparently decentralized structure is foreign to the notion of
national representative government that has served the developed world

8 William Tabb, *Economic Governance in the Age of Globalization*, New York 2004,
p. 193.
9 Ha-Joon Chang, "Kicking Away the Ladder: Infant Industry Promotion in
Historical Perspective," *Oxford Development Studies* 31:1 (2003), p. 21.
10 Stefan Andreasson, "Economic Reforms and 'Virtual Democracy' in South
Africa," *Journal of Contemporary African Studies* 21:3 (September 2003), p. 385.

well, while it is very amenable to the operations of a global hegemony. The dominant international perspective [i.e., Washington's] becomes the *de facto* paradigm for development, so that the whole world rapidly becomes unified in the broad direction of what is supported by donors and international organizations.[11]

Urban Africa and Latin America were the hardest hit by the artificial depression engineered by the IMF and the White House – indeed, in many countries the economic impact of SAPs during the 1980s, in tandem with protracted drought, rising oil prices, soaring interest rates, and falling commodity prices, was more severe and long-lasting than the Great Depression. Third World cities, especially, were trapped in a vicious cycle of increasing immigration, decreasing formal employment, falling wages, and collapsing revenues. The IMF and World Bank, as we have seen, promoted regressive taxation through public-service user fees for the poor, but made no counterpart effort to reduce military expenditure or to tax the incomes or real estate of the rich. As a result, infrastructure and public health everywhere lost the race with population increase. In Kinshasa, writes Theodore Trefon, "the population refers to basic public services as 'memories.'"[12]

The balance sheet of structural adjustment in Africa, reviewed by Carole Rakodi, includes capital flight, collapse of manufactures, marginal or negative increase in export incomes, drastic cutbacks in urban public services, soaring prices, and a steep decline in real wages.[13] Across the continent people learned to say "I have the crisis" in the same way one says, "I have a cold."[14] In Dar-es-Salaam, public-service expenditure per person fell 10 percent per annum during the 1980s, a virtual demolition of the local state.[15] In Khartoum, liberalization and

11 *Challenge*, p. 48.
12 Theodore Trefon, "Introduction: Reinventing Order," in Trefon, *Reinventing Order in the Congo*, p. 1.
13 Rakodi, "Global Forces, Urban Change, and Urban Management in Africa," in Rakodi, *Urban Challenge*, pp. 50, 60–61.
14 Achille Mbembe and Janet Roitman, "Figures of the Subject in Times of Crisis," in Enwezor et al., *Under Siege*, p. 112.
15 Michael Mattingly, "The Role of the Government of Urban Areas in the Creation of Urban Poverty," in Sue Jones and Nici Nelson (eds), *Urban Poverty in Africa: From Understanding to Alleviation*, London 1999, p. 21.

structural adjustment, according to local researchers, manufactured 1.1 million "new poor," most out of the decimated ranks of the public sector.[16] In Abidjan, one of the few tropical African cities with an important manufacturing sector and modern urban services, submission to the SAP regime punctually led to deindustrialization, the collapse of construction, and a rapid deterioration in public transit and sanitation; as a result, urban poverty in Ivory Coast – the supposed "tiger" economy of West Africa – doubled in the year 1987–88.[17] In Balogun's Nigeria, extreme poverty, increasingly urbanized in Lagos, Ibadan, and other cities, metastasized from 28 percent in 1980 to 66 percent in 1996. "GNP per capita is about $260 today," the World Bank reports, "below the level at independence 40 years ago and below the $370 level attained in 1985."[18] Overall, geographer Deborah Potts points out, wages have fallen so low in African cities that researchers can't figure how the poor manage to survive: this is the so-called "wage puzzle."[19]

In Latin America, beginning with General Pinochet's neoliberal coup in 1973, structural adjustment was closely associated with military dictatorship and the repression of the popular Left. One of the most striking results of this hemispheric counter-revolution was the rapid urbanization of poverty. In 1970, Guevarist *foco* theories of rural insurgency still conformed to a continental reality where the poverty of the countryside (75 million poor) overshadowed that of the cities (44 million poor). By the end of the 1980s, however, the vast majority of the poor (115 million) were living in urban *colonias, barriadas*, and *villas miserias* rather than on farms or in rural villages (80 million).[20]

According to ILO research, urban poverty in Latin America rose by an extraordinary 50 percent just in the first half of the decade, 1980 to 1986.[21] The average incomes of the working population fell by 40 percent in Venezuela, 30 percent in Argentina, and 21 percent in Brazil

16   Adil Mustafa Ahmad and Atta El-Hassan El-Batthani, "Poverty in Khartoum," *Environment and Urbanization* 7:2 (October 1995), p. 205.

17   Sethuraman, "Urban Poverty and the Informal Sector", p. 3

18   World Bank, *Nigeria: Country Brief*, September 2003.

19   Potts, "Urban Lives," p. 459.

20   UN, *World Urbanization Prospects*, p. 12.

21   Potts, "Urban Lives," p. 459.

and Costa Rica.[22] In Mexico informal employment almost doubled between 1980 and 1987, while social expenditure fell to half its 1980 level.[23] In Peru the 1980s ended in an SAP-induced "hyper-recession" that cut formal employment from 60 to 11 percent of the urban work-force in three years and opened the doors of Lima's slums to the occult revolution of Sendero Luminoso.[24]

Meanwhile, broad sections of the educated middle class, accustomed to live-in servants and European vacations, suddenly found themselves in the ranks of the new poor. In some cases, downward mobility was almost as abrupt as in Africa: the percentage of the urban population living in poverty, for example, increased by 5 percent in a single year (1980–81) in both Chile and Brazil.[25] But the same adjustments that crushed the poor and the public-sector middle class offered lucrative opportunities to privatizers, foreign importers, *narcotraficantes*, military brass, and political insiders. Conspicuous consumption reached hallucinatory levels in Latin America and Africa during the 1980s as the *nouveaux riches* went on spending sprees in Miami and Paris while their shantytown compatriots starved.

Indices of inequality reached record heights in the 1980s. In Buenos Aires the richest decile's share of income increased from 10 times that of the poorest in 1984 to 23 times in 1989. In Rio de Janeiro, inequality as measured in classical GINI coefficients climbed from 0.58 in 1981 to 0.67 in 1989.[26] Indeed, throughout Latin America, the 1980s deepened the canyons and elevated the peaks of the world's most extreme social topography. According to a 2003 World Bank report, GINI coefficients are 10 points higher in Latin America than Asia; 17.5 points higher than the OECD; and 20.4 points higher than Eastern Europe. Even the most egalitarian country in Latin America,

22 Alberto Minujin, "Squeezed: The Middle Class in Latin America," *Environment and Urbanization* 7:2 (October 1995), p. 155.

23 Agustín Escobar and Mercedes González de la Rocha, "Crisis, Restructuring and Urban Poverty in Mexico," *Environment and Urbanization* 7:1 (April 1995), pp. 63–64.

24 Henry Dietz, *Urban Poverty, Political Participation, and the State: Lima, 1970–1990*, Pittsburgh 1998, pp. 58, 65.

25 A. Oberai, *Population Growth, Employment and Poverty in Third World Mega-Cities*, p. 85.

26 Luis Ainstein, "Buenos Aires: A Case of Deepening Social Polarization," in Gilbert, *The Mega-City in Latin America*, p. 139.

Uruguay, has a more unequal distribution of income than any European country.[27]

Adjustment from Below

Everywhere in the Third World, the economic shocks of the 1980s forced individuals to regroup around the pooled resources of households and, especially, the survival skills and desperate ingenuity of women. As male formal employment opportunities disappeared, mothers, sisters, and wives were typically forced to bear far more than half the weight of urban structural adjustment: "While the burdens of survival [for the family] are enormous," writes an Indian scholar, "those of the women are even greater."[28] As geographer Sylvia Chant emphasizes, poor urban women under SAPs had to work harder both inside and outside the home to compensate for cuts in social service expenditures and male incomes; simultaneously new or increased user fees further limited their access to education and healthcare.[29] Somehow they were expected to cope. Indeed, some researchers argue that SAPs cynically exploit the belief that women's labor-power is almost infinitely elastic in the face of household survival needs.[30] This is the guilty secret variable in most neoclassical equations of economic adjustment: poor women and their children are expected to lift the weight of Third World debt upon their shoulders.

Thus, in China and the industrializing cities of Southeast Asia, millions of young women indentured themselves to assembly lines and factory squalor. "Women," according to recent research, "make up 90 percent of the 27 or so million workers in Free Trade Zones."[31] In

27 World Bank, *Inequality in Latin America and the Caribbean: Breaking with History?*, New York 2003, np.

28 U. Kalpagam, "Coping with Urban Poverty in India," *Bulletin of Concerned Asian Scholars* 17:1 (1985), p. 18.

29 Sylvia Chant, "Urban Livelihoods, Employment and Gender," in Robert Gwynne and Cristóbal Kay (eds), *Latin America Transformed: Globalization and Modernity*, London 2004, p. 214.

30 Caroline Moser with Linda Peake, "Seeing the Invisible: Women, Gender and Urban Development," in Richard Stren (ed.), *Urban Research in Developing Countries – Volume 4: Thematic Issues*, Toronto 1996, p. 309.

31 Women's Global Network for Reproductive Rights, *A Decade After Cairo*, p. 12.

Africa and most of Latin America (Mexico's northern border cities excepted), this option did not exist. Instead, deindustrialization and the decimation of male formal-sector jobs, often followed by male emigration, compelled women to improvise new livelihoods as piece-workers, liquor sellers, street vendors, lottery ticket sellers, hairdressers, sewing operators, cleaners, washers, ragpickers, nannies, and prostitutes. In a region where urban women's labor-force participation had always been lower than in other continents, the surge of Latin American women into tertiary informal activities during the 1980s was especially dramatic.

In her detailed study of "adjustment from below," social anthropologist Caroline Moser describes the impact of eight successive SAPs between 1982 and 1988 on a formerly upwardly mobile shantytown on the swampy edge of Guayaquil. Although open unemployment doubled in Ecuador, the major impact of the 1980s crisis was an explosion of underemployment estimated at fully half the workforce in both Guayaquil and Quito. In the *barrio* Indio Guayas, husbands who had previously enjoyed full-time work found themselves casualized and idle for up to a half a year; households, as a consequence, were forced to send more members out to work, both women and children. The female participation rate increased from 40 to 52 percent after the onset of the SAPs, but, with a decline in factory employment, women were forced to compete with each other for jobs as domestics or as street vendors. Despite this total mobilization of all household resources, living conditions, especially children's nutrition, declined dramatically. Moser found that almost 80 percent of the *barrio*'s children suffered some symptom of malnutrition. Healthcare, now largely privatized and more expensive, was no longer within reach of the formerly optimistic families of Indio Guayas.[32]

The Guayaquil experience was mirrored in Guadalajara during the neoliberal aftermath of the debt crisis of 1982. In a city that had traditionally been Mexico's capital of small-scale family-owned factories and workshops, the free fall in wages and the collapse of social expenditure in the early 1980s was followed, after the GATT agreement of 1986, by ruthless foreign competition. Guadalajara's

32 Caroline Moser, "Adjustment from Below: Low-Income Women, Time, and the Triple Role in Guayaquil, Ecuador," in Sarah Radcliffe and Sallie Westwood (eds), *"Viva": Women and Popular Protest in Latin America*, London 1993, pp. 178–85.

specialized niche – the small workshop production of mass consumer goods – couldn't survive the full onslaught of East Asian imports. The result – according to research by Augustín Escobar and Mercedes González – was simultaneously a huge increase in informal employment (by at least 80 percent between 1980 and 1987), emigration to California and Texas, and even more importantly, the restructuring of formal jobs "with precarious employment becoming the norm. Jobs are no longer secure, part-time employment becomes more common, outcontracting to smaller firms becomes general practice, and workers and employees are asked to perform more duties in order to remain in work." The household response, as in Guayaquil, was to send more females into domestic service, and also take their kids out of school to go to work. These short-term survival strategies, Escobar and González warned, would ultimately impair long-term economic mobility. "Worsening economic conditions limit the capacity of urban working-class households to implement long-term social mobility strategies, since it forces them to mobilize their inner resources and make extensive use of their labour force for basic survival."[33]

As in Africa and Asia, many Latin American urban families also "adjusted to adjustment" by sending dependent members back to the countryside, where subsistence was cheaper. "In Costa Rica," writes Cedric Pugh, "men and women split their households, with women and children often being constrained to migrate to poorer regions where housing outlays could be economized. Sometimes this added to separation and divorce with long-term consequences for living standards and the demand for housing among split households."[34]

The urban African experience has been even more harrowing since women and children have had to negotiate the AIDS holocaust (itself partly due to the poverty-enforced prostitution of poor women) and frequently, drought and civil war as well as structural adjustment. In Harare the 1991 SAP raised the cost of living 45 percent in a single year and 100,000 people ended up in hospital wards suffering from effects of malnutrition. As both Nazneen Kanji and Christian Rogerson have

33 Escobar and González, "Crisis, Restructuring and Urban Poverty in Mexico," pp. 63–73.
34 Pugh, "The Role of the World Bank in Housing," p. 55.

recounted in separate studies, ruthless competition has become the norm in the informal market economy – especially for market women and street vendors – as women struggle to provide food for their families: "Generally speaking, the incomes generated from these enterprises, the majority of which tend to be run by women, usually fall short of even minimum income standards and involve little capital investment, virtually no skills training, and only constrained opportunities for expansion into a viable business."[35] Meanwhile, as infant mortality doubled, AIDS spread and children's nutrition declined, desperate mothers in Harare sent young children back to the countryside or regrouped previously independent family members into extended households to save on rent and electricity.[36] Tens of thousands of older childen were forced to drop out of school in order to work or scavenge, with little hope of ever returning to education. Often the myriad pressures were too overwhelming and family solidarity itself collapsed. According to one group of researchers, "what may once have been a unit that supported and sustained its members has now become a unit in which members compete for survival."[37]

Rather than see their families destroyed, however, slum-dwellers in the late 1970s and 1980s, generally with women in the forefront, resurrected and reshaped that classical protest of the urban poor, the food riot. The slums of Africa, Latin American, and South Asia did not go gently into the IMF's good night – instead they exploded. In their pathbreaking study of grassroots resistance to structural adjustment (*Free Markets and Food Riots*, 2004), John Walton and David Seddon catalogued 146 "IMF riots" in 39 debtor countries from 1976 to 1992.[38] Whatever elements of a "human face" – the so-called "social dimensions of adjustment" – could be attributed to SAPs in the early

35 Rogerson, "Globalization or Informalization?," p. 347.

36 Nazneen Kanji, "Gender, Poverty and Structural Adjustment in Harare, Zimbabwe," *Environment and Urbanization* 7:1 (April 1995), pp. 39, 48–50; Drakakis-Smith, *Third World Cities*, p. 148 (malnutrition). Also see Deborah Potts and Chris Mutambirwa, "Basics Are Now a Luxury," pp. 73–75.

37 B. Rwezaura et al., quoted in Miriam Grant, "Difficult Debut: Social and Economic Identities of Urban Youth in Bulawayo, Zimbabwe," *Canadian Journal of African Studies* 37:2/3 (2003), pp. 416–17.

38 John Walton and David Seddon, *Free Markets and Food Riots: The Politics of Structural Adjustment*, Oxford 1994, pp. 39–45.

1990s were largely retrofitted in response to this extraordinary eruption
of global protest.

> The international dimensions of austerity are recognized symbolically in
> attacks on travel agencies, foreign automobiles, luxury hotels, and inter-
> national agency offices. Protests take varied forms, often appearing as
> classic food riots (Morocco, Brazil, Haiti) and at other times as peaceful
> protest demonstrations that turned violent (Sudan, Turkey, Chile) or as
> general strikes (Peru, Bolivia, India). Frequently, however, protest
> initiated with one of these tactics is transformed to another – demon-
> strations turn to riot, spontaneous violence is rechanneled in political
> organization.
>
>   The food riot as a means of popular protest is a common, perhaps
> even universal, feature of market societies – less a vestige of political-
> industrial evolution than a strategy of empowerment in which poor and
> dispossessed groups assert their claims to social justice. In the modern
> system of states and international economic integration, the explosive
> point of popular protest has moved, with most of the world's popula-
> tion, to the cities where the processes of global accumulation, national
> development, and popular justice intersect.[39]

The first wave of anti-IMF protests peaked between 1983 and 1985,
only to be followed by a second wave after 1989. In Caracas in
February 1989 a hugely unpopular IMF-dictated increase in fuel prices
and transit fares sparked a riot by angry bus riders and radical university students, and police batons quickly turned the confrontation into a
semi-insurrection. During the week-long *Caracazo*, tens of thousands
of poor people came down from their hillside *barrios* to loot shopping
centers, burn luxury cars, and build barricades. At least 400 were killed.
A month later Lagos erupted after student protests against the IMF: 50
died in three days of looting and street fighting in a city where most
poor people probably shared the boiling anger of "the King" in Chris
Abani's novel *Graceland*:

---

39 Ibid., p. 43.

De majority of our people are honest, hardworking people. But dey are at de mercy of dese army bastards and dose tiefs in the IMF, de World Bank and de U.S. ... Now we, you and I and all dese poor peple, owe de World Bank ten million dollars for nothing. Dey are all tiefs and I despise dem – our people and de World Bank people![40]

The Utopian Decade?

According to both neoclassical theory and World Bank projections, the 1990s should have righted the wrongs of the 1980s and allowed Third World cities to regain lost ground and bridge the chasms of inequality created by the SAPs – the pain of adjustment should have been followed by the analgesic of globalization. Indeed, the 1990s, as *The Challenge of Slums* wryly notes, were the first decade in which global urban development took place within almost utopian parameters of neoclassical market freedom.

During the 1990s, trade continued to expand at an almost unprecedented rate, no-go areas opened up and military expenditures decreased. ... All the basic inputs to production became cheaper, as interest rates fell rapidly along with the price of basic commodities. Capital flows were increasingly unfettered by national controls and could move rapidly to the most productive areas. Under what were almost perfect economic conditions according to the dominant neoliberal economic doctrine, one might have imagined that the decade would have been one of unrivalled prosperity and social justice.[41]

However, according to the UN's *Human Development Report 2004*, "an unprecedented number of countries saw development slide backwards in the 1990s. In 46 countries people are poorer today than in 1990. In 25 countries more people are hungry today than a decade ago."[42] Throughout the Third World a new wave of SAPs and self-imposed neoliberal programs accelerated the demolition of state employment,

40 Abani, *Graceland*, p. 280.
41 *Challenge*, p. 34.
42 United Nations Development Programme, *Human Development Report 2004*, New York 2004, p. 132.

local manufacturing, and home-market agriculture. The big industrial metropolises of Latin America – Mexico City, São Paulo, Belo Horizonte, and Buenos Aires – suffered massive losses of manufacturing jobs. In São Paulo the manufacturing share of employment fell from 40 percent in 1980 to 15 percent in 2004.[43] The cost of servicing debt (which in a country like Jamaica ate up 60 percent of the budget in the late 1990s) absorbed resources for social programs and housing assistance: it is the "social abandonment" of the urban poor, in the words of Don Robotham.[44]

The World Bank, for its part, applauded the disappearing role of the local state in *Urban Policy and Economic Development: An Agenda for the 1990s* (1991), a document that reconceptualized the public sector as a simple "enabler" of the marketplace. "With a central focus on the revalorization of market mechanisms," explains geographer Cecilia Zanetta in a review of the Bank's urban programs in Mexico and Argentina, "sound urban policies were now defined as those aimed at eliminating barriers that restricted the productivity of urban economic agents, both formal and informal, so as to maximize their contribution to the national economy."[45] This fetishization of "urban productivity," in fact, led to massive pressure to privatize utilities and urban services, regardless of impacts on employment or equitable distribution. As far as the World Bank was concerned, there was no chance that public-sector employment would regain lost ground in the 1990s.

The boom in exports all too frequently benefited only a tiny stratum. One of the most extreme cases was Angola, a major producer of oil and diamonds. In Luanda, where in 1993 a staggering 84 percent of the population was jobless or underemployed, inequality between the highest and lowest income deciles "increased from a factor of 10 to a factor of 37 between 1995 and 1998 alone."[46] In Mexico the percentage of the population living in extreme poverty increased from 16

43 Henry Chu, "Jobless in São Paulo," *Los Angeles Times*, 30 May 2004.

44 Don Robotham, "How Kingston Was Wounded," in Jane Schneider and Ida Susser (eds), *Wounded Cities: Destruction and Reconstruction in a Globalized World*, Oxford 2003, pp. 111–24.

45 Zanetta, *The Influence of the World Bank on National Housing Policies*, p. 25.

46 Paul Jenkins, Paul Robson, and Allan Cain, "Luanda," *Cities* 19:2 (2002), p. 144.

percent in 1992 to 28 percent in 1999, despite the much-hyped "success stories" of the border *maquiladoras* and NAFTA.[47] Likewise in Colombia, where urban wages declined, but coca acreage tripled during the regime of César Gaviria (elected in 1990), the drug cartels, according to an OECD report, "were among the most consistently favorable to his neoliberal policies."[48] Global inequality, as measured by World Bank economists across the entire world population, reached an incredible GINI coefficient level of 0.67 by the end of the century – this is mathematically equivalent to a situation where the poorest two-thirds of the world receive zero income, and the top third receives everything.[49]

Global turmoil at the the end of the decade, moreover, could be mapped with uncanny accuracy to cities and regions that experienced the sharpest increases in inequality. Throughout the Middle East and Muslim South Asia, a widening gulf between urban rich and poor corroborated the arguments of Islamists and even more radical Salafists about the irreformable corruption of ruling regimes. A final assault on the "socialist" remnants of the FLN state in Algeria began in 1995 with the privatization of 230 firms and the firing of 130,000 state workers; poverty shot up from 15 percent in 1988 to 23 percent in 1995.[50] Likewise, in Tehran, as the Islamic Revolution backed away from its original pro-poor policies, poverty sharply rose from 26 to 31 percent between 1993 and 1995.[51] In Egypt, despite five years of economic growth, 1999 World Bank data showed no decrease in household poverty (defined as an income of $610 or less per year) but did register a fall in per capita consumption.[52] Pakistan similarly faced a dual crisis of declining industrial competitiveness, as its textile exports were imperiled by China, and agricultural productivity declined due to

47 Zanetta, *The Influence of the World Bank on National Housing Policies*, p. 64.
48 Forrest Hylton, "An Evil Hour: Uribe's Colombia in Historical Perspective," *New Left Review* 23 (September–October 2003), p. 84
49 Shaohua Chen and Martin Ravallion, "How Did the World's Poorest Fare in the 1990s?" World Bank working paper, Washington, D.C., 2000, p. 18.
50 Laabas Belkacem, "Poverty Dynamics in Algeria," Arab Planning Institute, working paper, Kuwait (June 2001), pp. 3, 9.
51 Djavad Salehi-Isfahani, "Mobility and the Dynamics of Poverty in Iran: What Can We Learn from the 1992–95 Panel Data?," World Bank working paper (November 2003), p. 17.
52 Soliman, *A Possible Way Out*, p. 9.

chronic underinvestment in irrigation. As a result, the wages of casual and informal labor fell, poverty soared at a pace which the *National Human Development Report* characterized as "unprecedented in Pakistan's history," and urban income inequality, as measured by the GINI coefficient, increased from 31.7 percent in 1992 to 36 percent in 1998.[53]

The biggest event of the 1990s, however, was the conversion of much of the former "Second World" – European and Asian state socialism – into a new Third World. In the early 1990s those considered to be living in extreme poverty in the former "transitional countries," as the UN calls them, rocketed from 14 million to 168 million: an almost instantaneous mass pauperization without precedent in history.[54] Poverty, of course, did exist in the former USSR in an unacknowledged form, but according to World Bank researchers, the rate did not exceed 6 to 10 percent.[55] Now, according to Alexey Krasheninnokov, in his report to UN-HABITAT, 60 percent of Russian families live in poverty, and the rest of the population "can only be categorized as middle class by a considerable stretch." ("Middle-class" Russians, for example, spend 40 percent of their income on food as compared to a global middle-income standard of less than one-third.)[56]

Although the worst "transitional poverty" is hidden from view in derelict regions of the ex-Soviet countryside, the cities display shocking new extremes of overnight wealth and equally sudden misery. In St. Petersburg, for example, income inequality between the richest and poorest decile soared from 4.1 in 1989 to 13.2 in 1996.[57] Moscow may now have more billionaires than New York, but it also has more than one million squatters, many of them illegal immigrants from the Ukraine (200,000), China (150,000), Vietnam, and Moldavia; these people live in primitive conditions in abandoned buildings, rundown dormitories, and former barracks. Sweatshop firms, often praised in

53 Akmal Hussain, *Pakistan National Human Development Report 2003: Poverty, Growth and Governance,* Karachi 2003, pp. 1, 5, 7, 15, 23.

54 *Challenge,* p. 2.

55 Braithwaite, Grootaert, and Milanovic, *Poverty and Social Assistance in Transition Countries,* p. 47.

56 Alexey Krasheninnokov, "Moscow," UN-HABITAT Case Study, London 2003, pp. 9–10.

57 Tatyana Protasenko, "Dynamics of the Standard of Living During Five Years of Economic Reform," *International Journal of Urban and Regional Research* 21:3 (1997), p. 449.

the West as the vanguard of capitalism, "prefer to employ [these] outlaws, to pay them miserable salaries, and house 10 to 15 in one room apartments," while not paying any payroll taxes at all.[58] Russian researchers estimate that the informal or shadow economy probably equals 40 percent of the turnover of the formal economy.[59]

In the old Soviet Union urban housing was rationed but virtually free – 2 to 3 percent of household income was typically expended for rent and utilities – and depended upon a unique social infrastructure of district heating, subways, and workplace-based culture and recreation. Since the late 1990s, however, the government of Vladimir Putin has accepted IMF stipulations to raise payments for housing and heating to market level, despite a fall in incomes.[60] Simultaneously, there has been massive neglect, disinvestment, even abandonment of the crucial district infrastructures and factory-based social services, and as a result, older apartment blocks – indeed, whole neighborhoods, and some-times entire cities – have regressed to slum conditions. Many working-class residential areas are characterized by broken pipes, over-flowing sewers, faulty lighting, and, most dangerously, no winter heat. Millions of poor urban Russians, as a result, suffer conditions of cold, hunger, and isolation uncannily reminiscent of the siege of Leningrad during the Second World War.

Russian-style transitional poverty also exists in urban Eastern Europe, most notably in Bulgaria and Albania. In Sofia, hammered by deindustrialization and plant closures, poverty and inequality exploded in 1995–96, especially amongst Roma and Turkish minorities, older women, and large families: 43 percent of Bulgarians now live below the poverty line, and Sofia probably has the largest slum population in Europe. It also has Europe's most wretched slum, "Cambodia" in Fakulteta, where 35,000 Roma (90 percent of them unemployed) live under ghetto conditions that recall the misery of Dalits in India.[61] Europe's poorest city, however, is Elbasan (population 110,000), the

58 Krasheninnokov, "Moscow," p. 10.
59 Protasenko, "Dynamics of the Standard of Living During Five Years of Economic Reform," p. 449.
60 Ibid.
61 World Bank, "Bulgaria: Poverty During the Transition," quoted by Social Rights Bulgaria, 29 June 2003, www.socialrights.org.

former heavy industrial center of Albania which now survives only thanks to the remittances of its many emigrants in Italy and Greece. Tirana, meanwhile, is surrounded by burgeoning peri-urban shantytowns, with some poor people squatting in the ubiquitous pillboxes built by the paranoid Hoxha dictatorship.[62]

Success Stories?

Globalization's two great success stories in the 1990s were the continuing jobs-and-income boom in China's coastal cities and the emergence of an "India Shining" of high-tech enclaves and office parks. In both cases, development was no illusion: the forest of sky cranes around Shanghai, as well as new shopping malls and Starbucks in Bangalore, testify to economic dynamism, but these market miracles were purchased at high costs in increased economic inequality.

Since the late 1970s, the distribution of income and wealth in China's cities has gone from the most egalitarian in Asia to one of the most egregiously unequal. Indeed, as Azizur Khan and Carl Riskin point out in a seminal study, "the increase in urban inequality was proportionately greater than the increase in rural inequality."[63] Juxtaposed with the *nouveaux riches* are the new urban poor: on one hand, deindustrialized traditional workers, and on the other, unregistered labor migrants from the countryside. Chinese city folk no longer "eat from the same big pot" as in austere but secure Maoist times. In September 1997 President Jiang Zemin told a Communist Party conference that "workers should change their ideas about employment." In a dynamic market society, he argued, cradle-to-grave social security was no longer feasible.[64] This has meant the downsizing or even loss of a social safety net for the tens of millions of industrial workers and state employees restructured out of their jobs in recent years.

62 World Bank, "Albania: Growing Out of Poverty," working paper, 20 May 1997, p. 41.

63 Azizur Rahman Khan and Carl Riskin, *Inequality and Poverty in China in the Age of Globalization*, Oxford 2001, p. 36. As the authors emphasize, Chinese urban income statistics do not include the huge floating population of rural migrants, thus creating a bias toward underestimation of inequality.

64 Pamela Yatsko, *New Shanghai: The Rocky Rebirth of China's Legendary City*, Singapore 2003, p. 113.

Between 1996 and 2001 the number of state-owned industrial companies was reduced by 40 percent and a staggering 36 million workers were made redundant. Officially there was little rise in unemployment, but this was statistical sleight of hand, because laid-off state workers were put into a special "off post" category that didn't count them as jobless since they still received some social security benefits through their work unit. In reality, urban unemployment is estimated to be between 8 percent and 13 percent. An unusually high percentage of redundant workers are women because, according to journalist Pamela Yatsko, the bureau chief for the *Far Eastern Economic Review*, "the government estimated that laid-off women would be less of a security threat than jobless men." Former female industrial workers – welders, lathe operators, and shipbuilders – are now forced to hunt for low-paying service-sector jobs as maids, waitresses, nannies, or street vendors.[65]

Yet Mao's ex-heroes of history retain, for the most part, the privileges of official urban status and usually some security of tenure. The "peasant flood," however, enjoys official social rights only in the impoverished villages from which they have fled. An estimated 3 million migrant workers in Shanghai, for example, currently lack medical insurance, social welfare, or benefits of any kind. Migrants have also become the scapegoats for the contradictions of the new urban market economy. Some observers have compared the caste-like discrimination against rural migrants in contemporary urban China to that of "Black people in South Africa before the 1990s or of blacks and Asians in the United States throughout the first half of the twentieth century."[66] Indeed, Yatsko found recurrent scenes in Shanghai during the late 1990s that were disturbingly reminiscent of the evil city of the 1930s.

> The city, like others in China, only allows migrants to do certain low-status jobs, barring them from better jobs and kicking them out of the city if they cannot prove they are employed. Migrants mix little with the Shanghainese, who hold their country cousins in contempt and automatically blame them first when a crime is committed in the city. The

65 Ibid., pp. 113–15.
66 Solinger, *Contesting Citizenship in Urban China*, p. 5.

majority of migrant workers are men who find work on the city's omnipresent construction sites. They sleep at night in makeshift barracks on the site, rent cheap accommodation on the city's outskirts, or grab a slab of pavement if they have not yet found a job. Migrant women sometimes work as maids for Shanghai families or in decrepit barbershops in bad parts of town, washing hair for 10 yuan (US \$1.20) a head and, in some cases, providing sexual services for a bit more. Smudge-faced migrant waifs in rags, with or without their mothers, regularly beg for spare change outside popular watering holes, particularly those frequented by foreigners.[67]

Chinese officials, not unjustifiably, extol the indices of national economic progress, especially the incredible 10 percent yearly increase in GDP since 1980; they are less forthcoming about poverty and deprivation. By official admission, Chinese social indicators are highly unreliable. In 2002 the leading government think tank, the Development Research Center of the State Council, warned that urban poverty had been radically underestimated. It proposed raising the official figure from 14.7 million to at least 37.1 million, although it acknowledged that this revision still failed to include tens of millions of laid-off employees or the 100 million "floating workers" still counted as farmers.[68]

Urban poverty in India is more honestly acknowledged and publicly debated than in China, but local social scientists and social-justice activists trying to focus public attention on the underside of the recent economic growth have also had to swim against the current of celebratory official rhetoric As any reader of the business press knows, the drastic neoliberal restructuring of the Indian economy after 1991 produced a high-tech boom and stock-market bubble whose frenzied epicenters were a handful of Cinderella cities: Bangalore, Pune, Hyderabad, and Chennai. GDP grew at 6 percent during the 1990s, while the capitalization of the Bombay Stock Exchange doubled almost every year – and one result was one million new millionaires, many of them Indian engineers and computer scientists returned from Sunnyvale and Redmond. Less publicized, however, was the accompanying growth in poverty: India gained 56 million more paupers in the course of the "boom." Indeed, as Jeremy Seabrook underlines, the early 1990s may have been "the worst time for the poor since Independence," as deregulated food grain prices soared 58 percent between 1991 and 1994.[69]

Growth has been stupendously lopsided, with enormous speculative investment in the information technology sector leaving agriculture to stagnate and infrastructure to decay. Rather than taxing new million-aires, the neoliberal Janata government financed itself with the massive privatization of state industry, thanks to which Enron now sells elec-tricity near Bombay at three times the rate of the public utility. Neoliberal policies, like those in China, have wreaked havoc in the neg-lected Indian countryside, where three quarters of households lack access to sanitation and unpolluted drinking water, and the poor shout futilely for "Bijli, Sadaak, Paani" ("Electricity, Roads, and Water"). As Praful Bidwai reported in the *Asian Times* in 2000:

> Infant mortality rates are rising even in states like Kerala and Maharashtra, which have relatively good social indicators.... The gov-ernment is cutting spending on rural development, including agricultural programs, and rural employment and anti-poverty schemes, as well as on health, drinking water supply, education and sanitation. Income growth in the rural areas, where 70 percent of Indians live, averaged 3.1 in the 1980s. It has sharply declined to 1.8 percent. Real wages of rural workers decreased last year by more than 2 percent.[70]

While the urban middle classes indulge their new tastes for California-style tract homes and health clubs, the defeated rural poor have been killing themselves in droves. In Andhra Pradesh alone, wrote journalist Edward Luce in July 2004, "500 of its farmers have committed suicide this year alone, often by drinking the pesticide that was purchased with debts they could not repay."[71] Increased despair in the countryside, in

69 Seabrook, *In the Cities of the South*, p. 63.
70 Praful Bidwai, "India's Bubble Economy Booms as Poverty Grows," *Asia Times*, 17 March 2000.
71 *Financial Times*, 24/25 July 2004.

turn, has dislodged vast numbers of poor farmers and laborers whose only alternative has been migration to the slum outskirts of high-tech boomtowns like Bangalore.

As the headquarters of India's software and computer-service industries, as well as a major center for the manufacture of military aircraft, Bangalore (population 6 million) prides itself on its California-style shopping malls, golf courses, *nouvelle cuisine* restaurants, five-star hotels, and English-language cinemas. Dozens of tech campuses display logos for Oracle, Intel, Dell, and Macromedia, and local universities and technical institutes graduate 40,000 skilled workers and engineers each year. Bangalore advertises itself as a "prosperous garden city," and its southern suburbs are indeed a middle-class Shangri-la. Meanwhile, draconian urban renewal programs have driven underprivileged residents from the center to the slum periphery, where they live side by side with poor migrants from the countryside. An estimated 2 million poor people, many of them scorned members of the scheduled castes, squat in 1000 or so fetid slums, mostly on government-owned land. Slums have grown twice as fast as the general population, and researchers have characterized Bangalore's periphery as "the dumping ground for those urban residents whose labour is wanted in the urban economy but whose visual presence should be reduced as much as possible."[72]

Half of Bangalore's population lacks piped water, much less cappuccino, and there are more ragpickers and street children (90,000) than software geeks (about 60,000). In an archipelago of 10 slums, researchers found only 19 latrines for 102,000 residents.[73] Solomon Benjamin, a Bangalore-based consultant for the UN and the World Bank, reports that "children suffered heavily from diarrhoea and worm infestations, a high proportion were malnourished, and infant mortality rates in the slums were much higher than the state average." By the millennium, moreover, India's and Bangalore's neoliberal bubble had burst: although software continued to grow, "employment prospects in

72 Hans Schenk and Michael Dewitt, "The Fringe Habitat of Bangalore," in *Living in India's Slums*, p. 131.
73 Schenk, "Living in Bangalore's Slums" and "Bangalore: An Outline," in *Living in India's Slums*, pp. 23, 30–32, 44, 46; H. Ramachandran and G. S. Sastry, "An Inventory and Typology of Slums in Bangalore," in ibid., p. 54; Benjamin, "Governance, Economic Settings and Poverty in Bangalore," p. 39; www.agapeindia.com/street_children.htm for ragpickers and waifs.

almost all other sectors, especially the public sector, have shrunk rapidly or face unstable prospects. Thus the granite, steel and tinted glass offices in Bangalore, most of them belonging to software companies, pose a stark contrast to ill-maintained factories facing falling orders and tighter credit conditions."[74] Ruefully, a leading Western economic consultant was forced to concede that "Bangalore's high tech [boom] is a drop in the bucket in a sea of poverty."[75]

74 Benjamin, "Governance, Economic Settings and Poverty in Bangalore," pp. 36–39.

75 William Lewis quoted in Bernard Wysocki, "Symbol Over Substance," *Wall Street Journal*, 25 September 2000

8

A Surplus Humanity?

A proletariat without factories, workshops, and work, and
without bosses, in the muddle of the odd jobs, drowning in
survival and leading an existence like a path through embers.

Patrick Chamoiseau[1]

The brutal tectonics of neoliberal globalization since 1978 are analogous to the catastrophic processes that shaped a "Third World" in the
first place, during the era of late-Victorian imperialism (1870–1900). At
the end of the nineteenth century, the forcible incorporation into the
world market of the great subsistence peasantries of Asia and Africa
entailed the famine deaths of millions and the uprooting of tens of
millions more from traditional tenures. The end result (in Latin
America as well) was rural "semi-proletarianization," the creation of a
huge global class of immiserated semi-peasants and farm laborers
lacking existential security of subsistence. As a result, the twentieth
century became an age not of urban revolutions, as classical Marxism
had imagined, but of epochal rural uprisings and peasant-based wars of
national liberation.[2]

Structural adjustment, it would appear, has recently worked an
equally fundamental reshaping of human futures. As the authors of

1 Patrick Chamoiseau, *Texaco*, New York 1997, p. 314.
2 See my *Late Victorian Holocausts: El Niño Famines and the Making of the Third World*, London 2001, especially pp. 206–09.

The Challenge of Slums conclude: "Instead of being a focus for growth and prosperity, the cities have become a dumping ground for a surplus population working in unskilled, unprotected and low-wage informal service industries and trade." "The rise of [this] informal sector," they declare bluntly, "is ... a direct result of liberalization." Some Brazilian sociologists call this process – analogous to the semi-proletarianization of landless peasants – *passive proletarianization*, involving the "dissolving of traditional forms of (re)production, which for the great majority of direct producers does not translate into a salaried position in the formal labor market."[3]

This informal working class, without legal recognition or rights, has important historical antecedents. In modern European history, Naples, even more than Dublin or London's East End, was the exemplar of an urban informal economy. In this "most shocking city of the nineteenth century," as Frank Snowden calls it in his brilliant study, a "chronic super-abundance of labour" survived by miracles of economic improvisation and the constant subdivision of subsistence niches. A structural dearth of formal jobs – permanent unemployment was estimated at 40 percent – was transformed into an overwhelming spectacle of informal competition. The street scene in *Risorgimiento* Naples (described below by Snowden) was a colorful but tragic anticipation of contemporary Lima or Kinshasa.

> It was characteristic of the ailing local economy that tens of thousands of people subsisted by peddling their wares amidst the filth of the city lanes and alleys. It was these impoverished entrepreneurs who gave Naples its feverish activity as a great emporium. These men and women were not workers, but "ragged-trousered capitalists" who filled a bewildering variety of roles that baffled all efforts at quantification. A local authority termed them "micro-industrialists." The elite of the streets were newspaper vendors who practiced only one trade year-round and enjoyed a stable renumeration. The other huxters were "gypsy merchants," authentic nomads of the marketplace who moved from activity to activity as opportunity dictated. There were sellers of vegetables,

3 *Challenge*, pp. 40, 46; Thomas Mitschein, Henrique Miranda, and Mariceli Paraense, *Urbanização Selvagem e Proletarização Passiva na Amazônia – O Caso de Belém*, Belém 1989 (quoted in Browder and Godfrey, *Rainforest Cities*, p. 132).

chestnuts and shoe laces; purveyors of pizzas, mussels and recycled clothes; vendors of mineral water, corn cobs and candy. Some of the men completed their activity by acting as messenger-boys, distributors of commercial leaflets or private dustmen who emptied cesspits or removed domestic waste for a few *centesimi* a week. Others acted as professional mourners paid to follow the hearses bearing the bodies of substantial citizens to the cemetery at Poggioreale. By their presence, hired paupers swelled the attendance, allowing the genteel classes to confirm their popularity and their sense of power.[4]

Today there are hundreds, even thousands, of Napleses. In the 1970s, to be sure, Manuel Castells and other radical critics could persuasively criticize the "myth of marginality" that correlated slum housing with economic informality by pointing to the large numbers of industrial workers and public employees forced to live in substandard housing in cities such as Caracas and Santiago.[5] Moreover, in Latin America at least, the dominant urban labor-market trend during the previous era of import-substitution industrialization had been the relative *reduction* in informal employment – from 29 percent in 1940 to 21 percent in 1970 for the region as a whole.[6]

Since 1980, however, economic informality has returned with a vengeance, and the equation of urban and occupational marginality has become irrefutable and overwhelming: informal workers, according to the United Nations, constitute about two-fifths of the economically active population of the developing world.[7] In Latin America, adds the Inter-American Development Bank, the informal economy currently employs 57 percent of the workforce and supplies four out of five new "jobs."[8] (Indeed, the *only* jobs created in Mexico between 2000 and 2004 were in the informal sector.) Other sources claim that more than half of urban Indonesians, 60 to 75 percent of Central Americans, 65

4 Snowden, *Naples in the Time of Cholera*, Cambridge 1995, pp. 35–36.
5 Castells, *The City and the Grassroots*, pp. 181–83.
6 Orlandina de Oliveira and Bryan Roberts, "The Many Roles of the Informal Sector in Development: Evidence from Urban Labor Market Research, 1940–1989," in Cathy Rakowski (ed.), *Contrapunto: The Informal Sector Debate in Latin America*, Albany 1994, p. 56.
7 *Challenge*, pp. 40, 46.
8 Cited in *The Economist*, 21 March 1998, p. 37.

percent of the populations of Dhaka and Khartoum, and 75 percent of Karachians subsist in the informal sector.[9]

Smaller cities, like Huancayo in Peru or Allahabad and Jaipur in India, tend to be even more informalized, with three-quarters or more of their workforces existing in the shadowlands of the off-the-books economy.[10] Likewise, in China millions of rural immigrants cling to urban life by the most precarious (and usually illegal) of handholds. According to Aprodicio Laquian, "Most of the jobs found in small towns and cities are in the informal sector: food stalls and restaurants, beauty parlours and barber shops, dressmaking salons, or petty trading. While these informal-sector jobs tend to be labour-intensive and can absorb significant numbers, there are questions about their economic efficiency and productive potential."[11]

In most sub-Saharan cities, formal job creation has virtually ceased to exist. An ILO study of Zimbabwe's urban labor markets under "stagflationary" structural adjustment in the early 1990s found that the formal sector was creating only 10,000 jobs per year in the face of an urban workforce increasing by more than 300,000 per annum.[12] Similarly, an OECD study of West Africa predicts that a shrinking formal sector will employ one-quarter or less of the labor force by 2020.[13] This corresponds to grim UN projections that informal employment will somehow have to absorb 90 percent of urban Africa's new workers over the next decade.[14]

9 *Challenge*, p. 103; Rondinelli and Kasarda, "Job Creation Needs in Third World Cities," *Third World Cities*; Hasan, "Introduction," in Khan, *Orangi Pilot Project*, p. xl (cites Karachi Master Plan of 1989); Ubaidur Rob, M. Kabir, and M. Mutahara, "Urbanization in Bangladesh," in Gayl Ness and Prem Talwer (eds), *Asian Urbanization in the New Millennium*, Singapore 2005, p. 36.

10 Rondinelli and Kasarda, p. 107.

11 Laquian, "The Effects of National Urban Strategy and Regional Development Policy on Patterns of Urban Growth in China," p. 66.

12 Guy Mhone, "The Impact of Structural Adjustment on the Urban Informal Sector in Zimbabwe," "Issues in Development" discussion paper #2, Geneva n.d., p. 19.

13 Cour and Snrech, *Preparing for the Future*, p. 64.

14 *Challenge*, p. 104.

Myths of Informality

Altogether, the global informal working class (overlapping with but non-identical to the slum population) is about one billion strong, making it the fastest-growing, and most unprecedented, social class on earth. Since anthropologist Keith Hart, working in Accra, first broached the concept of an "informal sector" in 1973, a huge literature has wrestled with the formidable theoretical and empirical problems involved in studying the survival strategies of the new urban poor. Although large informal sectors certainly existed in Victorian cities, as well as in comprador Shanghai and urban colonial India ("an overwhelming and enduring reality," writes Nandini Gooptu), the current macroeconomic role of informality is revolutionary.[15]

Among researchers, there is a base consensus that the 1980s crisis – during which informal-sector employment grew two to five times faster than formal-sector jobs – has inverted their relative structural positions, establishing informal survivalism as the new primary mode of livelihood in a majority of Third World cities. Even in rapidly industrializing urban China, "there has been a proliferation of rudimentary informal activities which provide means of survival to the urban poor."[16] Part of the informal proletariat, to be sure, is a stealth workforce for the formal economy, and numerous studies have exposed how the subcontracting networks of Wal-Mart and other mega-companies extend deep into the misery of the *colonias* and *chawls*. Likewise, there is probably more of a continuum than an abrupt divide between the increasingly casualized world of formal employment and the depths of the informal sector. Yet at the end of the day, the majority of the slum-dwelling laboring poor are truly and radically homeless in the contemporary international economy. Researchers accordingly have been forced to scrap the optimistic "Todaro model" embraced by modernization theorists and Alliance for Progress ideologues in the 1960s, according to which the informal sector is simply a school of urban skills from which most rural immigrants eventually graduate to formal-sector jobs.[17] Instead of

15 Gooptu, *The Politics of the Urban Poor in Early Twentieth-Century India*, p. 2.
16 Khan and Riskin, *Inequality and Poverty in China in the Age of Globalization*, p. 40.
17 See the classic formulation: M. Todaro, "A Model of Labor Migration and Urban Unemployment in Less Developed Countries," *American Economic Review* 59:1 (1969), pp. 138–45.

upward mobility, there is seemingly only a down staircase by which redundant formal-sector workers and sacked public employees descend into the black economy.

Yet there has been much resistance to drawing the straightforward conclusion that the growth of informality is an explosion of "active" unemployment, what the ILO's Oberai characterizes as the "substitution of underemployment and disguised unemployed for increases in open unemployment."[18] Apostles of self-help and NGO-scale programs indeed blanch when veteran researchers such as Jan Breman (who has spent 40 years studying poverty in India and Indonesia) conclude that upward mobility in the informal economy is largely a "myth inspired by wishful thinking."[19] Instead, innumerable studies – often sponsored by the World Bank and other pillars of the so-called Washington Consensus – have sought consolation in the belief that the informal sector is potentially the urban Third World's *deus ex machina*.

Hernando de Soto, of course, is internationally famous for arguing that this enormous population of marginalized laborers and ex-peasants is a frenzied beehive of proto-capitalists yearning for formal property rights and unregulated competitive space: "Marx would probably be shocked to find how in developing countries much of the teeming mass does not consist of oppressed legal proletarians but of oppressed extralegal small *entrepreneurs*."[20] De Soto's bootstrap model of development, as we have seen, is especially popular because of the simplicity of his recipe: get the state (and formal-sector labor unions) out of the way, add micro-credit for micro-entrepreneurs and land titling for squatters, then let markets take their course to produce the transubstantiation of poverty into capital. (De Soto-inspired optimism, in its most absurd version, has led some development-aid bureaucrats to redefine slums as "Strategic Low-Income Urban Management Systems.")[21] This semi-utopian view of the informal sector, however, grows out of a nested set of epistemological fallacies.

18 Oberai, *Population Growth, Employment and Poverty in Third-World Mega-Cities*, p. 64.
19 Jan Breman, *The Labouring Poor: Patterns of Exploitation, Subordination, and Exclusion*, New Delhi, p. 174.
20 Quoted in Donald Krueckeberg, "The Lessons of John Locke or Hernando de Soto: What if Your Dreams Come True?," *Housing Policy Debate* 15:1 (2004), p. 2.
21 Michael Mutter, UK Department for International Development, quoted in *Environment and Urbanization* 15:1 (April 2003), p. 12.

First, neoliberal populists have failed to heed anthropologist William House's 1978 warning in his case studies of Nairobi slums about the need to distinguish micro-accumulation from sub-subsistence: "The simple dichotomy of the urban economy in less developed countries into formal sector and informal sector is clearly inadequate. The informal sector can be further categorized into at least two subsectors: an intermediate sector, which appears as a reservoir of dynamic entrepreneurs, and the community of the poor, which contains a large body of residual and under-employed labor."[22]

Alejandro Portes and Kelly Hoffman, following House, recently evaluated the overall impact of SAPs and neoliberalization upon Latin American urban class structures since the 1970s. They carefully distinguished between an *informal petty bourgeoisie* ("the sum of owners of microenterprises, employing less than five workers, plus own-account professionals and technicians") and the *informal proletariat* ("the sum of own-account workers minus professionals and technicians, domestic servants, and paid and unpaid workers in microenterprises"). They found a strong correlation in virtually every country between expansion of the informal sector and the shrinkage of public-sector employment and the formal proletariat: de Soto's heroic "microentrepreneurs" are usually displaced public-sector professionals or laid-off skilled workers. Since the 1980s they have grown from about 5 percent to more than 10 percent of the economically active urban population: a trend reflecting "the *forced entrepreneurialism* [their emphasis] foisted on former salaried employees by the decline of formal sector employment."[23]

Second, the employees, paid and unpaid, of the informal sector have been almost as invisible in Third World labor-market studies as shantytown renters in most housing research.[24] Despite the stereotype of the heroic self-employed, however, most participants in the informal economy work directly or indirectly for someone else (via the

22 See William House, "Nairobi's Informal Sector: Dynamic Entrepreneurs or Surplus Labor?," *Economic Development and Cultural Change* 32 (January 1984), pp. 298–99; also "Priorities for Urban Labour Market Research in Anglophone Africa," *The Journal of Developing Areas* 27 (October 1992).

23 Alejandro Portes and Kelly Hoffman, "Latin American Class Structures: Their Composition and Change during the Neoliberal Era," *Latin American Research Review* 38:1 (2003), p. 55.

24 Oberai, *Population Growth, Employment and Poverty in Third-World Mega-Cities*, p. 109.

consignment of goods or the rental of a pushcart or rickshaw, for example).

Third, "informal employment" by its very definition, as Jan Breman reminds us, is the absence of formal contracts, rights, regulations, and bargaining power. Petty exploitation (endlessly franchised) is its essence, and there is growing inequality *within* the informal sector as well as between it and the formal sector.[25] De Soto's "Invisible Revolution" of informal capital is really about myriad invisible networks of exploitation. Thus Breman and Arvind Das describe the relentless micro-capitalism of Surat:

> In addition to the blatant exploitation of labour, what characterizes the informal sector is the crude technology, low capital investment, the excessively manual nature of production within it. At the same time, the sector is also marked by high rates of profit and enormous capital accumulation assisted by the fact that the informal sector is ... not registered, let alone taxed. One of the most telling pictures of this sector is the sight of the "gentlemanly" owner of a garbage shop, sitting in his well-ironed clothes by his gleaming motorcycle, amidst the piles of waste that the rag-pickers have painfully sorted out for him to profit from. Rags to riches, indeed![26]

Fourth – and this is a corollary of the previous two points – informality ensures extreme abuse of women and children. Again, it is Breman, in his magisterial study of the working poor in India, who drags the skeleton out of the closet: "Out of public view, it is usually the weakest and smallest shoulders that have to bear the heaviest burdens of informalization. The image of shared poverty does not do justice to the inequality with which this form of existence, too, is permeated within the sphere of the household."[27]

Fifth, in contrast to the wishful thinking of bootstrap ideologues, the informal sector – as observed by Frederic Thomas in Kolkata – generates jobs not by elaborating new divisions of labor, but by fragmenting existing work, and thus subdividing incomes:

25 Breman, *The Labouring Poor*, pp. 4, 9, 154, 196.
26 Jan Breman and Arvind Das, *Down and Out: Labouring Under Global Capitalism*, New Delhi 2000, p. 56.
27 Breman, *The Labouring Poor*, p. 231.

... three or four persons dividing a task which could be as well done by one, market women sitting for hours in front of little piles of fruit or vegetables, barbers and shoeshiners squatting on the sidewalk all day to serve only a handful of customers, young boys dodging in and out of traffic selling tissues, wiping car windows, hawking magazines or cigarettes individually, construction workers waiting each morning, often in vain, in the hope of going out on a job.[28]

The surpluses of labor transformed into informal "entrepreneurs" are often astonishing. A 1992 survey of Dar-es-Salaam estimated that the majority of the city's more than 200,000 petty traders were not the famed *Mama Lishe* (female food vendors) of ethnographic lore but simply unemployed youth. The researchers noted: "In general, informal petty business is the employment of last resort for the most economically vulnerable city residents."[29] Moreover, informal and small-scale formal enterprises ceaselessly war with one another for economic space: street vendors versus small shopkeepers, jitneys versus public transport, and so on.[30] As Bryan Roberts says about Latin America at the beginning of the twenty-first century, "the 'informal sector' grows, but incomes drop within it."[31]

Competition in urban informal sectors has become so intense that it recalls Darwin's famous analogy about ecological struggle in tropical nature: "Ten thousand sharp wedges [i.e., urban survival strategies] packed close together and driven inwards by incessant blows, sometimes one wedge being struck, and then another with greater force." Space for new entrants is provided only by a dimunition of per capita earning capacities and/or by the intensification of labor despite declining marginal returns. This effort to "provide everyone with some niche, however small, in the overall system" proceeds by the same kind of overcrowding and "gothic elaboration" of niches that Clifford Geertz, borrowing a term from art history, famously characterized as "involution" in the agricultural economy of colonial Java. *Urban*

28 Thomas, *Calcutta Poor*, p. 114.
29 William Kombe, "Institutionalising the Concept of Environmental Planning and Management," in Westendorff and Eade, *Development and Cities*, p. 69.
30 Sethuraman, "Urban Poverty and the Informal Sector," p. 8.
31 Bryan Roberts, "From Marginality to Social Exclusion: From Laissez Faire to Pervasive Engagement," *Latin American Research Review* 39:1 (February 2004), p. 196.

involution, thus, seems an apt description of the evolution of informal employment structures in most Third World cities.[32]

Tendencies toward urban involution, to be sure, existed during the nineteenth century. The European urban-industrial revolutions were incapable of absorbing the entire supply of displaced rural labor, especially after continental agriculture was exposed to the devastating competition of the North American prairies and Argentine pampas from the 1870s. But mass emigration to the settler societies of the Americas and Australasia, as well as Siberia, provided a dynamic safety valve that prevented the rise of mega-Dublins and super-Napleses, as well as the spread of the kind of underclass anarchism that had taken root in the most immiserated parts of Southern Europe. Today, by contrast, surplus labor faces unprecedented barriers to emigration to rich countries.

Sixth, because they contend with such desperate conditions, it is perhaps not surprising that the poor turn with fanatic hope to a "third economy" of urban subsistence, including gambling, pyramid schemes, lotteries, and other quasi-magical forms of wealth appropriation. For example, in their study of the household economy of the Klong Thoey slum in the port of Bangkok, Hans-Dieter Evers and Rüdiger Korff discovered that fully 20 percent of neighborhood income was redistributed through gambling and share games.[33] Throughout the urban Third World, moreover, religious devotion revolves around attempts to influence fortune or importune good luck.

Seventh, under such conditions, it is not surprising that initiatives such as micro-credit and cooperative lending, while helpful to those informal enterprises managing to tread water, have had little macro impact on the reduction of poverty, even in Dhaka, the home of the world-famous Grameen Bank.[34] Indeed, stubborn belief in "leveraging the micro-enterprise," writes Jaime Joseph, a veteran community

32 Clifford Geertz, *Agricultural Involution: The Processes of Ecological Change in Indonesia*, Berkeley 1963, pp. 80–82. T. McGhee uses the "urban involution" metaphor in "Beachheads and Enclaves: The Urban Debate and the Urbanization Process in Southeast Asia since 1945," in Y. M. Yeung and C. P. Lo (eds), *Changing South-East Asian Cities: Readings on Urbanization*, London 1976.

33 Evers and Korff, *Southeast Asian Urbanism*, p. 143.

34 Serajul Hoque, "Micro-credit and the Reduction of Poverty in Bangladesh," *Journal of Contemporary Asia* 34:1 (2004), pp. 21, 27.

organizer in Lima, has become something of an urban cargo cult amongst well-meaning NGOs: "There has been much emphasis placed on small or micro-enterprises as the magic solution in offering economic development for the urban poor. Our work over the last 20 years with small businesses, which are multiplying in the megacity, shows that most of them are simply survival tactics with little or no chances for accumulation."[35]

Eighth, increasing competition within the informal sector depletes social capital and dissolves self-help networks and solidarities essential to the survival of the very poor – again, especially women and children. An NGO worker in Haiti, Yolette Etienne, describes the ultimate logic of neoliberal individualism in a context of absolute immiseration:

> Now everything is for sale. The woman used to receive you with hospitality, give you coffee, share all that she had in her home. I could go get a plate of food at a neighbor's house; a child could get a coconut at her godmother's, two mangoes at another aunt's. But these acts of solidarity are disappearing with the growth of poverty. Now when you arrive somewhere, either the woman offers to sell you a cup of coffee or she has no coffee at all. The tradition of mutual giving that allowed us to help each other and survive – this is all being lost.[36]

Similarly, in Mexico, Mercedes de la Rocha "warns that persistent poverty over two decades has effectively brought the poor to their knees." Sylvia Chant continues: "While the mobilization of household, family, and community solidarity served as vital resources in the past, there is a limit to how many favors people can call on from one another and how effective these exchanges are in the face of huge structural impediments to well-being. In particular, there are worries that the disproportionate burdens that have fallen on women have stretched their personal reserves to capacity and there is no further 'slack' to be taken up."[37]

35 Jaime Joseph, "Sustainable Development and Democracy in Megacities," in Westendorff and Eade, *Development and Cities*, p. 115.

36 Quoted in Bell, *Walking on Fire*, p. 120.

37 Paraphrased in Sylvia Chant, "Urban Livelihoods, Employment and Gender," in Gwynne and Kay, pp. 212–14.

Ninth, and finally, under such extreme conditions of competition, the neoliberal prescription (as set out in the World Bank's *1995 World Development Report*) of making labor even more flexible is simply catastrophic.[38] De Sotan slogans simply grease the skids to a Hobbesian hell. Those engaged in informal-sector competition under conditions of infinite labor supply usually stop short of a total war of all against all; conflict, instead, is usually transmuted into ethnoreligious or racial violence. The godfathers and landlords of the informal sector (invisible in most of the literature) intelligently use coercion, even chronic violence to regulate competition and protect their investments. As Philip Amis emphasizes: "There are barriers to entry in terms of capital, and often political terms, which create a tendency towards monopoly in the successful areas of the informal sector; these are difficult to get into."[39]

Politically, the informal sector, in the absence of enforced labor rights, is a semifeudal realm of kickbacks, bribes, tribal loyalties, and ethnic exclusion. Urban space is never free. A place on the pavement, the rental of a rickshaw, a day's labor on a construction site, or a domestic's reference to a new employer: all of these require patronage or membership in some closed network, often an ethnic militia or street gang. Whereas traditional formal industries such as textiles in India or oil in the Middle East tended to foster interethnic solidarity through unions and radical political parties, the rise of the unprotected informal sector has too frequently gone hand in hand with exacerbated ethnoreligious differentiation and sectarian violence.[40]

38 Breman, *The Labouring Poor*, pp. 5, 201.
39 Philip Amis, "Making Sense of Urban Poverty," *Environment and Urbanization* 7:1 (April 1995), p. 151.
40 I think Manuel Castells and Alejandro Portes, however, went too far in a 1989 essay that suggests that the proletariat is "fading away" in the face of the "increasing heterogeneity of work situations and, thus, of social conditions." (Castells and Portes, "World Underneath: The Origins, Dynamics and Effects of the Informal Economy," in Portes, Castells, and Lauren Benton (eds), *The Informal Economy: Studies in Advanced and Less Developed Countries*, Baltimore 1989, p. 31.) Informal workers, in fact, tend to be massively crowded into a few major niches where effective organization and "class consciousness" might become possible if authentic labor rights and regulations existed. It is the lack of economic citizenship, rather than livelihood heterogeneity *per se*, that makes informal labor so prone to clientalist subordination and ethnic fragmentation. I thus echo Jan Breman when he says that main issue in the informal sector is the formalization of the rights and protections of labor, not property (p. 201).

A Museum of Exploitation

If the informal sector, then, is not the brave new world envisioned by its neoliberal enthusiasts, it is most certainly a living museum of human exploitation. There is nothing in the catalogue of Victorian misery, as narrated by Dickens, Zola, or Gorky, that doesn't exist somewhere in a Third World city today. I allude not just to grim survivals and atavisms, but especially to primitive forms of exploitation that have been given new life by postmodern globalization – and child labor is an outstanding example.

Although children are rarely discussed by ideologues of bootstrap capitalism, their extralegal labor, often on behalf of global exporters, constitutes an important sector of most informal urban economies. The Convention on the Rights of the Child – ratified by all countries except the United States and Somalia – bans the most egregious abuses, but as Human Rights Watch and UNICEF have discovered, it is rarely enforced in poorer cities or across the divide of racial and caste prejudice. The full extent of contemporary child labor, of course, is zealously hidden from view and defies any straightforward measurement; nonetheless, what has been exposed is shocking.

A recent study of slum children in Dhaka, for instance, discovered that "nearly half of boys and girls aged 10 to 14 were performing income-generating work," and "only 7 percent of girls and boys aged 5 to 16 years attended school." Dhaka has the largest number of child laborers in Asia (about 750,000), and their earnings provide half the income in poor, female-headed households and nearly a third in male-headed families.[41] Although Mumbai boasts of its high levels of school attendance, Arjun Appadurai finds that its "gigantic restaurant and food service economy [is] almost completely dependent on a vast army of child labor."[42] In Cairo and other Egyptian cities, children under twelve are perhaps 7 percent of the workforce; this includes the

41 Jane Pryer, *Poverty and Vulnerability in Dhaka Slums: The Urban Livelihoods Study*, Aldershot 2003, p. 176; Victoria de la Villa and Matthew S. Westfall (eds), *Urban Indicators for Managing Cities: Cities Data Book*, Manila 2001 (number of child laborers).
42 Arjun Appadurai, "Deep Democracy: Urban Governmentality and the Horizon of Politics," *Environment and Urbanization* 13:2 (October 2001), p. 27.

thousands of street children who gather and resell cigarette butts (a pack a day otherwise costs half of a poor man's monthly salary).[43]

The world capital of enslaved and exploited children, however, is probably the Hindu sacred city of Varanasi (population 1.1 million) in Uttar Pradesh. Famed for its textiles as well as for its temples and holy men, Varanasi (Benares) weaves its carpets and embroiders its *saris* with the bonded labor of more than 200,000 children under the age of 14.[44] In exchange for tiny loans and cash payments, incredibly poor rural Dalits and Muslims sell their children – or their entire families – to predatory textile contractors. According to UNICEF, thousands of children in the carpet industry are "kidnapped or lured away or pledged by their parents for paltry sums of money."

> Most of them are kept in captivity, tortured and made to work for 20 hours a day without a break. Little children are made to crouch on their toes, from dawn to dusk every day, severely stunting their growth during formative years. Social activists in the area find it hard to work because of the strong Mafia-like control that the carpet loom owners have on the area.[45]

Varanasi's silk *sari* industry, investigated by Human Rights Watch, is no better: "The children work twelve or more hours a day, six and a half or seven days a week, under conditions of physical and verbal abuse. Starting as young as age five, they earn from nothing at all to around 400 rupees (US $8.33) a month." In one workshop, researchers discovered a 9-year-old chained to his loom; everywhere they saw young boys covered with burn scars from the dangerous work of boiling silkworm cocoons, as well as little girls with damaged eyesight from endless hours of embroidering in poor lighting.[46]

Another notorious center of child labor is India's glass capital: Firozabad (population 350,000), also in Uttar Pradesh. It is bitterly ironic that the glass bangles beloved by married women are made by

---

43 Nedoroscik, *The City of the Dead*, p. 64.
44 Zama Coursen-Neff, *Small Change: Bonded Child Labor in India's Silk Industry* (Human Rights Watch Report 15:2, January 2003), p. 30.
45 UNICEF, *The State of the World's Children 1997*, Oxford 1998, p. 35.
46 Coursen-Neff, *Small Change*, pp. 8, 30.

50,000 children working in some 400 of the subcontinent's most infernal factories:

> Children work on all types of jobs, such as carrying molten loams of glass stuck on the tips of iron rods, which are just two feet away from their bodies; drawing molten glass from tank furnaces in which the temperature is between 1500 and 1800 degrees centigrade and the arm is almost touching the furnace because the arm of a child is so small; joining and annealing the glass bangles where the work is done over a small kerosene flame in a room with little or no ventilation because a whiff of air can blow out the flame. The whole factory floor is strewn with broken glass and the children run to and fro carrying this burning hot glass with no shoes to protect their feet. Naked electric wires are to be seen dangling everywhere because the factory owners could not be bothered to install insulated internal wiring.[47]

Worldwide, however, the largest sector of urban child labor is unquestionably domestic service. A very large segment of the urban middle class in the Third World directly exploits poor children and teenagers. For example, "a survey of middle-income households in Colombo showed that one in three had a child under 14 years of age as a domestic worker" – the same percentage as Jakarta. In Port-au-Prince, as well as in San Salvador and Guatemala City, it is not rare to find seven- or eight-year-old domestics working ninety-hour weeks, with one day off each month. Likewise, in Kuala Lumpur and other Malaysian cities, where domestics are usually young Indonesian girls, the standard working stint is 16 hours per day, 7 days a week, with no scheduled rest.[48]

While poor urban children are still treated as slaves or indentured labor, some of their fathers remain little more than draught animals. The rickshaw has always been a notorious emblem of the degradation of labor in Asia. Invented in Japan in the 1860s, it allowed "human animals" to replace mule carts and horse-drawn carriages as the chief means of transportation in the great cities of East and South Asia.

---

47 *State of World's Children*, p. 37.

48 Ibid., p. 30; Human Rights Watch, "Child Domestics: The World's Invisible Workers," June 10, 2004, p. 3.

Except in Japan, rickshaws survived even the competition of street-cars after the First World War because of their convenience, low cost, and role as status "passports" of the petty bourgeoisie. ("People tended to think," wrote the 1920s Beijing novelist Xi Ying, "'if you don't even have a private rickshaw, what on earth are you?'")[49] Pulling a rickshaw was reckoned the harshest form of urban labor, and, in Shanghai at least, most pullers (lucky to earn the equivalent of ten cents a day) perished of heart attacks or tuberculosis within a few years.[50]

Revolutionaries, of course, denounced the rickshaw and promised a day of liberation for hundreds of thousands of rickshaw coolies, but in some parts of Asia, this day has been long postponed. Indeed, informal man-powered transit, including old-fashioned rickshaws and bicycle-based pedicabs (invented in 1940), probably employs and exploits more poor men today than in 1930. The ILO has estimated that there are more than 3 million rickshaw-pullers on the streets of Asia.[51] In Dhaka ("God's Own City," an urban planner told Jeremy Seabrook, because "it runs automatically"), the rickshaw sector is the "second-largest provider of employment in the city, second only to the million-or-so employed by the garment industry." The 200,000 *rickshawallahs* – the unsung Lance Armstrongs of the Third World – earn about a dollar per day for pedaling an average of 60 kilometers in Dhaka's nightmarish traffic and pollution.[52] As the male occupation of last resort in a city of growing poverty, there is violent competition between licensed and unlicensed rickshaw-pullers, with the latter living in fear of the police who regularly seize and burn their illegal "vehicles."[53]

Similarly in Calcutta, where Jan Breman has aptly described rickshaw-pulling as "urban share-cropping," 50,000 Bihari immigrants are the backbone of the industry. Most live away from their families,

49 David Strand, *Rickshaw Beijing: City People and Politics in the 1920s*, Berkeley 1989, p. 28. See also James Warren, *Rickshaw Coolie: A People's History of Singapore, 1880–1940*, Singapore 2003.

50 Stella Dong, *Shanghai: The Rise and Fall of a Decadent City*, New York 2000, pp. 162–63.

51 Sethuraman, "Urban Poverty and the Informal Sector," p. 7.

52 Seabrook, *In the Cities of the South*, pp. 35–37.

53 See the article in *Housing by People in Asia* 15 (published by Asian Coalition for Housing Rights) (October 2003).

sometimes for decades, huddled together in sheds or stables, depend-ent upon small tight-knit groups to regulate employment. They are not, Breman stresses, the "independently operating small entrepreneurs [of myth], busily thrusting their way upwards via accumulation, but dependent proletarians who live on the defensive." Their small symbolic compensation is that they are not the worst-off: that distinc-tion belongs to the *thelas*, so low and heavy they must be pulled by a man and his whole family.[54]

The most ghoulish part of the informal economy, even more than child prostitution, is the surging world demand for human organs, a market created in the 1980s by breakthroughs in kidney transplant surgery. In India, the impoverished periphery of Chennai (Madras) has become world renowned for its "kidney farms." According to a *Frontline* investigation, "for eight years between 1987 and 1995, the slum in Bharathi Nagar in Villivakkam, a Chennai suburb, was the hub of the kidney trade in Tamil Nadu. At the height of the boom, partly fueled by foreigners flocking to South India for kidneys, the slum was called Kidney Nagar or Kidney-bakkam." The area's slum-dwellers were mostly drought refugees struggling to survive as rickshaw-pullers or day laborers. Journalists estimated that more than 500 people, or one person per family, had sold their kidneys for local transplants or for export to Malaysia; a majority of the donors were women, including "many deserted women ... forced to sell their kidneys to raise money to support themselves and their children."[55]

Cairo's slums have also been mined in recent years for human body parts. "Most clients in these procedures," explains Jeffrey Nedoroscik, "are wealthy Persian Gulf Arabs. Whereas there are other countries in the Middle East that have transplant centers, few of them have the enormous numbers of poor who are willing to sell their organs. In the past, laboratories would send recruiters into Cairo's slums and poor areas such as the City of the Dead to enlist potential donors."[56]

54 Breman, *The Labouring Poor*, pp. 149–54.
55 Other poor communities, like the twin towns of Pallipalayam and Kumarapalayam, were also involved in the Tamil Nadu kidney trade. Many of the donors were powerloom weavers coping with layoffs and overseas competition. "One-Kidney Communities" (Investigation), *Frontline* 14:25 (13–26 December 1997).
56 Nedoroscik, *The City of the Dead*, p. 70.

The Little Witches of Kinshasa

How far can the elastic fabric of informalization be stretched to provide shelter and livelihood for the new urban poor? One great city, officially expelled from the world economy by its Washington overseers, struggles for bare subsistence amidst the ghosts of its betrayed dreams: Kinshasa is the capital of a naturally rich and artificially poor country where, as President Mobutu himself once put it, "everything is for sale and everything can be bought." Of the world's megacities, only Dhaka is as poor, and Kinshasa surpasses all in its desperate reliance upon informal survival strategies. As an anthropologist observes with some awe, it is the simultaneous "miracle and nightmare" of a vast city where the formal economy and state institutions, apart from the repressive apparatus, have utterly collapsed.[57]

Kinshasa is a city universally described by its own inhabitants as "*cadavre, épave*" (cadaver, a wreck) or "*Kin-la-poubelle*" (Kinshasa, the rubbish heap).[58] "Today it is estimated," writes the anthropologist René Devisch, "that less than 5 percent of the Kinois earn a regular salary."[59] Residents survive by their "ubiquitous vegetable plots and their wits, buying and selling, smuggling and haggling." "Article 15" (the penal code for theft) has become the city charter, and *se débrouiller* ("to cope in spite of all") is the unofficial civic slogan.[60] Indeed, with its figure-foreground reversal of formality and informality, Kinshasa almost reinvents the categories of political economy and urban analysis. As the anthropologist Filip De Boeck, who studies children in the Congo, asks:

> What does it mean to be a city of an estimated 6 million inhabitants in which there is hardly any car traffic or public transportation for the simple reason that, at frequent intervals, there is not a drop of fuel

57 René Devisch, "Frenzy, Violence, and Ethical Renewal in Kinshasa," *Public Culture* 7:3 (1995) p. 603.

58 Thierry Mayamba Nlandu, "Kinshasa: Beyond Dichotomies," conference paper, Conference on Urban Poverty, *African News Bulletin-Bulletin d'Information Africaine Supplement*, issue 347 (1998), p. 2.

59 René Devisch, "Parody in Matricentered Christian Healing Communes of the Sacred Spirit in Kinshasa," *Contours* 1:2 (Fall 2003), p. 7.

60 Wrong, *In the Footsteps of Mr. Kurtz*, p. 152.

available for weeks or even months? Why continue the social convention of referring to a banknote as "money" when one is confronted daily with the fact that it is just a worthless slip of paper? ... What is the use of distinguishing between formal and informal or parallel economies when the informal has become the common and the formal has almost disappeared?[61]

The Kinois negotiate their city of ruins with an irrepressible sense of humor, but even flak-jacketed irony yields before the grimness of the social terrain: average income has fallen to under $100 per year; two-thirds of the population is malnourished; the middle class is extinct; and one in five adults is HIV-positive.[62] Three-quarters are likewise unable to afford formal healthcare and must resort instead to Pentecostal faith-healing or indigenous magic.[63] And, as we shall see in a moment, the children of poor Kinois are turning into witches.

Kinshasa, like the rest of Congo–Zaire, has been wrecked by a perfect storm of kleptocracy, Cold War geopolitics, structural adjustment, and chronic civil war. The Mobutu dictatorship, which for 32 years systematically plundered the Congo, was the Frankenstein monster created and sustained by Washington, the IMF, and the World Bank, with the Quai d'Orsay in a supporting role. The World Bank – nudged when needed by the State Department – encouraged Mobutu to use the collateral of his nation's mineral industries to borrow vast sums from foreign banks, knowing full well that most of the loans were going straight to private Swiss bank accounts. Then the IMF, starting with the first SAP in 1977, stepped in to make sure that ordinary Congolese paid off the debt with interest. The early conditionalities (enforced by an IMF team at Banque du Zaire and French personnel at the Ministry of Finance) decimated the civil service: a quarter-million public employees – the largest formal occupational group in the

61 Filip De Boeck, "Kinshasa: Tales of the 'Invisible City' and the Second World," in Enwezor et al., *Under Siege*, p. 258.

62 James Astill, "Congo Casts out its Child Witches," *Observer*, 11 May 2003.

63 Lynne Cripe et al., "Abandonment and Separation of Children in the Democratic Republic of the Congo," US Agency for International Development evaluation report conducted by the Displaced Children and Orphans Fund and Leahy War Victims Contract (April 2002), pp. 5–7.

economy – were laid off without benefits. Those who remained punctually turned to embezzlement and graft ("Article 15") on an epic scale, with Mobutu's public endorsement.

A decade later, with the Congo's once-impressive infrastructure rusted or looted, the IMF imposed a new SAP. Tshikala Biaya describes how the 1987 agreement "sought to give 'legal power' to the informal sector and make it a new milch cow which would replace the welfare state that the IMF and the World Bank had just destroyed." The Club of Paris rolled over Mobutu's debt in exchange for further retrenchment in the public sector, more market openness, privatization of state companies, removal of exchange controls, and increased export of diamonds. Foreign imports flooded Zaire, home industries closed down, and another 100,000 jobs were lost in Kinshasa. Hyperinflation promptly destroyed the monetary system and any semblance of economic rationality.[64]

"Money," wrote René Devisch, "appeared to be a mysterious and fantastic entity, retaining no relation to either labor or production. People came to seek refuge in an economy of fortune."[65] The Kinois, indeed, were caught up in a desperate frenzy of betting: French horse races, lotteries organized by the big breweries, bottle cap games by the soft drink companies, and, most fatefully, a pyramidal money scheme, secretly controlled by the military. (A similar quasi-magical "pyramidmania" would sweep Albania with equally devastating results in 1996–97, sucking up and destroying half the impoverished nation's GDP.)[66] Initial investors won radios or appliances from South Africa, inducing everyone else to gamble that they could board the scheme and then disembark before it crashed – but there were few survivors of the inevitable disaster. As Devisch explains, "With such a large part of the population of Kinshasa involved in these financial schemes, the effects of the collapse on the economy, and especially the informal sector, were

64 Tshikala Biaya, "SAP: A Catalyst for the Underdevelopment and Privatization of Public Administration in the Democratic Republic of Congo, 1997–2000," *DPMN Bulletin* 7:3 (December 2000).

65 Devisch, "Frenzy, Violence, and Ethical Renewal in Kinshasa," p. 604.

66 See analyses by World Bank researchers: Carlos Elbirt, "Albania under the Shadow of the Pyramids;" and Utpal Bhattacharya, "On the Possibility of Ponzi Schemes in Transition Economies," in *Transition Newsletter* (newsletter published by the World Bank Group) (January–February 2000), (www.worldbank.org/transition-newsletter/janfeb600/pgs24–26.htm).

disastrous. The bitter frustration of the people led to an imaginary yet vicious mentality of sorcery."[67]

The immediate aftermath, amidst continuing inflation, was the great urban *jacquerie* of September 1991 when Kinshasa's slum-dwellers – with the Army's connivance – engaged in a massive, festive pillaging of factories, stores, and warehouses. Devisch describes the "euphoric and perverse unleashing of anomie, of the inert violence internalized by the people under the pressures of galloping inflation and a bankrupt labor market."[68] Other disasters punctually followed. In January 1993 Kinshasa was again pillaged, but this time by soldiers alone. The banking system collapsed, public administration more or less disappeared, enterprises resorted to using barter, and minor public employees discovered that their salaries were now worth only one-eighth of their 1988 value in real terms. According to De Boeck, "The withdrawal in November 1993 of the IMF and the World Bank from the country attested to the fact that Congo was no longer participating in the world economy."[69] With the national economy in ruins and the Congo's wealth locked in Swiss bank vaults, Mobutu was finally overthrown in 1997; "liberation," however, only led to foreign interventions and an endless civil war that the USAID estimated had taken more than 3 million lives (mostly from starvation and disease) by 2004.[70] The rapine by marauding armies in the eastern Congo – resembling scenes from Europe's Thirty Years War – propelled new waves of refugees into overcrowded Kinshasa slums.

In the face of the death of the formal city and its institutions, ordinary Kinois – but above all, mothers and grandmothers – fought for their survival by "villagizing" Kinshasa: they reestablished subsistence agriculture and traditional forms of rural self-help. Every vacant square meter of land, including highway medians, was planted in cassava, while women without plots, the *mamas miteke*, went off to forage for roots and grubs in the brush.[71] With the successive

67 Devisch, "Frenzy, Violence, and Ethical Renewal in Kinshasa," p. 604.

68 Ibid., p. 606.

69 De Boeck, "Kinshasa," p. 258.

70 3.8 million is the actual estimate of Anthony Gambino, retiring director of the USAID mission to the Congo (Mvemba Dizolele, "Eye on Africa: SOS Congo," UPI, 28 December 2004).

71 De Boeck, "Kinshasa," p. 266.

collapses of the world of work and then of the fantasy universe of gambling, people returned to a reliance upon village magic and prophetic cults. They sought release from the "disease of the whites," "*yimbeefu kya mboongu*": the fatal illness of money.[72] In the place of abandoned factories and looted stores, tiny churches and prayer groups set up shop under crude but brightly painted signs. In huge slums like Masina (locally known as "The Republic of China" because of its density), Pentecostalism spread at a tropical velocity: "At the end of 2000, it was reported that there were 2,177 religious sects newly constituted in Kinshasa, many who meet during all-night prayer sessions."[73]

As Devisch and others have emphasized, the Pentecostal phenomenon is variegated and complex, encompassing a spectrum of indigenous and imported forms. Some churches, for example, were founded by Catholic laymen or ex-seminarians, who, lacking the financial means or education to enter the priesthood, instead created lucrative franchises of American-style preaching based on faith-healing and the gospel of prosperity.[74] Others, like the Mpeve Ya Nlongo church, are female-led healing communes, where trances, prophetic dreams, and "celestial tongues" are used to access both the Holy Ghost and tribal ancestors in anticipation of a "world to come" that will eliminate poverty and inequality. "These mother-centered communities," writes Devisch, "speak of the need to have moral centers for the future of the city, the care for value, a sense of nesting and domestication."[75] In any case, Kinshasa's Pentecostal revival corresponded to grassroots spiritual renewal – a reenchantment of a catastrophic modernity – in a historical context where politics has become utterly discredited.

But the Kinois' talents for self-organization and *se débrouiller* have real material limits as well as a darker side. Despite heroic efforts, especially by women, traditional social structure is eroding. In the face of absolute immiseration, anthropologists describe the dissolution of the

72 Devisch, "Frenzy, Violence, and Ethical Renewal in Kinshasa," p. 625.
73 Abdou Maliq Simone, p. 24.
74 Sedecias Kakule interviewed in "Democratic Republic of the Congo: Torture and Death of an Eight-Year-Old Child," Federation Internationale de L'Acat (Action des Christiens pour L'Abolition de la Torture) (FIATCAT), (October 2003).
75 René Devisch, précis of talk ("'Pillaging Jesus:' The Response of Healing Churches of Central Africa to Globalization"), *Forum for Liberation Theology, Annual Report 1997–98*.

gift exchanges and reciprocity relations that order Zairean society: unable to afford bride price or become breadwinners, young men, for example, abandon pregnant women and fathers go AWOL.[76] Simultaneously, the AIDS holocaust leaves behind vast numbers of orphans and HIV-positive children. There are huge pressures on poor urban families – shorn of their rural kinship support networks, or conversely, overburdened by the demands of lineage solidarity – to jettison their most dependent members. As a researcher for Save the Children grimly notes: "The capacities of Congolese families and communities to assure basic care and protection for their children seem to be breaking down."[77]

This crisis of the family, moreover, has coincided with both the Pentecostal boom and a renascent fear of sorcery. Many Kinois, according to Devisch, interpret their fate within the larger urban catastrophe as "a type of curse or *ensorcellement*."[78] As a result, literal, perverse belief in Harry Potter has gripped Kinshasa, leading to the mass-hysterical denunciation of thousands of child "witches" and their expulsion to the streets, even their murder. The children, some barely more than infants, have been accused of every misdeed and are even believed, in the Ndjili slum at least, to fly about at night in swarms on broomsticks. Aid workers emphasize the novelty of the phenomenon: "Before 1990, there was hardly any talk of child witches in Kinshasa. The children who are now being accused of witchcraft are in the same situation: they become an unproductive burden for parents who are no longer able to feed them. The children said to be 'witches' are most often from very poor families"[79]

The charismatic churches have been deeply complicit in promoting and legitimizing fears about bewitched children: indeed, the Pentecostals portray their faith as God's armor against witchcraft. Hysteria amongst both adults and children (who have developed intense phobias about cats, lizards, and the long dark nights of power blackouts) has been exacerbated by the widespread circulation of lurid

76 Review of lecture by Filip De Boeck, "Children, the Occult and the Street in Kinshasa," *News from Africa* (February 2003).
77 Mahimbo Mdoe quoted in Astill, "Congo Casts Out its 'Child Witches'."
78 Devisch, "Frenzy, Violence, and Ethical Renewal in Kinshasa," p. 608.
79 "DRC: Torture and Death of an Eight-Year-Old Child," October 2003.

Christian videos showing the confessions of "witch children" and subsequent exorcisms, sometimes involving starvation and scalding
water.[80] USAID researchers directly blame the industry of "self-made
preachers" who "set up their pulpits and mete out predictions for those
seeking an easy fix for their grief and misfortune."

> When prophecies fail, the preachers might easily blame continued misery
> on spurious causes, such as witchcraft, often turning on children as the
> source because they are easy to blame and least able to defend them-
> selves. A family seeking the advice of their preacher might, for example,
> be told that their handicapped child is causing their continued misery,
> citing the child's disability as a clear indication that he or she is a witch.[81]

De Boeck, on the other hand, claims that the sects are sustaining an
informal moral order amidst general collapse, and that "the church
leaders do not themselves produce these accusations, but merely
confirm and thereby legitimize them." The pastors organize public confessions and exorcisms (cure d'âmes): "The child is placed in the middle
of a circle of praying, often entranced women who regularly lapse into
glossolalia, a sign of the Holy Spirit." But families often refuse to take
children back once they have been accused, and they are then forced
into the street. "I am Vany and I am three years old," one child told De
Boeck. "I was ill. My legs started to swell. And then they started saying
that I was a witch. It was true. The preacher confirmed it."[82]

Witch children, like possessed maidens in seventeenth-century
Salem, seem to hallucinate the accusations against them, accepting their
role as sacrificial receptacles for family immiseration and urban anomie.
One boy told photographer Vincen Beeckman:

> I've eaten 800 men. I make them have accidents, in planes or cars. I even
> went to Belgium thanks to a mermaid who took me all the way to the

80 See "Christian Fundamentalist Groups Spreading over Africa," German
campaign of Friends of People Close to Nature, 17 June 2004 (www.fpcn-global.org).
81 Cripe et al., "Abandonment and Separation of Children in the Democratic
Republic of Congo," p. 16.
82 See extracts from Filip De Boeck, "Geographies of Exclusion: Churches and
Child-Witches in Kinshasa," BEople 6 (March–August 2003).

port of Antwerp. Sometimes I travel by broomstick, other times on an avocado skin. At night, I'm 30 and I have 100 children. My father lost his job as an engineer because of me – then I killed him with the mermaid. I also killed my brother and sister. I buried them alive. I also killed all of my mother's unborn children.[83]

Beeckman contends that because there is no functioning child welfare system in Kinshasa, the family expulsion of accused witches is not just rationalization for abandonment, but also "a chance to place them in a religious community, where they will receive some sort of education and food to live on, or to get them into one of the centres run by an international NGO." But most child witches, especially the sick and HIV-positive kids, simply end up in the street, becoming part of the urban army, at least 30,000 strong, composed of "runaways, child abuse victims, children displaced by war, child soldiers who have deserted, orphans and unmarried."[84]

The child witches of Kinshasa, like the organ-exporting slums of India and Egypt, seem to take us to an existential ground zero beyond which there are only death camps, famine, and Kurtzian horror. Indeed, an authentic Kinois, Thierry Mayamba Nlandu, in a poignant but Whitmanesque ("the shanties, too, sing Kinshasa ...") reflection, asks: "How do these millions survive the incoherent, miserable life of Kinshasa?" His answer is that "Kinshasa is a dead city. It is not a city of the dead." The informal sector is not a *deus ex machina*, but "a soulless wasteland," yet also "an economy of resistance" that confers honor on the poor "where otherwise the logic of the market leads to total despair."[85] The Kinois, like the inhabitants of the Martinican slum called "Texaco" in Patrick Chamoiseau's famed novel of the same name, hold on to the city "by its thousand survival cracks" and stubbornly refuse to let go.[86]

83 Vincen Beeckman, "Growing Up on the Streets of Kinshasa," *The Courier ACP EU* (September–October 2001), pp. 63–64.
84 Beeckman, "Growing Up on the Streets of Kinshasa," p. 64.
85 Thierry Mayamba Nlandu, "Kinshasa: Beyond Chaos," in Enwezor et al., p. 186.
86 Chamoiseau, *Texaco*, p. 316.

Epilogue

Down Vietnam Street

The promise is that again and again, from the garbage,
the scattered feathers, the ashes and broken bodies,
something new and beautiful may be born.

John Berger[1]

The late-capitalist triage of humanity, then, has already taken place. As
Jan Breman, writing of India, has warned: "A point of no return is
reached when a reserve army waiting to be incorporated into the labour
process becomes stigmatized as a permanently redundant mass, an
excessive burden that cannot be included now or in the future, in
economy and society. This metamorphosis is, in my opinion at least,
the real crisis of world capitalism."[2] Alternately, as the CIA grimly
noted in 2002: "By the late 1990s a staggering one billion workers rep-
resenting one-third of the world's labor force, most of them in the
South, were either unemployed or underemployed."[3] Apart from the de
Sotan cargo cult of infinitely flexible informalism, there is no official
scenario for the reincorporation of this vast mass of surplus labor into
the mainstream of the world economy.

1 John Berger, "Rumor," preface to Tekin, *Berji Kristin*, p. 8.
2 Breman, *The Labouring Poor*, p. 13.
3 Central Intelligence Agency, *The World Factbook*, Washington, D.C. 2002,
p. 80.

The contrast with the 1960s is dramatic: forty years ago ideological warfare between the two great Cold War blocs generated competing visions of abolishing world poverty and rehousing slum-dwellers. With its triumphant Sputniks and ICBMs, the Soviet Union was still a plausible model of breakneck industrialization via heavy industries and five-year plans. On the other side, the Kennedy administration officially diagnosed Third World revolutions as "diseases of modernization," and prescribed – in addition to Green Berets and B-52s – ambitious land reforms and housing programs. To immunize Colombians against urban subversion, for example, the Alliance for Progress subsidized huge housing projects such as Ciudad Kennedy (80,000 people) in Bogotá and Villa Socorro (12,000 people) in Medellín. The *Allianza* was advertised as a Western Hemisphere Marshall Plan that would soon lift pan-American living standards to southern European, if not *gringo*, levels. Meanwhile, as we have seen, charismatic nationalist leaders like Nasser, Nkrumah, Nehru, and Sukarno retailed their own versions of revolution and progress.

But the promised lands of the 1960s no longer appear on neoliberal maps of the future. The last gasp of developmental idealism is the United Nations' Millennium Development Goals (MDGs) campaign (caricatured as "Minimalist Development Goals" by some African aid workers) that aims to cut the proportion of people living in extreme poverty in half by 2015, as well as drastically reducing infant and maternal mortality in the Third World. Despite episodic expressions of rich-country solidarity like the Make Poverty History and Live 8 events during the July 2005 Gleneagles G8 Summit, the MDGs will almost certainly not be achieved in the foreseeable future. In their *Human Development Report 2004*, top UN researchers warned that at current rates of "progress" sub-Saharan Africa would not reach most MDGs until well into the twenty-second century. The chief partners in Africa's underdevelopment, the IMF and World Bank, repeated the same pessimistic assessment in their *Global Monitoring Report* issued in April 2005.[4]

With a literal "great wall" of high-tech border enforcement blocking large-scale migration to the rich countries, only the slum remains as a

4 *Human Development Report 2004*, pp. 132–33; Tanya Nolan, "Urgent Action Needed to Meet Millennium Goals," *ABC Online*, 13 April 2005.

fully franchised solution to the problem of warehousing this century's surplus humanity. Slum populations, according to UN-HABITAT, are currently growing by a staggering 25 million per year.[5] Moreover, as emphasized in an earlier chapter, the frontier of safe, squattable land is everywhere disappearing and new arrivals to the urban margin confront an existential condition that can only be described as "marginality within marginality," or, in the more piquant phrase of a desperate Baghdad slum-dweller, a "semi-death."[6] Indeed, *peri-urban poverty* – a grim human world largely cut off from the subsistence solidarities of the countryside as well as disconnected from the cultural and political life of the traditional city – is the radical new face of inequality. The urban edge is a zone of exile, a new Babylon: it was reported, for example, that some of the young terrorists – born and raised in Casablanca's peripheral *bidonvilles* – who attacked luxury hotels and foreign restaurants in May 2003 had never been downtown before and were amazed at the affluence of the *medina*.[7]

But if informal urbanism becomes a dead-end street, won't the poor revolt? Aren't the great slums – as Disraeli worried in 1871 or Kennedy fretted in 1961 – just volcanoes waiting to erupt? Or does ruthless Darwinian competition – as increasing numbers of poor people compete for the same informal scraps – generate, instead, self-annihilating communal violence as yet the highest form of "urban involution"? To what extent does an informal proletariat possess that most potent of Marxist talismans: "historical agency"?

These are complex questions that must be explored via concrete, comparative case studies before they can be answered in any general sense. (At least, this is the approach that Forrest Hylton and I have adopted in the book we are writing on the "governments of the poor.") Portentous post-Marxist speculations, like those of Negri and Hardt, about a new politics of "multitudes" in the "rhizomatic spaces" of globalization remain ungrounded in any real political sociology. Even within a single city, slum populations can support a bewildering variety

5 UN-HABITAT, "Sounding the Alarm on Forced Evictions," press release, 20th Session of the Governing Council, Nairobi, 4–8 April 2005.

6 Quoted in James Glanz, "Iraq's Dislocated Minorities Struggle in Urban Enclaves," *New York Times*, 3 April 2005.

7 See accounts at www.maroc-hebdo.press.ma and www.bladi.net.

of responses to structural neglect and deprivation, ranging from charismatic churches and prophetic cults to ethnic militias, street gangs, neoliberal NGOs, and revolutionary social movements. But if there is no monolithic subject or unilateral trend in the global slum, there are nonetheless myriad acts of resistance. Indeed, the future of human solidarity depends upon the militant refusal of the new urban poor to accept their terminal marginality within global capitalism.

This refusal may take atavistic as well as avant-garde forms: the repeal of modernity as well as attempts to recover its repressed promises. It should not be surprising that some poor youth on the outskirts of Istanbul, Cairo, Casablanca, or Paris embrace the religious nihilism of al Salafia Jihadia and rejoice in the destruction of an alien modernity's most overweening symbols. Or that millions of others turn to the urban subsistence economies operated by street gangs, *narcotraficantes*, militias, and sectarian political organizations. The demonizing rhetorics of the various international "wars" on terrorism, drugs, and crime are so much semantic apartheid: they construct epistemological walls around *gecekondus*, *favelas*, and *chawls* that disable any honest debate about the daily violence of economic exclusion. And, as in Victorian times, the categorical criminalization of the urban poor is a self-fulfilling prophecy, guaranteed to shape a future of endless war in the streets. As the Third World middle classes increasingly bunker themselves in their suburban themeparks and electrified "security villages," they lose moral and cultural insight into the urban badlands they have left behind.

The rulers' imagination, moreover, seems to falter before the obvious implications of a world of cities without jobs. True, neoliberal optimism is dogged by a certain quotient of Malthusian pessimism, perhaps best illustrated by the apocalyptic travel writing of Robert D. Kaplan (*The Ends of the Earth* and *The Coming Anarchy*). But most of the deep thinkers at the big American and European policy think tanks and international relations institutes have yet to wrap their minds around the geopolitical implications of a "planet of slums." More successful — probably because they don't have to reconcile neoliberal dogma to neoliberal reality — have been the strategists and tactical planners at the Air Force Academy, the Army's RAND Arroyo Center, and the Marines' Quantico (Virginia) Warfighting Laboratory. Indeed, in the absence of other paradigms, the Pentagon has evolved its own distinctive perspective on global urban poverty.

The Mogadishu debacle of 1993, when slum militias inflicted 60 percent casualties on elite Army Rangers, forced military theoreticians to rethink what is known in Pentagonese as MOUT: "Military Operations on Urbanized Terrain." Ultimately a National Defense Panel review in December 1997 castigated the Army as unprepared for protracted combat in the nearly impassable, maze-like streets of poor Third World cities. All the armed services, coordinated by the Joint Urban Operations Training Working Group, launched crash programs to master street-fighting under realistic slum conditions. "The future of warfare," the journal of the Army War College declared, "lies in the streets, sewers, highrise buildings, and sprawl of houses that form the broken cities of the world.... Our recent military history is punctuated with city names – Tuzla, Mogadishu, Los Angeles [!], Beirut, Panama City, Hué, Saigon, Santo Domingo – but these encounters have been but a prologue, with the real drama still to come."[8]

To help develop a larger conceptual framework for MOUT, military planners turned in the 1990s to Dr. Strangelove's old alma mater, the Santa Monica-based RAND Corporation. RAND, a nonprofit think tank established by the Air Force in 1948, was notorious for wargaming nuclear Armageddon in the 1950s and for helping to strategize the Vietnam War in the 1960s. These days RAND does cities: its researchers ponder urban crime statistics, inner-city public health, and the privatization of public education. They also run the Army's Arroyo Center, which has published a small library of studies on the social contexts and tactical mechanics of urban warfare.

One of the most important RAND projects, initiated in the early 1990s, has been a major study of "how demographic changes will affect future conflict." The bottom line, RAND finds, is that the urbanization of world poverty has produced "the urbanization of insurgency" – the title of their report. "Insurgents are following their followers into the cities," RAND warns, "setting up 'liberated zones' in urban shantytowns. Neither U.S. doctrine, nor training, nor equipment is designed

---

8 Major Ralph Peters, "Our Soldiers, Their Cities," *Parameters* (Spring 1996), pp. 43–50.

for urban counterinsurgency." The RAND researchers focus on the example of El Salvador during the 1980s, where the local military, despite massive support from Washington, was unable to stop FMLN guerrillas from opening an urban front. Indeed, "had the Farabundo Martí National Liberation Front rebels effectively operated within the cities earlier in the insurgency, it is questionable how much the United States could have done to help maintain even the stalemate between the government and the insurgents."[9] The mega-slum, the researchers clearly imply, has become the weakest link in the new world order.

More recently, a leading Air Force theorist made similar points in the *Aerospace Power Journal*: "Rapid urbanization in developing countries," writes Captain Troy Thomas in the Spring 2002 issue, "results in a battlespace environment that is decreasingly knowable since it is increasingly unplanned." Thomas contrasts modern, hierarchical urban cores, whose centralized infrastructures are easily crippled by either air strikes (Belgrade) or terrorist attacks (Manhattan), with the sprawling slum peripheries of the Third World, organized by "informal, decentralized subsystems," where no blueprints exist and "points of leverage in the system are not readily discernable." Using the "sea of urban squalor" that surrounds Karachi as a prime example, Thomas portrays the challenge of "asymmetric combat" within "non-nodal, non-hierarchical" urban terrains against "clan-based" militias propelled by "desperation and anger." He also cites the slum peripheries of Kabul, Lagos, Dushanbe (Tajikistan), and Kinshasa as other potential nightmare battlefields, to which other military writers frequently add Port-au-Prince. Thomas, like other MOUT planners, prescribes high-tech gear plus realistic training, preferably in "our own blighted cities," where "massive housing projects have become uninhabitable and industrial plants unusable. Yet they would be nearly ideal for combat-in-cities training."[10]

Who, exactly, is the enemy that future robo-soldiers, trained in the slums of Detroit and LA, will stalk in the labyrinth of Third World

9 Jennifer Morrison Taw and Bruce Hoffman, *The Urbanization of Insurgency: The Potential Challenge to U.S. Army Operations*, Santa Monica 1994 (on-line summary at www.rand.org/pubs/monograph_reports/2005/MR398.SUM.pdf).

10 Captain Troy Thomas, "Slumlords: Aerospace Power in Urban Fights," *Aerospace Power Journal* (Spring 2002), pp. 1–15 (online edition).

cities? Some experts simply shrug their shoulders and answer "whatever." In an influential article on "Geopolitics and Urban Armed Conflict in Latin America," written in the mid-1990s, Geoffrey Demarest, a leading researcher at Fort Leavenworth, proposed a strange cast of "anti-state actors," including "psychopathic anarchists," criminals, cynical opportunists, lunatics, revolutionaries, labor leaders, ethnic nationals, and real-estate speculators. In the end, however, he settled on the "dispossessed" in general, and "criminal syndicates" in particular. In addition to advocating the use of research tools borrowed from architecture and urban planning to help predict future subversion, Demarest added that "security forces should address the sociological phenomenon of excluded populations." He was particularly concerned with "the psychology of the abandoned child," since he believes – along with many advocates of the so-called "youth bulge" theory of crime – that slum children are the secret weapon of anti-state forces.[11]

In summary, the Pentagon's best minds have dared to venture where most United Nations, World Bank or Department of State types fear to go: down the road that logically follows from the abdication of urban reform. As in the past, this is a "street without joy," and, indeed, the unemployed teenage fighters of the 'Mahdi Army' in Baghdad's Sadr City – one of the world's largest slums – taunt American occupiers with the promise that their main boulevard is "Vietnam Street." But the war planners don't blench. With coldblooded lucidity, they now assert that the "feral, failed cities" of the Third World – especially their slum outskirts – will be the distinctive battlespace of the twenty-first century. Pentagon doctrine is being reshaped accordingly to support a low-intensity world war of unlimited duration against criminalized segments of the urban poor. This is the true "clash of civilizations."

MOUT doctrine – according to Stephen Graham, who has written extensively on the geography of urban warfare – is thus the highest stage of Orientalism, the culmination of a long history of defining the

---

11 Geoffrey Demarest, "Geopolitics and Urban Armed Conflict in Latin America," *Small Wars and Insurgencies* 6:1 (Spring 1995), n.p. (internet text). On the rise of "strategic demography" and the criminalization of youth, see the important paper by Anne Hendrixson, *Angry Young Men, Veiled Young Women: Constructing a New Population Threat*, Corner House Briefing 34, Sturminster Newton 2004.

West by opposition to a hallucinatory Eastern Other. According to Stephen Graham, this dichotomizing ideology – now raised to "moral absolutism" by the Bush administration – "works by separating the 'civilised world' – the 'homeland' cities which must be 'defended' – from the 'dark forces,' the 'axis of evil,' and the 'terrorists' nests' of Islamic cities, which are alleged to sustain the 'evildoers' which threaten the health, prosperity, and democracy of the whole of the 'free' world."[12]

This delusionary dialectic of securitized versus demonic urban places, in turn, dictates a sinister and unceasing duet: Night after night, hornetlike helicopter gunships stalk enigmatic enemies in the narrow streets of the slum districts, pouring hellfire into shanties or fleeing cars. Every morning the slums reply with suicide bombers and eloquent explosions. If the empire can deploy Orwellian technologies of repression, its outcasts have the gods of chaos on their side.[13]

12 Stephen Graham, "Cities and the 'War on Terror'," forthcoming in *Theory, Culture and Society*, draft, 2005, p. 4.
13 See Mike Davis, "The Urbanization of Empire: Megacities and the Laws of Chaos," *Social Text* 81 (Winter 2004).

Acknowledgments

While I was in the university library, Forrest Hylton was behind a barricade in the Andes. His generous and incisive comments on this text, and, more generally, his firsthand knowledge of Latin American urbanism, have been invaluable. He and I are working on a Verso sequel to the present book that will explore the history and future of slum-based resistance to global capitalism. His own forthcoming books on Colombia and Bolivia are brilliant examples of committed and visionary scholarship.

Tariq Ali and Susan Watkins deserve special thanks for persuading me to turn "Planet of Slums" (*New Left Review* 26, March/April 2004) into a book. Perry Anderson, as always, provided friendship and advice of the highest order. Ananya Roy in the Department of Planning at UC Berkeley invited me up to discuss the NLR article, and I am very grateful for her hospitality and stimulating comments. At Verso, the wonderful Jane Hindle was my original editor; more recently, I've enjoyed working with Giles O'Bryen and Tom Penn. Although I have never met either of them, my admiration for Jan Breman (*The Labouring Poor in India*, Oxford 2003) and Jeremy Seabrook (*In the Cities of the South*, Verso 1996) should be obvious from the frequency with which I quote from their magnificent books.

Having made my son Jack the hero of a recent "science-adventure" trilogy, it is time to dedicate a book to his big sister Roisin. Every day she makes me proud in a hundred different ways. (Don't worry, my little ones, Cassandra Moctezuma and James Connolly, your time will soon come.)

Index